The Shaping of an Arab Statesman

The Shaping of an Arab Statesman

Sharif Abd al-Hamid Sharaf
and the Modern Arab World

Edited by Patrick Seale

Quartet Books
London Melbourne New York

First published by Quartet Books Limited 1983
A member of the Namara Group
27/29 Goodge Street, London W1P 1FD

Copyright © 1983 by Leila Sharaf

British Library Cataloguing in Publication Data

The Shaping of an Arab statesman.
  1. Sharaf, Abdul Hamid
  2. Statesmen—Jordan—Biography
  I. Seale, Patrick
  956.95044'092'4   DS154.52.S/

  ISBN 0-7043-2341-9

Typeset by MC Typeset, Rochester, Kent
Printed by Nene Litho, bound by
Woolnough Bookbinding both of
Wellingborough, Northants.

Contents

The Contributors

Patrick Seale writes on Middle East affairs for the *Observer* and other journals

Peter Mansfield is a historian and journalist specializing in the Arab world

Robert Stephens is the Diplomatic Correspondent of the *Observer*

Adeed Dawisha is Deputy Director of Studies at the Royal Institute of International Affairs, London

Suleiman Mousa is a senior official at the Ministry of Culture in Amman

Roger Owen is a Fellow of St Antony's College, Oxford

Umayya S. Tukan is on the staff of the Central Bank of Jordan

Rami G. Khouri edits the *Jordan Times* in Amman

Edward Said is Parr Professor of English and Comparative Literature at Columbia University, New York, and a member of the Palestine National Council

Prince Hassan bin Talal is the Crown Prince of Jordan

Hisham Sharabi is Professor of History at the Center of Contemporary Arab Studies, Georgetown University, Washington

Al-Sadig al-Mahdi is a former Prime Minister of the Sudan and a leading figure in Islamic circles

Hazem Nuseibeh is Jordan's Ambassador to the United Nations

Malcolm Kerr is President of the American University of Beirut

Michael Gilsenan is Reader in Anthropology at University College, London

Foreword

This volume stands as a modest memorial to a distinguished Jordanian, the Sharif Abd al-Hamid Sharaf. His sudden and premature death at the age of forty in 1980, when he was serving as Prime Minister, robbed his country and Arab politics of one of its brightest sons.

Much of his adult life was spent struggling with the many problems which press upon Jordan: relations with often importunate Great Powers; the relentless Palestine tragedy which affects Jordan more intimately than any other Arab state; at home the growing pains of a young nation – the whole set in an unstable, often brutal, context of inter-Arab disputes and repeated wars with Israel.

The Sharif was not only an active politician but also an intellectual. How better to honour him, it was thought, than to invite a number of eminent writers, many of whom had known him personally, to explore in a series of essays some of the themes and ideas he cared about, so as to paint a contemporary portrait of Jordan and the Arab world to which he contributed so much and to which, had he lived, he could have contributed so much more.

P.S.

The Shaping of an Arab Statesman

Abd al-Hamid Sharaf

Patrick Seale

The Middle East is a part of the world where, in the absence of strong institutions, men put their personal imprint on events. The style of government is shaped, the tone of society set, even to a large extent the quality of life determined by the man at the top. Because these are countries in transition, still groping for an identity and a destiny, a single individual can point them in a new direction, just as a river whose bed is not yet established will forge a different course under the pressure of a fresh and powerful head of water. Abd al-Hamid Sharaf, to whom King Hussein gave great responsibility in Jordan at an early age, was such a leader, with the gifts and personality to rally his countrymen behind a new vision. But it was not to be. After only six months in the premiership he was cut down by a heart attack on 3 July 1980, five days before his forty-first birthday. Great public servant though he undoubtedly was, having given almost half his brief life to the interests of Jordan, his career had the poignancy of crowning promise unfulfilled. The ideas which poured unstoppably from him never had time to be translated into the bricks and mortar of the new society of his hopes. He will be remembered less for his actual achievements than for his giving Jordanians – and indeed Arabs everywhere – an inspiring glimpse of peaceful and yet radical change.

Sharaf always believed that a small country, if it were to justify its existence, had to have a dream transcending the day-to-day running of affairs. In an Arab landscape of widespread disillusion and frustration, particularly after the 1967 defeat, his dream for Jordan was that it should be a model for other countries – a model of a reformed society granting the individual the respect and attention he, and she, deserved.

The creative paradox of this tall, elegant, somewhat reserved man was that he was both an aristocrat and a genuine radical, a figure with precedents in the annals of revolutionary Europe but less common in the Third World today. Yet it was precisely this conjunction of opposites which gave him his special authority. As a Sharif – that is to say, the son of a family which traced its descent from the Prophet – and as a Hashemite, he was born to leadership, related to King Hussein and to King Faisal II of Iraq, killed in the 1958 revolution. But in the Arab world in which Abd al-Hamid grew up, something more than lineage was needed to match the appeal of a Nasser or the seductions of Arab nationalism. At the American University of Beirut, that forcing house of politics, he gained his spurs in the radical movement, thus winning a legitimacy with the anti-establishment Left which lasted the whole of his life.

Born into a princely house, tempered in a radical furnace, he was further moulded by nearly a decade's exposure to liberal America. So familiar did he there become with Western modes of thinking that, to a degree unusual for an Arab politician, he could join in intimate and trustful dialogue with his Western counterparts.

It is hard to think of another Arab statesman who enjoyed equal credibility with three such diverse and often antagonistic categories: the traditional Arab establishment, the anti-establishment Left, and the West's political elites.

Abd al-Hamid Sharaf undoubtedly had pride of race, as was evident from his bearing, but it was a pride without complacency. His branch of the Hashemite family had more than its share of hardship and suffering and his own early childhood was spent as a refugee.

His father, Sharif Sharaf, was fifty-nine when the boy was born, but in spite of this great age difference and the fact that the fortunes of war kept them much apart, the father was a hero to the son who was brought up on tales of the Hijaz, of Hashemite family history, of noble deeds in tribal wars. Above all he revered his father as an Arab nationalist.

Sharif Sharaf was born in 1880 in Taif, an ancient city in the mountains of western Arabia, and was the city's last Hashemite prince, or governor, from 1914 to 1925 when it was lost together with the whole of the Hijaz to the Saudis. Being an Arab chieftain in the early years of the century, he lived much in the saddle, and, when Sharif Hussein raised the standard of the Arab Revolt against the Turks, it was natural that he should be in the thick of it. T. E. Lawrence in his *Seven Pillars of Wisdom* awarded him top marks.

He was a powerful man, perhaps the most capable of all the Sherifs in the army, but devoid of ambition: acting out of duty, not from impulse. He was rich, and had been for years chief justice of the Sherif's [Hussein's] court. He knew and handled tribesmen better than any man, and they feared him, for he was severe and impartial, and his face was sinister, with a left eyebrow which drooped (the effect of an old blow) and gave him an air of forbidding hardness . . . I found him good to work with, very clear-headed, wise and kind, with a pleasant smile – his mouth became soft then, while his eyes remained terrible – and a determination to do fittingly always.

When the House of Hashem was defeated by Ibn Saud, Sharif Sharaf found refuge in Iraq in 1926 where Prince Faisal had become king under the umbrella of the British mandate. Sharaf and his household took Iraqi nationality. His youngest child, Abd al-Hamid, born in Baghdad in 1939, was the last of a family which included a much older half-brother, two sisters, and a full brother. Until the Second World War life was uneventful. A man of modest and austere tastes, Sharif Sharaf had little truck with the royal court dominated from 1939 onwards by his self-important cousin, the Regent Abd al-Ilah.

It was perhaps for this reason that when a group of nationalist army officers in association with Rashid Ali al-Gaylani, the leading anti-British politician of the time, seized power and deposed the regent in April 1941, their choice fell on Sharif Sharaf to replace him.

Although the Rashid Ali rebellion lasted only a few weeks before it was put down by British force, it remains to this day in nationalist sentiment a high point of Arab endeavour, the only serious indigenous challenge to Britain's hold over the Middle East in the Second World War. Sharaf's association with it confirmed his nationalist credentials, a legacy his son inherited.

But there was a heavy price to be paid. When Rashid Ali's regime collapsed on 29 May, its leaders, including Sharif Sharaf, fled to Tehran, but this haven proved shortlived. Before the end of the year Persia was occupied by British and Soviet forces, the Iraqi nationalists scattered into new exile and some, Sharaf among them, were arrested. His family were not to see him again until 1947. Interned by the British in Rhodesia for three years, he was eventually handed over to the Iraqis to serve another three-year sentence. Meanwhile his wife and children lived the uncertain life of wartime refugees, first in Istanbul for eighteen months, then briefly in Berlin until air raids and food shortages drove them on to Sofia, where again they could not settle but returned to Istanbul. In November 1945 King Abdullah invited them to Transjordan where they made their home in a villa in the grounds of the royal palace.

Abd al-Hamid was eight when his father joined them from his prison cell in Iraq, and fifteen when his father died in 1955. As the only male member of the family then in Jordan, the boy had to walk alone behind the coffin. Though he knew his father only for a few brief years, his influence on him was profound. From Sharif Sharaf he learned to practise a certain personal austerity, to admire unselfish public service, and to disdain the vulgar display of wealth. Father and son even shared the same diversions – reading, horse-riding and intelligent jokes.

Closest to Abd al-Hamid were his two elder sisters, Shaikha and Sakina, who in effect brought him up after his mother's death in 1950. The wartime years in Europe had been hard but also liberating for the sisters, who chafed at seclusion in an Islamic royal household in what was then little more than a village. They too had inherited the family brains – and the family stoicism. So the tone of the house in which Abd al-Hamid grew up was reserved, disciplined, intellectual, loving, but not very sociable. As a result he may have missed a natural element of childhood – fun and irresponsibility – and, as a grown man, made up for it with pranks and games.

First at English mission schools, then at an Islamic college, he was always top of the class, excelling also at drawing. A White Russian émigré, 'Colonel' George Alief, was engaged as his art tutor. From drawings of horses and cowboys he graduated to caricatures with which he regaled his friends throughout his life. Shortly after his sixteenth birthday he was sent off to Lebanon to become the youngest freshman of his year at the American University of Beirut.

Beirut in 1955 offered exhilarating freedoms to this boy fresh out of his sisters' quiet and sober household. The AUB was an extra-ordinary institution in those years, providing a rigorous grounding in American liberal studies in the classrooms and, outside them, in the leafy university gardens and the student cafes beyond the gates, a crash course in the fearsome complexities of Arab politics. It was a highly exciting moment to be an Arab. President Nasser was just beginning to inspire men with the hope of a reborn Arabism defiantly independent of the Western powers which had controlled Middle East destinies for so long. He had swung Arab opinion against the Western-sponsored Baghdad Pact, he had smashed the Western arms monopoly by buying weapons from the East, his 'Voice of the Arabs', broadcasting daily from Cairo, resounded across the air waves, and within a few months he was to bring the Arab world cheering to its feet with his takeover of the Suez Canal.

The students of the AUB, drawn from all over the area, were swept by these events into a high fever of debate and demonstra-tion. On campus the Ba'th Party, pioneers of Arab unity and quick to see in the Egyptian leader the instrument for realizing their pan-Arab dreams, were making most of the running. Their princi-pal rivals were the Communist Party, which regarded Arab nationalism of any sort as an obstacle to proletarian international-ism, and the Parti populaire syrien (PPS), which preached the unity of the Levant as a surer safeguard than pan-Arab unity for its varied minorities. These parties were not sedate discussion clubs. Each was more like a secret society, with its cell structure, clandestine recruitment, news-sheets and street fighters. The young Sharaf was attracted to none of them. But, heir to an Arab nationalist tradition, he could in no way keep aloof from the political ferment. The fact that his father had joined Rashid Ali and been punished by the Hashemite establishment in Iraq inclined him in a radical direction. The home he found was yet another conspiratorial outfit which was in later years to make a considerable mark in the Arab world. This was the Movement of Arab Nationalists (MAN).

In its early years at least, MAN was very secret indeed, rarely if

ever breaking cover and forbidding its members to talk shop
outside their clandestine cells. In this it resembled the other
organizations – indeed it deliberately modelled itself on the CP. It
was a time of secrecy when outsiders sensed that much was going
on but could not easily know who belonged to what. This underground ferment reflected the public crisis in Arab political society at
the time, with the collapse of traditional parties, with Nasser beginning to show his hand, and with emerging new forces competing
for supremacy. MAN was one of these. It had been formally
established only in 1954, but its roots reached back to the loss of
much of Palestine to the Jews in 1948, an event which gave a group
of chance-met students at the AUB a cause for life. There were four
of them with equal claim to be founders of the MAN – two
Palestinians, George Habash from Lydda and Wadih Haddad from
Safad; a Kuwaiti, Ahmad al-Khatib; and Hani al-Hindi, of Syrian
origin but an Iraqi by birth whose father had fled home to Syria after
the crushing of the Rashid Ali revolt. Three of them, Habash,
Haddad and Khatib, had studied medicine, and Hindi political
science. All four graduated before Sharaf reached Beirut, but their
organization continued to thrive, both there and elsewhere, and in
Beirut bore the imprint of the founders.

It was still earnestly puritanical – no dancing, no dating, no
football – and, without any ideology except nationalism, it was
totally obsessed with revenging the catastrophe of Palestine.
Palestine defined MAN's attitude to everything else. It loathed the
Left because Arab Communists, taking the lead from Russia, had
approved the partition of Palestine. Moreover the Communists
opposed Arab unity, without which, MAN believed, there could
be no Palestinian liberation. In fact MAN's founders were right-
wing nationalists, a tendency perhaps encouraged by their
American education. In contrast with today's young Muslim
activists, they did not think in religious terms, they attended neither
mosque nor church, and never considered which of them was
Muslim, which Christian. Over the years the movement attracted
sympathizers of two different sorts. While the backbone consisted
of poor Palestinians active in the refugee camps, the leadership was
dominated by young men of social position who wanted to play a
role in the nationalist struggle but had no time for left-wing
policies. Abd al-Hamid Sharaf was such a one.

During his first year at the AUB, MAN, like the Ba'th, joined the

Nasser bandwagon, but the movement was still too unimportant to attract the Egyptian leader's attention. Only when the Ba'th fell out with Nasser in 1959 did MAN move into the privileged slot as his principal ally in Arab Asia. By then Sharaf had lived through a few interesting moments. His move up the party ladder was rapid, from membership of a *halakah* (link), a sort of political seminar for candidates, through a *khaliyeh* (cell), with responsibilities for recruitment and supervision, to a *rabitah* (bond), grouping several cells, and finally to membership of a *shu'beh* (district command), directly linked to the *qiyyadah* or supreme leadership. The *shu'beh* of which he was a part was responsible for controlling MAN's university recruits.

His intellectual gifts were soon recognized. For a couple of years from 1958, when he was nineteen, he was one of a two-man 'ideological committee' entrusted with editing the party news-paper, *Al-Hurriyyah* (Freedom), and defining the movement's doctrinal stance. His associate in this enterprise was a brilliant, self-taught Lebanese Shi'ite, Muhsin Ibrahim, who in later years moved rapidly left to become one of the most prominent left-wing activists and ideologues of the Arab world. In their days together on the ideological committee, Abd al-Hamid had a tempering influ-ence on the fiery Muhsin. Jointly they faced the problem that MAN's intellectual resources were thin. In contrast to the corpus of Marxist doctrine which the Communists could call on, and to Michel Aflaq's visionary theories which inspired the Ba'th, MAN could fall back only on the writings of Sati' al-Husri, the pioneer spokesman between the world wars of secular pan-Arab national-ism whose major contribution was to give a nationalist stamp to the educational system in Iraq. To help fill the ideological void, Abd al-Hamid and Muhsin produced a stream of pamphlets and articles.

When the sixteen-year-old Sharaf had left Amman for Beirut to begin his university life, he was a loyal Jordanian who had enjoyed King Hussein's hospitality and was now benefiting from a govern-ment scholarship. But his radical activities in Beirut soon came to the attention of the authorities in Amman. It became known that this young Hashemite had been carried aloft by cheering anti-Hashemite students. The king was not amused. MAN was staunchly republican, robustly pro-Nasser, passionately opposed to the Western connection at a time when, after Suez, King Hussein with Western support was wrestling to retain his throne against the assaults of such nationalist officers as General Ali Abu Nuwar. In 1958 the pressures on Jordan became intense, first as a result of the union of Syria and Egypt, then with the murderous overthrow of the Hashemite monarchy in Iraq. To hold the radical forces in check, American marines landed in Beirut and British troops in Jordan.

Sharaf lived these events in his own nervous system. As a Hashemite but also a radical nationalist, he was torn in opposite directions. The killing of his royal relations in Baghdad was a shock – softened only by the fact that this was the branch of the family which had persecuted his father. When the Iraqi revolution occurred he was spending the summer holidays in Amman – and soon found himself in custody. Such was his estrangement from the regime and the security authorities' suspicion of him. But the king, always more inclined to forgive than to punish, soon let him out again. He returned to Beirut and his secret activities, took a BA degree in philosophy in 1959 (when his government scholarship ended), and stayed away from Jordan for the next three years.

In 1959, still at the AUB, Sharaf enrolled for a master's degree in international relations, which he was awarded in 1962. Without a scholarship, he helped keep himself by doing translations. His situation was eased when his sisters left Amman in their turn and eventually joined him and his elder brother, Fawaz, in a flat in Ras Beirut. But by then he had long known the young woman who was to become his wife.

Leila Najjar, a little dynamo of a girl, was, like Sharaf, extremely bright and, like him, a student at the AUB and a committed member of MAN. The daughter of a doctor, Leila was of Druze stock, a member of one of Lebanon's most ancient mountain communities. She and Abd al-Hamid were both eighteen when, in 1957, they met at the Arab Cultural Club, in effect a front organization run by MAN to attract and sort out likely candidates for membership. Leila was accepted in 1958 when Abd al-Hamid had already climbed high in the hierarchy, but she soon followed him up the ladder of responsibilities. Eventually she became the chairwoman of a national committee for women's activities. Through all these divergences of activity, the two young people kept closely in touch. Although they did not marry until 1965, theirs was a university romance which never dimmed.

Militants together, they began from 1961 onwards to lose their faith together, but it was less they who altered than the movement. From ideological discussion and social work, MAN was passing into the harsh, often brutal, world of revolutionary Arab politics. What really changed MAN's nature was the sharpened contest with the Ba'th once the United Arab Republic was created in 1958. Architects of the Egyptian–Syrian union, the Ba'th had been successful because of their links with influential Syrian army officers and their mass support. MAN felt it must travel the same road and started to establish clandestine links with army officers in many Arab countries. When Nasser quarrelled with the Ba'th in 1959, he turned MAN into an instrument to fight his former allies and pushed it further into activism.

But Sharaf was no revolutionary. He was repelled by the idea of violence. A small incident may serve to illustrate the point. MAN was in 1960 debating whether or not to drop the call for 'revenge' (against Israel) from its party slogans. Leila, still a Pasionaria, opposed the change, only to be teasingly rebuked by Abd al-Hamid as a 'savage Druze'.

MAN's lurch to the left in 1961 must also have contributed to Sharaf's disillusion. In the wake of Syria's defection from the UAR that year, which effectively put an end to Egypt's pan-Arab hopes, Nasser tried to regain the initiative by abruptly switching the focus of his policies from Arab unity to socialism. Most of his formerly right-wing disciples in MAN faithfully followed suit, but others, having no taste for intellectual somersaults, dropped out. Among them was Abd al-Hamid. The way was open for a reconciliation with King Hussein.

Sharaf and his brother Fawaz returned to Amman in 1961. A little earlier, a cousin, Sharif Zaid ibn Shaker, had also been at odds with the authorities and had had to give up his position in the army, but had subsequently been reconciled to the king. (He is now commander-in-chief of the armed forces.) Through his agency, the Sharaf brothers were accepted back on friendly terms. They were welcomed back to the family and to the service of their country. Fawaz was appointed to the Foreign Ministry and is at the time of writing ambassador in Bonn. Abd al-Hamid too was given a job in the Foreign Ministry, as Director of Arab Affairs at the age of twenty-three. The radical chapter was over, the reformer's had begun.

Sharaf owed the State of Jordan seven years of service for the funds spent on his education. In fact he was to repay the debt nearly three times over, spending the rest of his life in public office.

What is striking is how effortlessly, without apparent anxiety or self-doubt, he took to ever higher official responsibilities as if coming into his birthright. The hallmark of the man was his ability to perform complex and demanding tasks without being visibly stretched and with the gentlemanly nonchalance of those who do not question their right to lead.

Almost without apprenticeship he was catapulted by the king, who early recognized his promise, into top jobs. In 1963 he became director-general of broadcasting, the following year assistant to the head of the Royal Diwan, and after another twelve months, when he was barely twenty-six, Minister of Information and Culture in the government of Wasfi Tal, a post he held through two testing years until the June War of 1967. In these five years Sharaf was transformed from a graduate student into a valued member of the inner counsels of the Hashemite State. He had a ring-side seat from which to observe, and to be moulded by, crucial developments in the Arab world: the quarrelsome aftermath of the collapse of the Syrian–Egyptian union; the long drawn out agony of the Yemen war and the erosion of Nasser's prestige; the disappointing experiment of Ba'th rule in Iraq and Syria; and, finally, the crippling inter-Arab rivalries which gave Israel its chance in the blitzkrieg of June 1967 to destroy Arab power for a generation.

These events planted the seeds of a radical critique of Arab society which was to bear fruit a decade later when he became the king's most trusted adviser.

If on his upward progress Sharaf was shy about anything, it was about his youthfulness, but he disarmed criticism by his mastery of the subject in question, his wide reading, his intellectual approach – and also by a highly developed sense of mischief and an irreverent tendency to crack jokes. A trip abroad to Rome in 1963, when he was director of the radio station, gave him a chance to be his age. He joined a Jordanian friend studying painting there and for a few days lived as a poor student, sharing a room in a cheap hotel and living off pasta.

But these were years of achievement as well as of promise. In his tenure as Minister of Information and Culture he founded an institute of fine art, a national gallery (housed in a modest villa), a

music school, a separate department of art and culture in the
Ministry of Information, a national theatre troupe and Jordan's first
television station. He was fond of saying that it would do the Arabs
more good to produce one talented pianist than a hundred
ambassadors discoursing about 'the cause'. He believed that the
Arabs' cultural backwardness, as much as their military weakness,
was responsible for their defeat by Israel and for the discredit in
which they were held by the West.

In 1965 Sharaf was a member of the Jordanian delegation to the
non-aligned conference due to be held in Algiers. But as the dele-
gates were assembling, President Ben Bella was overthrown by the
army chief, Houari Boumedienne, and the conference was called
off. Thus unexpectedly released from work, Sharaf took the
opportunity to telegraph Leila Najjar in Beirut and ask her to meet
him in Paris and get married. The choice of a foreign capital was
deliberate. It may not have been considered entirely suitable for a
Hashemite to marry a Druze, and for their part the Druze certainly
had objections. To this day matters of personal status, such as
marriage, remain firmly in the hands of Lebanon's various ethnic
and religious communities, powers which are exercised in a
restrictive manner. A Muslim girl, for example, cannot marry
outside her religion. As a Druze Leila could not have got permission
in Lebanon to marry Sharaf. Dr Najjar, however, was tolerant, and
along with her brother and sisters accompanied his daughter to the
ceremony in Paris. But the honeymoon in London was interrupted
by a cable from Jordan's Prime Minister, Wasfi Tal, informing
Sharaf that he had been appointed Minister of Information, and the
newly-weds returned speedily to Amman. It was to be a good
marriage, rare as gold in any country. It was also a marriage of
equals, rare in the Arab world. Leila was to be Sharaf's greatest asset
for the rest of his life.

The West presents many Arab intellectuals with a painful dilemma.
Their natural affinity, their tastes and inclinations draw them
westwards, yet the West is indifferent, if not actively hostile, to
their national aspirations. The Soviet East has few seductions for
them, yet it puts its money, its arms and its diplomacy behind their
causes. It is no exaggeration to say that Sharaf lived with this
dilemma for the full nine years of his service in the United States,

from 1967 to 1976. He felt at home in America. There was much about American life that he enjoyed. He made many close friends. But as a representative of an Arab country he had to suffer the vagaries of America's Middle East policy under three presidents, see Israel always preferred, witness at the close of his life Egypt weened by Kissinger's diplomacy from the Arab camp leaving his own country with little practical chance of ever recovering its lost territory. Was America then a friend or an enemy? At any rate it was a model, but not always one to be followed. His natural liking for debate, free speech, the free practice of politics was undoubtedly confirmed by his American experience, but there were certain aspects of American democracy that he found less attractive, notably the working of the lobbies at the very centre of the legislative system, and among them the seemingly all-powerful pro-Israeli lobby. Professional frustrations apart, however, the American years were of great value. By exposing him to important events and to international colleagues often of high quality, they gave his mind an added sophistication and a sharper cutting edge.

He and Leila, still a very young couple, were sent to take over the Jordan embassy in Washington in the stormy aftermath of the Six Day War. It was not Sharaf's first visit to the United States. As a new AUB graduate in 1959 he had been awarded a 'leadership grant' to spend three months touring America and had enjoyed the experience very much. It was an indication of his intellectual appetites that no sooner had he returned as ambassador in 1967 than he enrolled as a doctoral student at Georgetown University, choosing to write his thesis on the Jarring peace mission as an example of international mediation. Jeane Kirkpatrick, then his teacher, was later to describe him as the brightest student she had ever taught in the School of Political Studies.

No ambassador can entirely escape the social round, but Sharaf did not enjoy diplomatic junketing, too often finding it frivolous and shallow. He preferred small dinner parties with well chosen guests and good talk. He liked the company of academics and journalists. When the Sharafs entertained he was conscious of the need not to be too lavish, sensitive to the fact that Jordan was a poor country taking aid from the United States. It fell to him to purchase an ambassadorial residence on behalf of his government and he typically chose an unostentatious house on Chevy Chase Circle. His distaste for display lasted throughout his life.

Take any decade in Arab politics and you can be sure to find it full of turmoil. But Sharaf's decade in America was a particularly historic one in which the course of Arab affairs was violently redirected. On arrival in Washington he had immediately to deal with the consequences of the 1967 War, a war which cut Jordan in half, destroyed Nasser's credibility and with it the hopes of a whole generation of Arab nationalists, and which could not but be felt a profound humiliation for every Arab. To Jordan – and to its ambassador – fell the difficult task of acting as a bridge between the Arabs and the West, seeing that many leading Arab states had severed relations with Washington.

Out of the rubble of war grew the Palestinian guerrilla movements, reviving Arab morale but in their impatient and rebellious vitality posing a challenge to their host Arab countries. To save its political order Jordan was compelled to take on the militias in an anguished fratricidal struggle in 1970–71, from which it emerged victorious but the target of bitter abuse and criticism from its brother Arabs. Although outside Jordan and distant from the battle on the ground, Sharaf had to summon cool nerve and dignity to face the diplomatic fall-out of his country's isolation. In the middle of this trying period, in 1971, he was transferred from the Washington embassy to take up the post of Jordan's permanent representative at the United Nations, where his skill and tact were to play a large part in effecting a reconciliation between the Hashemite kingdom and its Arab critics. Within a few months of his arrival in New York, Sharaf had captured the trust of his fellow Arab ambassadors and the chairmanship of their Information Committee.

In Washington Sharaf had served his country well, making many influential friends in Congress and various government agencies, particularly among the 'Arabists' of the State Department. But at the United Nations he was truly in his element, although these were years when Jordan faced new challenges. Jordan played no part in the October war and was held on the margin of the complex negotiations which led to Israel's disengagement agreements with Egypt and Syria. The two agreements with Egypt of 1973 and 1975 – and particularly the latter – were viewed with mounting alarm in the Arab world where they were rightly seen as removing Egypt from the battlefield and thus destroying any future Arab military option. The true significance of these developments was that, after twenty years of active involvement in the affairs of Arab Asia

(1955-75), Egypt was now distancing itself to pursue the narrower path of its national interests. But with the removal of its weight, Arab Asia became far more vulnerable to Israeli power – and to its own disruptive rivalries and tensions, as was tragically demonstrated in Lebanon. To protect Jordan from the engulfing turbulence took nimble footwork. These were among the problems with which Sharaf would have to wrestle when he returned to high office in Jordan in 1976.

The years in New York were the last in which the Sharafs had the comparative space and leisure to be themselves. They relished the freedom of living in New York and the intellectual opportunities it offered. Sharaf biked and ran and played with his two boys, Nasser and Faris, in Central Park, browsed in bookshops, went to concerts and theatres, but his great love was the cinema. He had an encyclo-paedic knowledge of films, read the specialist magazines, some-times slipped out from tedious receptions to go to the movies. He used to say that if he had not been a politician, he would have liked to be a film director (he could equally have been a first-class journalist or an academic). But although he loved New York, he never identified culturally with the United States. As with many other Arab intellectuals, attraction was countered by distaste for some aspects of American life and especially for American conven-tional attitudes towards the Middle East. At times Sharaf saw America as a dinosaur, small of brain and beefy of body, whose embrace could be smothering even for its friends.

In July 1976, ten days after his thirty-seventh birthday, Sharaf was asked by the king to assume the responsibilities of head of the Royal Diwan – in effect to become the king's closest adviser on the whole range of domestic and foreign affairs.

He was to prove that most valuable of advisers, one not afraid to speak his mind. As a man with intimate personal knowledge of radical thinking, as a diplomat with long high-level experience in the West, and above all as a Hashemite, he was able to defend positions which from another adviser might have been overruled. There was a profound sympathy between the king and Sharaf. Each seemed able to pick up and develop the other's ideas – a creative partnership which for four years was of great value to Jordan.

Sharaf's personal qualities commanded respect. He was a man so even-tempered, calm and rational that he was not easy to quarrel with. Like all truly persuasive men, he had a genuine interest in dialogue. No one could doubt the power of his intellect, the extent of his knowledge, the openness of his mind, or his capacity for work, but he was so modest and free from self-importance that these qualities lay lightly upon him. What made his personality not simply impressive but also lovable was an impish sense of fun which came bubbling out in quips and puns and sometimes irreverence. Once when he was already Prime Minister, he attended an open-air graduation ceremony at Yarmouk University. As tends to happen on formal occasions, the rhetoric was floridly long-winded. To cut it short, Sharaf angled his wrist so as to reflect a shaft of sunlight from the glass of his watch into the speaker's eyes. The king, seated at his side, suddenly became aware that his Prime Minister was playing a practical joke.

Sharaf saw himself as a pragmatic modern nationalist. He believed in Arab unity, not in its old romantic Nasserist sense, but rather as the outcome of steady, step-by-step cooperation. Jordan's well-being in his view lay, first, in establishing sound working relations with the Palestinians both inside and outside Jordan, and then in having balanced relations with its principal Arab neighbours, Iraq, Syria and Saudi Arabia.

In his years at the Royal Diwan his greatest service to his king and country was to help steer Jordan through the treacherous waters of regional politics after Anwar Sadat's visit to Jerusalem. To him it was common sense that if the Arabs were ever to evolve an effective strategy towards Israel, they had to end their petty quarrels and reach a general consensus. Arab solidarity was the basis of his Arab policy and in his view the key to peace. It was a policy which stood him in good stead when the great test came over Camp David. Jordan faced enormous pressure to join the American-sponsored peace process. But the risks were too high and the inducements too few. The king and his chief adviser concluded that it was necessary to oppose Camp David, to attend the Baghdad summit in November 1978, and to commit Jordan to the majority Arab position, whatever the painful strains on relations with the West.

It was a striking testimony of the king's faith in Sharaf's judgment that he should call him to the premiership in December 1979, at the close of a momentous year in the politics of the region. In that year King Hussein's close friend, the Shah of Iran, had been swept from power by Islamic revolution; Sadat had signed his peace treaty with Israel, uniting most of the Arab world against him; Islamic radicalism had surfaced violently in Saudi Arabia itself, in the seizure of the Great Mosque at Mecca; and American hostages had begun their long ordeal in Tehran. Arab rejectionism, Islamic fundamentalism, Palestinian despair, Western pressure – such were among the forces with which Jordan had to come to terms. Jordan's continued prosperity and stability are proof enough that the policy decisions taken at that time were sound.

What Sharaf did as premier was to introduce radical policies at home to match the challenges abroad. From his first day in office everyone was aware that a fresh, young, modern, liberal leader was now in charge. Men with a radical past were included in his cabinet. Jordanians had the novel experience of seeing a Prime Minister in his shirt-sleeves arguing the toss with the public. One of his earliest moves was to set up a bureau of complaints attached to his own office, giving the humblest citizen access to him. But beneath the informal style and the innovations lay a coherent programme of domestic reform. This was outlined in a sweeping political manifesto, itself a new departure in Jordanian politics.

What, then, were Sharaf's political themes? From the torrent of his ideas, three may be picked out as central to his thinking.

The first of these was undoubtedly the theme of participation. Sharaf was a democrat who was profoundly disturbed by the lack of institutions and the exercise of whim in Arab society. He was of course aware that Jordan in its turbulent environment could not adopt a representational system such as he had seen in the West, but he was certain that a process of democratization had to be started. When head of the Royal Diwan he had advised the king to initiate the successful experiment of a National Consultative Council as a platform, in the absence of an elected forum, for the discussion of national issues. As premier he strove to make the NCC more independent and authoritative. At the same time he worked to decentralize power, eager to introduce more regional self-government throughout the country and to give under-secretaries and directors-general of ministries real executive responsibility. He believed strongly in the freedom of the press, although he acknowledged the need for public opinion to be guided. He wanted people to argue issues through and he enjoyed doing it himself. A newspaper editor recalls how Sharaf at the end of a busy day would telephone him at 11 p.m. to suggest they discuss some controversial subject over a hamburger and a cup of coffee. Determined that Jordan's professional associations should play a bigger role in social development, Sharaf talked often to bankers and businessmen and tried, for instance, to get the Syndicate of Engineers to finance an engineering school for the university.

But where Sharaf showed himself to be more of a social thinker than simply a politician was in his understanding that for a healthy society it was the individual and not just the constitution which needed changing. This could be described as the second strand of his philosophy: the importance he gave to reforming the educational system, to promoting women's rights, and to defending the dignity of the individual. Many Jordanians remember that, as a newly appointed premier, he paid a visit to the prison and freed all prisoners who had served more than half their term and all those not sentenced for violent or political crimes. To the astonishment of the wardens, he insisted that his bodyguards remain outside the jail and his ADC leave his gun in the guardroom. Nor would he allow photographers to accompany him, arguing that to take pictures of men behind bars was an affront to their dignity.

The notion that the renaissance of Arab society starts with the re-education of Arab man is of course an old one, shared by both Sati' al-Husri and Michel Aflaq, to name only two of the more recent ideologues of Arab nationalism. Sharaf proposed to give it modern and practical application.

The third theme to which Sharaf gave attention concerned at its narrowest the uses and abuses of money and, more broadly, what could be called the quality of life. Thus he was very keen on the conservation of resources and launched a campaign to urge people to save water, petrol, electricity – what he termed rather conceptually the 'rationalization of consumption'. As in his private life, so in affairs of state he was opposed to gross and profligate consumerism and to the tendency of wealthy Jordanians to buy imported luxuries the country could ill afford. He wanted to reform the tax system, to make sure the privileged private sector contributed its share to government revenues, and to stamp out corruption and profiteering in the public service. Inevitably these views were not welcome to everyone.

In a word, Sharaf was a very radical Prime Minister who would certainly have left a permanent mark on his own society and might

even have created a model for export to the Arab world, had he
lived to see his ideas through.

Apart from King Hussein, who has directed Jordan's destinies for
thirty years, this small country has in recent times produced two
men of vision, both of them cut down before their time. One was
Wasfi Tal, the other Abd al-Hamid Sharaf. They were on the best of
terms and learned from each other. It must be said, however, that
Wasfi was an earthier, more home-grown product, who could
claim to know every hill-top, every chieftain, the name of every
camel. He was a leader rooted in Jordanian soil. Abd al-Hamid did
not know his country so intimately. He was not a man of the
masses. He was happier with ideas than with instincts, but he shared
with Wasfi a dream of what their country could become.

Just before dawn on 3 July 1980 Jordan's editors were wakened by
telephone calls requesting them to return to their newspapers and
stop the presses. There was widespread consternation. Was the
country in danger? Then came the news that their young, bold and
brave Prime Minister was dead. 'It was a very great shock,' one of
them recalls. 'As if in a dream I recast the front page and gave it to
the printers. Then I went out to my car and wept. He had given us a
vision of the future, a glimpse beyond the horizon. But his life
snapped, and now we must try to realize his dreams without him.'

Part I Jordan

Jordan and Palestine

Peter Mansfield

The lands of Palestine and Jordan cannot be defined in terms of precise geographical borders. But as an idea and inspiration they will survive as long as humanity.

They occupy the region lying between the Mediterranean and the Arabian Desert and stretching from the Litani river in the north to the Gaza valley in the south, which in ancient times straddled one of the great highways of the world, linking Asia with Africa and connecting the first civilized communities known to man.

It is a mountainous land of great beauty, with narrow plains and valleys. Rainfall is rarely abundant but sufficient to make it fertile compared with the great deserts to the south and east. The name Palestine is derived from the Philistines, a people who infiltrated and occupied the coastal plain in the twelfth century BC. (The Philistines, through no fault of their own, have suffered in history because of the custom initiated by German students in the nineteenth century of referring to anyone who had not been to a university – and was therefore presumably uncultured – as a Philistine.)

Before the arrival of the Philistines, the region was known as the Land of Canaan after its principal inhabitants. Other invaders or infiltrators, attracted by its fertile valleys and plains, were drawn in from the surrounding deserts and among them were the Israelites who came in from the east at about the same time as the Philistines arrived from the sea. Some two centuries later the Israelite tribes were united by David to form the first and only Kingdom of Israel in Palestine with Jerusalem as its capital. This united kingdom lasted just seventy years until it split into two, with the southern half – Judah – forming an alliance with Syria. This survived for 300 years while Israel, the northern half, lasted for 200. By 587 BC Jewish rule in Palestine came to an end for some 2,400 years.

After the destruction of the Kingdom of Judah Palestine came under the rule of pagans for nine centuries – first Babylonians, then Persians, then Greeks under Alexander the Great and finally the Romans under Pompey in 63 BC.

It was under pagan Roman rule that Jesus Christ was born, lived and died in Palestine, and some 300 years after his death the Roman Empire became Christianized. The Jews in Palestine rebelled twice against their Roman rulers – first in 66-70 AD when the Emperor Titus destroyed Jerusalem and finally in 132-135 AD under Hadrian when the Jews were either killed or scattered into exile.

But it was not only the Jews who challenged the Romans. The Nabataean Arabs, who dominated the caravan trade with Arabia from their rock-hewn capital in the secret valley of Petra in the south of modern Jordan, defied imperial Rome for decades. Their powerful and civilized merchant state for a time included Damascus and modern Lebanon and also stretched into Arabia along the east coast of the Red Sea. Their art and architecture were Hellenistic but their writing was a form of Aramaic and their speech was Arabic. The language and alphabet of the Nabataeans can be regarded as the parents of those of the Holy Quran. It is not fanciful to suggest that the Nabataean inheritance lies behind the individuality of modern Jordan.

Byzantine or Christian Roman rule lasted another three centuries until it was replaced by that of the new all-conquering faith which burst out of Arabia some six hundred years after the death of Jesus – Islam. In 638 AD Jerusalem surrendered to the Caliph Omar. The majority of the people of Palestine became Muslims by religion as they were already Arab by language and culture.

The Arabs ruled Palestine for five centuries until the establishment of the Latin Kingdom of Jerusalem in 1099 AD. After the recovery of the Holy City by Saladin in 1187 it came under the rule of the Sultans of Egypt for another 400 years. Then in 1517 AD the Ottoman Turks, the new great political and military power of

Islam, captured Palestine from the Arabs and ruled it for another 400 years.

The conquest of the Ottoman Turks, like that of the Muslim Arabs in the seventh century, did not mean any full-scale colonization or dispossession of the indigenous inhabitants. Palestine was linked administratively to Damascus until 1830 when it was placed under Sidon and then under Acre until, in the general administrative reorganization of 1887-88, Palestine was divided into the *mutassarifiyeh* of Nablus and Acre, part of the *Vilayet* or province of Beirut, while the autonomous *mutassarifiyeh* of Jerusalem, comprising about two-thirds of the population of Palestine, was placed under the direct authority of Constantinople. The overwhelming majority of the people were Arab peasants, Christian and Muslim, who worked the lands of the large landowning families. Economically, Palestine was a relatively stagnant but peaceful region of the Ottoman Empire. However, in the early part of the twentieth century the Palestinian Arabs shared in the general Arab renaissance. Their elite found opportunities for service in the Ottoman Empire. The small Jewish population (about 60,000 out of a total of about 700,000) lived mainly in the towns. But already by the beginning of the twentieth century, the people of Palestine were becoming seriously alarmed by the arrival of Zionist immigrants, mostly from Russia, who set up their own exclusive colonies in the countryside.

After the administrative reorganization of 1888, the land east of the River Jordan which was later Transjordan, was in theory administered from Damascus, capital of the *Vilayet* of Syria. But, thinly populated and with few resources, the region was largely autonomous under the great tribal confederations such as the Howeitat in the south and Bani Saqr in the north.

This relatively tranquil situation was transformed by the outbreak of the First World War in April 1914. By November the Ottoman Empire had joined Germany and Austro-Hungary against Britain, France and Russia and Britain at once adopted a strategy of allying itself with a revolt of the Arabs against the Ottomans. Modern Arab nationalism was still only a nascent movement but it was fed by the domineering and repressive policies of the Turks in their Arab provinces which greatly intensified after the outbreak of war. A leader for the Arab Revolt appeared in Hussein ibn Ali, thirty-seventh in line of descent from the Prophet Muhammad and

member of the Hashemite family of Arabia who held the prestigious post of Grand Sharif of Mecca. Negotiations followed
between Britain and the Sharif until the latter raised the flag of
revolt against the Turks in June 1916.

But the agreement between Britain and the Arabs on the future
shape of the Middle East after the defeat of the Ottoman Empire,
when the Arabs hoped to govern themselves, was far from clear.
Moreover it conflicted with two other undertakings of Britain: to
its principal ally France to divide the region into their respective
spheres of influence and to the Zionists to assist with the establishment of a Jewish National Home in Palestine. On 2 November 1917
the Sharif Hussein proclaimed himself 'King of the Arab Countries'
but this was unacceptable to Britain and France. As a compromise,
they agreed to recognize him as King of the Hijaz in January 1917.

The Arab irregular forces led by the Sharif Hussein's third son
Amir Faisal played a key role in the defeat of the Ottoman Turks.
Armed tribesmen, with a core of regular troops, carried out
guerrilla operations on the right flank of the British Expeditionary
Force from Egypt under General Allenby as it advanced into
Palestine. By a daring stroke they captured Aqaba in July 1917.
Allenby's advance took Jerusalem on 9 December and after a delay
because of the severe winter and stiff Turkish resistance, Damascus
fell on 1 October 1918. The Turks capitulated on 30 October and
the Ottoman Empire came to an end.

Wild Arab rejoicing greeted the liberation of Syria; the civilian
population had suffered desperately from famine and Turkish
repression. Faisal's troops entered the captured cities in triumph and
took over the administration. But Britain's obligations to its
principal ally immediately began to assert themselves. The whole of
Greater Syria was divided into Occupied Enemy Territory
Administration (OETA) regions. British OETA South covered
approximately the area of the subsequent Palestine mandate, the
French-administered OETA West comprised the whole Syrian and
Lebanese coastal area from Tyre to Cilicia. It was only in OETA
East – the Syrian interior – that Faisal and the Arabs maintained
some autonomy but France was determined that even this should
not last. Meanwhile, Iraq was placed under a single Anglo–Indian
administration with a British civil commissioner at its head.

Amir Faisal attempted to represent the interests of the Arabs at
the Paris Peace Conference where the future of the non-Turkish

provinces of the Ottoman Empire was decided. But he was in a weak position, heavily dependent on British power; neither Britain nor France recognized him as representing more than the Hijaz.

Nevertheless, Faisal and his Arab nationalist followers were determined to try to establish an independent Arab Syria. Elections were held wherever possible throughout Syria – that is where they were not blocked by the French – and a General Syrian Congress called for recognition of the independence of Syria (including Palestine) and Iraq. In March 1920 the Congress passed another resolution proclaiming the independence of Syria under Faisal as king.

Faisal's authority never extended to Palestine, where the British were firmly in control, but during 1919, when he was creating a rudimentary government in Damascus, he sent officials into Transjordan who, with the help of Faisal's prestige, succeeded in establishing a measure of order. But it was not to last. Britain and France reacted swiftly to block the Damascus resolutions. In May 1920 the Supreme Council of the League of Nations announced the partition of Greater Syria into the two French mandates of Lebanon and Syria and the British mandate of Palestine, while Iraq was to remain undivided as a British mandate. The British mandate for Palestine carried with it the obligation to carry out the terms of the Balfour Declaration. By July 1920 the French forces had occupied Damascus and driven Faisal into exile.

The French could not take over Transjordan because it came under British control. The first British High Commissioner included in his jurisdiction the entire area of Palestine and Transjordan. However, Britain administered Transjordan differently through a system of local self-goverment with British advisers. Three rudimentary governments were set up – one in Ajlun for the north, one in Amman for the centre and a third in Kerak for the south. From Ma'an southwards came under the rule of King Hussein as part of the independent Kingdom of Hijaz.

This was the situation when Faisal's elder brother Abdullah arrived in Ma'an in November 1920 at the head of some tribal forces. It was widely thought that he intended to advance into Syria to avenge his brother Faisal. Knowing that the British were already planning to help Faisal become King of Iraq – a throne he had expected for himself – he was staking out his own claim. As he advanced northwards to Amman and Ajlun, the people flocked to his support.

This was one more threat to Britain's Middle East plans which were already endangered by a full-scale revolt in Iraq and violent Arab opposition to Zionist encroachments in Palestine. Winston Churchill, the new Secretary of State for the Colonies, decided to act. At a conference in Cairo in March 1921 it was confirmed that Faisal should accede to the throne of Iraq. Churchill then proceeded to Jerusalem to reassure the Palestinian Arabs that Britain would not allow Palestine to be turned into a Jewish state and to confer with Abdullah. Churchill rejected Abdullah's various proposals for the incorporation of Transjordan either into Iraq or Palestine under an Arab administration, but agreed to a provisional arrangement whereby Britain recognized Abdullah as Amir of Transjordan with an annual British subsidy until Britain could persuade France to restore an Arab state in Syria with Abdullah at its head. Since the French had no such intention the provisional arrangement became permanent and the state of Transjordan came into existence. From 1927 onwards the British High Commissioner for Palestine received a separate commission for Transjordan.

The Amir Abdullah was then thirty-nine years old. His skills were political rather than military. Gifted and shrewd, he soon made his impoverished desert territory into a peaceful and relatively well-administered, if patriarchal, state with its own powerful identity. Although his claim to rule was based on Hashemite pan-Arabism he secured the fierce loyalty of most of the local tribal leaders to himself and his family.

The hand of the mandate was light in Transjordan. Britain's role was confined to providing a handful of advisers and helping to create a small trained defence force – the Arab Legion. Abdullah was able to secure one supreme advantage for Transjordan – its exclusion from the provisions of the Balfour Declaration. In 1922 a British Government White Paper excluded Transjordan from the area of Jewish settlement.

So it was that Transjordan's political development was entirely different from that of Palestine. Already in 1923 Transjordan was declared an independent state in principle, although the British continued to control finance and foreign affairs and a series of agreements gradually reduced the British role until the independent Hashemite Kingdom of Jordan came into existence in 1946.

In contrast the political situation in Palestine inexorably deterio-rated through the 1920s and 1930s as the British searched vainly to resolve two incompatible aims – the Palestinians' desire for a free Arab Palestine and the Zionist objective of a Jewish state. Although the Palestinian Arabs at the beginning of the mandate formed over ninety per cent of the population, their internal divisions and their lack of experience in international affairs made them politically weaker than the Zionists who were dedicated to the point of fanaticism and could always rally support for their cause in the British Parliament. The traditional leadership of Arab notables gradually lost their credit among the younger generation of Palestinians. One member of the Husseini family, Hajj Amin al-Husseini, acquired special prominence through his appointment as Mufti of Jerusalem in 1921 and President of the Supreme Muslim Council in the following year although the right of Hajj Amin and his family to leadership was strongly contested by others such as the Nashashibis.

The Palestinians gained sympathy and support throughout the Arab and Muslim worlds but this was not effective in countering the threat of Zionist political and economic power which grew steadily under the umbrella of the mandate. In desperation the Arab political parties joined in April 1936 to form an Arab Higher Committee, presided over by Hajj Amin. The Committee called a general strike and at the same time Arab rebels, joined by volunteers from Syria, took to the hills. A general Arab rebellion broke out which lasted intermittently until 1939 when it was put down by overwhelming British military force.

The Palestinian Arab community was shattered and exhausted by the rebellion. However, its position appeared to improve during the Second World War as the British Government decided that the pledges contained in the Balfour Declaration had been fulfilled. In a 1939 White Paper Jewish immigration was to be limited to 75,000 over the next five years after which it would be subject to Arab acquiescence. After ten years an end to the mandate and an independent Palestine would be considered.

Although the Palestinians distrusted the British Government and disliked the possibility that the mandate would be extended beyond ten years, they were conciliated enough to end their opposition for the duration of the War. They still formed over two-thirds of the population of Palestine and despite substantial transfers of land, the Zionists still owned less than seven per cent of Palestinian territory. The Zionists, on the other hand, detested and opposed the White

Paper. They were restrained only as long as Hitler's threat to Britain's survival continued. During the war they switched their main international base from Britain to the United States while in Palestine they built up their underground armies and arms supplies in preparation for the coming struggle against the British and the Arabs.

Transjordan was developing differently and separately during this period but it was far from insulated from events in Palestine. There were many ties of blood between the people of the two banks and owing to the higher levels of education among Palestinians, some were recruited as officials for the fledgling administration in Amman. Inevitably, Transjordanians felt emotionally involved in the unfolding tragedy of Palestine. However, an element of territorial nationalism was growing up in Transjordan as it did elsewhere in the former Arab provinces of the Ottoman Empire. A feeling of 'Transjordan for the Transjordanians' was eventually translated into a law confining government posts to Transjordanians. This was opposed by Arab nationalists who maintained that nothing should intensify the artificially imposed divisions between the Arabs but in practical terms the separate development of Transjordan had the support of the great majority of the population of the country. Moreover, a number of Arabs of the political elite of neighbouring lands – Palestine, Syria and the Hijaz – came and settled in Transjordan. The three Prime Ministers of the early years of the Kingdom were all of Syrian origin.

Abdullah – who became King Abdullah in 1946 – had come to Transjordan as a pan-Arab nationalist. This was the source of his prestige. He believed in the unity of the Arabs as much as did the nationalists of Jerusalem or Damascus. But he saw it in terms of unity under Hashemite leadership – that is of himself and his cousins in Iraq. He had never abandoned his family's claims in Syria. He did not include Egypt in this concept or the Arabian Peninsula which by 1925 had been lost by the Hashemites to Ibn Saud. While awaiting developments elsewhere in Greater Syria, he wisely preferred to build up his power base in Transjordan which, though smaller and poorer than Palestine or Syria, had the advantage that he could rule it effectively through his personal authority.

Abdullah's stand gave him many enemies among Arab nationalists who opposed the Hashemites. They ranged from the Husseini family in Palestine to republicans in Syria. He had his supporters in both countries but they did not predominate. A further blow to his aims was the establishment in 1945 of the Arab League with its headquarters in Cairo. It was no longer practical to exclude Egypt from plans for Arab unity.

When in 1947 an exhausted and despairing Britain handed the problem of Palestine over to the UN and a US-dominated Security Council voted to partition Palestine into Jewish and Arab states with Jerusalem and its surrounding area internationalized, war became inevitable. The Palestinian Arabs, who were still two-thirds of the population, rejected a decision which gave fifty-five per cent of the land to the Zionists and no one was prepared to enforce partition. Fighting broke out before the British mandate formally ended on 15 May 1948, causing a mass exodus of Palestinian Arabs, but the regular armies of Egypt, Syria, Iraq and Transjordan did not cross into Palestine before the British had withdrawn. Already the Zionists had proclaimed the State of Israel and been recognized by both the USA and USSR.

King Abdullah, like the other Arab leaders, had hoped that his regular forces would not be engaged but would secure the territory allotted to the Arabs under partition. The Arab Legion was well-trained but consisted only of a front-line force of 4,500 without reservists. For weapons it depended entirely on Britain and its Commander-in-Chief, General Glubb, was British. However, it soon became apparent that no steps were being taken by the UN to install an international regime in Jerusalem which was about to be overrun by the Zionists. With its Iraqi allies the Legion held the central sector of Palestine and maintained the siege of the Jewish population in Jerusalem until both sides accepted the first UN truce of June 1948. But the ceasefire broke down, the Arab siege of West Jerusalem was broken and sporadic fighting, with the Zionists increasingly gaining the upper hand, continued until Jordan and Israel signed an armistice agreement on 3 May 1949. Only an enclave of twenty-one per cent of Palestine remained in Arab hands – including Hebron, Bethlehem, Ramallah, Nablus and the Old City of Jerusalem.

Mistrust and rivalry between the Arab states, poor equipment and training of most of the Arab forces, the fierce determination and skill of the Zionists, backed by powerful international sympathy and support, combined to defeat the Arabs.

By the end of the war, Transjordan controlled what was left of

Arab Palestine (with the exception of Gaza), and King Abdullah determined to unite these West Bank territories with his Kingdom. (In June 1949 the name of the state was formally changed to the Hashemite Kingdom of Jordan.) The majority of the inhabitants of the enclave, defenceless and in imminent danger of being swallowed up by the Zionists, saw no alternative and in December 1948 a conference of some 2,000 Arab notables at Jericho invited King Abdullah to unite Palestine and Jordan. The move was bitterly opposed both by the Arab Higher Committee, which had set up its own all-Palestine Government in Gaza, and by the other Arab states, who tried unsuccessfully to block it. In the autumn of 1949 they united to challenge his hold over the Old City of Jerusalem by reverting to the 1947 partition resolution which provided for the internationalization of Jerusalem. But since the Israelis rejected internationalization the move failed. The Arab states never gave wholehearted support to the Gaza all-Palestine Government which, lacking any practical authority, soon became a phantom.

During the rest of 1949 King Abdullah tried to secure improved terms with the Israelis – including an outlet to the sea at Haifa – but the Israelis were in no mood to give up anything they had seized. Embittered and appalled by the disaster, most Arabs were in a rejectionist mood. King Abdullah's many enemies denounced his vain efforts to make peace with Israel. King Abdullah proceeded with the unification of the East and West Banks of Jordan. The act of union took place on 24 April 1950 after elections had been held on the two banks to a Chamber of Deputies which had been doubled in size to accommodate the Palestinians. Four leading Palestinians joined the cabinet. Reluctantly the other Arab states accepted the *de facto* existence of the united Kingdom of Jordan.

The new enlarged Kingdom faced almost impossibly difficult political and economic circumstances. The new population was larger than the original inhabitants of Transjordan and about half a million of them were destitute refugees from occupied Palestine. The new frontiers were mere armistice lines which often separated villagers from their lands, divided Jerusalem into two unequal halves and cut off the Kingdom from any access to the Mediterranean. While the majority of the new population accepted the act of unification they had done so in a state of political shock and to some extent because there was no alternative. Only some felt loyalty to King Abdullah while others were bitterly hostile. Some had reservations about being ruled by Transjordanians whom they regarded as less advanced than themselves. Transjordan, although formally independent, was in reality still under the heavy influence of Britain, which the Palestinians held chiefly to blame for their fate. Moreover, the deep-seated belief of the Palestinians, as of most Arabs, was that with right and justice on their side, they would eventually be allowed to return to their homes in Palestine.

The Jordanian Government's response to this sensitive situation was inevitably ambiguous. While it tried to carry out the political integration of the new population – both West Bankers and refugees – and was the only Arab state to offer the refugees full citizenship, it continued, like the other Arabs, to maintain that the refugees were primarily an international political and economic responsibility and would never abandon their Right of Return. Thus it both aimed to combat Palestinian separatism and maintain its right to speak for the Palestinians while proclaiming that one day an Arab Palestine would be restored. This unavoidable 'paradox of Jordan' has lasted until quite recent times; it was the basis for its political difficulties for some twenty-five years. From a desperately difficult starting-point, Jordan made remarkable social and economic progress in the 1950s and 1960s. A steady flow of Western aid, a relatively efficient administration and the skill and energy of the people combined to transform the country. Palestinian and Jordanian enterprise enabled Amman to blossom into a major city. But the anomaly of the country's Jordanian/Palestinian dual nature constantly threatened its very existence.

Both Jordan's precariousness and its durability were at once demonstrated when King Abdullah was assassinated in the al-Aqsa Mosque in Jerusalem on 20 July 1951. A member of the Husseini family was the most prominent of those implicated although not Hajj Amin, who then headed the shadowy all-Palestine Government in the Egyptian-controlled Gaza Strip.

Abdullah was succeeded by his eldest son Talal. Despite his ill-health, which caused him to abdicate a year later, he was able to carry out some domestic reforms and improve relations with the Arab states. The succession passed to his seventeen-year-old son Hussein who was still at school in England and came to the throne on attaining his majority in 1953.

The prospects for Jordan were hardly reassuring. Only some of the fifty per cent of the population who were Palestinian by birth gave their loyalty to the monarchy. Some held high positions in government and the administration while others prospered in business, trade and banking but even some of these clung to the hope of a restoration of Arab Palestine. The great majority – half a million of them refugees living in camps – had nothing else to look forward to. None without exception remained unaffected by the pan-Arab storm which swept the Arab world in the 1950s, finding its principal expression in Nasserism and Ba'th socialism. Many Transjordanians – especially the youth – were influenced by the same trends and the fact that the Jordan Government was still closely associated with Britain and the West, while Arab nationalism was increasingly neutralist, added to the government's difficulties.

The young king, who had to gain experience rapidly in order to survive, pursued a policy of alternately bowing to the storm and confronting it. He never wavered in his belief that the Hashemites were the true founders and inheritors of the pan-Arab cause. In December 1955 he gave up any idea of taking Jordan into the British-sponsored Baghdad Pact after serious rioting swept the country. A few months later he gained wild popularity by dismissing Glubb Pasha, the British commander of his army. Yet in April 1957, when the anti-Western Nasserist tide was at its height, he asked for the resignation of his own neutralist government, which had terminated the Anglo–Jordanian treaty and planned to establish relations with Moscow. With the help of loyal troops, the king foiled an attempted coup, imposed martial law and dissolved parliament and the political parties. Henceforward the United States became the main supplier of essential economic and military aid to Jordan.

The vicissitudes of Arab politics helped the king. Rivalry between Nasserism and Ba'thism and the collapse of the Syrian–Egyptian union in 1961 enabled the Jordanian monarchy to survive even the destruction of its principal ally – the Hashemite monarchy in Iraq.

Nevertheless, the problem of Jordan's internal security was desperately difficult. Any border incident in which a Palestinian individual or small group attempted to penetrate into Israel to carry out raids provoked immediate massive retaliation by the Israeli armed forces against civilians. Israel never acknowledged Jordan's efforts to prevent such incidents. The feelings aroused among the

Palestinians in Jordan caused demonstrations which bordered on revolt. The King had moments of deep pessimism. There were several attempts on his life and those of his ministers.

The other Arab states might dispute Jordan's right to represent the Palestinians, as they had done in the days of King Abdullah, but they were not agreed on any alternative. The Palestinians them-selves, during this period, were prepared to merge with the general pan-Arab cause. They spoke of the Arab liberation of Palestine rather than Palestine liberation. They did not at this stage think in terms of establishing their own movement with its own leadership. However, from the end of the 1950s this attitude began gradually to change. The Fatah guerrilla organization came secretly into exist-ence in 1958; experience of resisting the Israeli occupation of Gaza in 1956–57 had shown the different Palestinian political groups they were capable of common action. The concept of a 'Palestinian entity' began to take shape.

It was partly in recognition of this trend that the Arab heads of state agreed, with varying degrees of enthusiasm, to the establish-ment of the Palestine Liberation Organization in 1964 with Ahmed Shuqairy, Palestine representative at the Arab League, as Chairman of its Executive Committee, and to the creation of a Palestine Liberation Army. On Jordan's insistence, however, the PLO had no sovereignty over any territory and the PLA did not train or exercise in Jordan.

The situation was transformed by the 1967 War. Jordan joined in as the ally of Egypt. Despite previous hostility between King Hussein and President Nasser, Jordan could not remain neutral when Syria and Egypt were involved. As a result of the war Israel occupied the remaining twenty-one per cent of Palestine.

Economically the war was a shattering blow for Jordan. While most of the country's nascent industry was sited on the East Bank, much of its agriculture and most of the vital tourist industry were on the West Bank. Both the military and the political situations were unresolved. The 1967 defeat gave a wholly new impetus to the development of the PLO as an independent liberation movement. It was as if the Palestinians had collectively decided that they could no longer rely on the pan-Arab movement to further their cause.

In 1968 Yasser Arafat took over as Chairman of the PLO Executive. The quasi-parliament of the Palestine National Council took on new life and the various guerrilla organizations in the PLO, of which al-Fatah was the most important, began to develop their own military and civilian institutions – training camps, schools and medical services. Many of these were sited in Jordan and Palestinian commando raids into Israel caused daily artillery duels and heavy Israeli air and rocket attacks on Jordanian territory. The Jordanian authorities were divided in their attitude towards the Palestinian organizations. Some were in favour of compromise while others wanted to restrict and control their actions. In February 1968 King Hussein strongly denounced the commandos for provoking a heavy Israeli reprisal attack but his government afterwards compromised by taking the line that Jordan could not be held responsible for attacks on Israelis inside occupied Arab territory. In March the Jordanian army and Palestinian commandos cooperated in a major engagement known as the Battle of Kerameh in which they inflicted heavier losses on an Israeli raiding force than on any previous occasion. This was the high point of relations between Jordan and the Palestinian organizations.

Inside the occupied territories the situation was confused. Here Jordan and the PLO were now rivals for the loyalty of the Palestinians. Jordan continued to recognize and pay the salaries of government officials and teachers. The Arab citizens of East Jerusalem had a special need to hold on to their Jordanian citizenship in order to preserve their identity when Israel proceeded with the annexation of the rest of the city. The Israeli military authorities wanted to prevent them from developing their political links with either; at the same time they did not wish to see a local nationalist elite emerge. They tolerated and even encouraged the Arab *mukhtars* and mayors provided they confined themselves to municipal affairs and did not engage in politics. Commercial links with Jordan were permitted through the open-door policy across the River Jordan but at the same time the Israelis moved to tie the West Bank strategically and economically with Israel by planting Jewish settlements and building roads.

Against the bitter experience of Israeli military occupation, the Palestinian population, many of whom had been driven from their homes in 1948, had a new possibility. They could now be in contact with their fellows in Israel from whom they had been cut off for twenty years. 'Palestinianism' or Palestine national consciousness – as opposed to a wider Arab nationalism – greatly intensified among them. As yet, however, there was hardly any talk of establishing a small independent Palestinian state in the West Bank; only total liberation and the establishment of a non-sectarian democratic state in the whole of Palestine was considered.

Meanwhile, the Palestinian guerrilla organizations were consolidating their position in Jordan until they formed something of a state within a state. The trend was watched with anxiety by the king and with anger by some of his officers. Some of the Palestinians – especially the smaller extremist groups outside the PLO's control – cared little about Jordanian feelings. They were over-confident, believing that the trend in the Arab world was in their favour. The Jordanian authorities concentrated their criticism on the extreme left-wing Palestinian organizations. Inevitable clashes occurred in 1970, culminating in the civil war of September engaging all Palestinian commando forces in Jordan, with Syrian support, and the Jordanian armed forces. Arab leaders meeting in Cairo helped to end the fighting but Palestinian military power in Jordan was broken. In the following June the Palestinian commandos were driven out of the East Bank and their training camps closed.

This was the nadir of relations between Palestine and Jordan. In November 1971 the Prime Minister Wasfi Tal was assassinated in Cairo by three young members of the self-styled Black September organization, dedicated to revenge. The PLO denied that Black September was a branch of Fatah but the Jordanians were sceptical.

Some of King Hussein's Transjordanian supporters now favoured cutting the country's losses by letting the West Bank go and returning to Transjordan's pre-1948 borders. But this was unacceptable to the king who had not abandoned his belief in his responsibility to speak on behalf of the Palestinians or to try to recover Jerusalem from the Zionists. On the other hand he maintained that Jordan should continue to explore peace options.

The 1970–71 clashes left a bitter legacy but in removing the centre of PLO military and political activities from Jordan – mainly to Lebanon – it eliminated the direct cause of conflict between Jordan and the PLO. Yasser Arafat and the PLO leadership remained relentlessly hostile and when in March 1972 King Hussein announced his plans for a federal Palestinian/Jordanian state of the East and West Banks, to be known as the United Arab Kingdom and with twin capitals in Amman and Jerusalem, they denounced them. On the other hand the Jordanian Government had some success in strengthening its ties with the moderate Palestinian leadership in the occupied territories.

When in October 1973 Egypt and Syria launched their assault on Israel to recover their lost territory Jordan played a limited role. It avoided the direct involvement which would have brought the certain disaster predicted by the king but sent two armoured brigades to fight alongside Syria. This preserved the Jordanian armed forces from destruction but weakened Jordan's bargaining position in the aftermath of the war. Whereas for the first time since 1957 real US pressure was put on Israel to give up some of its conquests, the Israelis saw no reason to make any concessions to Jordan and summarily rejected King Hussein's suggestions that they should negotiate a disengagement agreement in the Jordan Valley along the lines of those that had been reached with Egypt and Syria. Any Israeli proposals for a settlement with Jordan included conditions which Jordan could not possibly accept – such as the retention of Israeli sovereignty over the whole of Jerusalem and permanent military occupation of part of the West Bank.

Meanwhile the PLO was making rapid progress in gaining international recognition, culminating in the UN General Assembly's decision to invite Yasser Arafat to address it in November 1974. He was accorded the honours of a head of state.

This trend was accompanied with a lively and sometimes fierce debate within the Palestinian liberation movement. The development of Palestinian national consciousness was unmistakable but this raised many practical questions such as whether a provisional Palestinian Government should be formed and whether the establishment of a Palestinian mini-state on any liberated territory was a desirable objective. Many leading Palestinians strongly opposed the mini-state as detracting from the overall objectives of the liberation of the whole of Palestine. But on one point virtually all Palestinians were agreed: any liberated territory should be independent.

The debate was sufficiently resolved for the Palestine National Council to affirm at its twelfth session in June 1974 that the PLO 'is struggling by all means, and first and foremost by armed struggle, to liberate the territory of Palestine and to establish the independent national authority of the Palestinian people in every part of Palestinian territory that is liberated'. This was a unique milestone in the history of Jordan/Palestine relations. King Hussein, while renouncing any claim to speak for all the Palestinians, still held that Jordan represented the true government of the people of the West

Bank and East Jerusalem. But when the Arab heads of state met in Rabat in October 1974 he found himself alone. Even Saudi Arabia, his closest ally, now regarded the PLO as the representative of all the Palestinians. Jordan finally accepted without reservation the summit's final resolution which endorsed the PNC's June resolution and recognized the PLO as the 'sole legitimate representative of the Palestinians'.

The way was now open for a gradual thaw in relations between Jordan and the PLO. The *rapprochement* was not immediate. The Lebanese civil war of 1975-76, in which the PLO became involved, intervened and it was not until 1977 that a senior PLO delegation visited Amman. But the trend towards the establishment of mutual trust has been greatly enhanced by Jordan's determination to stand by the Rabat summit resolution. King Hussein has dismissed any proposals emanating from Israel for a 'Jordanian solution' to the Palestinian problem whereby Jordan would negotiate on the Palestinians' behalf. Similarly, Jordan and the PLO have maintained almost identical attitudes towards the Camp David negotiations. Jordan has rejected as futile US and Egyptian efforts to include it in talks on Palestinian autonomy.

Within the occupied territories the acceptance of PLO leadership since 1974 has been unmistakable. Israeli efforts to suggest that the inhabitants only support the PLO out of fear have impressed no impartial observer. Similarly, attempts to find an 'alternative' Palestinian leadership among mayors and notables in the less politically conscious countryside have had very little success. When municipal elections were held in the West Bank in April 1976 and the PLO did not call for a boycott, the PLO made sweeping gains. The Israeli authorities have not since allowed any elections to take place.

In March 1977 the Palestine National Council, meeting for the first time since 1974, adopted a fifteen-point national programme which included the formula of an independent national state. Although the objective of the total liberation of Palestine from Zionism has never been abandoned, the establishment of a small Palestinian state in the West Bank and Gaza as an immediate goal is accepted by the majority of the Palestinian leadership both inside and outside the occupied territories. Most of these agree that such an independent state should have some kind of structured relationship with Jordan but they assert that a decision on this matter must be made by the Palestinians when they have their own state. King Hussein and the Jordanian Government endorse this view.

Because of Israel's intransigent refusal, backed at present by the United States, to accept an independent Palestine, its birth may still be long delayed. When it happens the new state is certain to live in close symbiosis with Jordan. More than half of the people of Jordan are still Palestinians by birth so that it is inconceivable that it should be otherwise. But it has been necessary for the concepts of Palestine and Jordan to be separated before they can be united.

Jordan and the Powers

Robert Stephens

Since the Hashemite Kingdom of Jordan now has more than a million Palestinians among its population and has borders which march with those of Syria, Iraq, Saudi Arabia and Israel, it can scarcely avoid playing a central role in Middle East politics and thus attracting the close and not always welcome attention of the Great Powers.

It has been heavily involved in two of the four Arab–Israeli wars, in 1948 and 1967. It has also been the cockpit of recurrent struggles by the Great Powers and their client states for influence in the Arab East. The Kingdom has often seemed nevertheless to stay on the sidelines waiting for its neighbours or the Powers to decide its fate. This impression may be largely an illusion; what is real in it may be explained by modern Jordan's relatively brief national existence, its geographic vulnerability, and the prudence of a poor relation. It may also reflect the hesitation created by Jordan's simultaneous and not always compatible roles of buffer state and of revisionist power seeking the recovery of lost lands which until very recently supported more than half its people.

Until 1956-57, with the Suez War and the abrogation of the Anglo–Jordan treaty, Britain was the dominant Great Power in Jordan's foreign relations. This British role continued on the surface until 1958 when at King Hussein's request British troops were called in for support against the possible repercussions of the revolution in

Iraq, the union of Syria with Egypt, and the Lebanese civil war.

By that time Jordan had already begun to move closer to the United States under Eisenhower's presidency. Although the king did not feel able at first publicly to endorse the Eisenhower Doctrine, he looked to Washington for diplomatic support and economic and military aid. The despatch of the US Sixth Fleet and US marines to the Lebanon was a proof of the strength of increasing American interest in the Middle East and especially in the Arab states.

The first severe test of American patronage came with the 1967 War and Jordan's loss of the West Bank. King Hussein was disappointed by the degree of United States support for Israel during the war and by its subsequent leisurely approach to making a Middle East peace. In response to American pressure Jordan accepted the Security Council resolution 242 as the basis for a quick peace settlement. But nothing happened. There was no comparable American pressure on Israel to make peace. Nevertheless Jordanian decision-makers remained in close relationship with the United States. Jordan, like other Arab states, suffered from the policy conflicts in Washington over Arab–Israeli peace-making between the State Department and Dr Kissinger. Even when he himself became Secretary of State, Kissinger believed that discrediting Russia and her radical allies in the Middle East was more important than pressing for a peace settlement that Arab moderates could accept.

After the 1973 October War Jordan followed the American lead to the Geneva peace conference, but to no avail as far as the West Bank was concerned.

Things began to change with the Carter presidency. Even before the Camp David peace agreements in 1978 the Carter administration put intense pressure on Jordan through its control of Jordan's arms supplies. The Jordanians found Brzezinski, President Carter's national security adviser, particularly harsh to deal with.

The rift between Amman and Washington became deeper after the signature of the Camp David agreements between Egypt, Israel and the United States. King Hussein joined with the other leaders of the Arab League states at the Arab summit in Baghdad in condemning Egypt's moves for a separate peace with Israel and suspending her from membership of the Arab League. The anti-Camp David front included other 'moderate' Arab regimes having friendly relations with the United States. Most important among them was Saudi Arabia which has increasingly taken over the role formerly played by King Hussein as a kind of unofficial spokesman in Washington for collective Arab views, particularly when, as in Nasser's day, American relations with Egypt, the biggest Arab power, were bad.

Jordan's opposition to the Camp David agreements, including the role they allocated to Jordan in deciding the future of the West Bank, meant a further weakening if not an end of the Jordanian special relationship with America. By the late 1970s Jordan had begun to demonstrate a greater independence financially from the United States with the help of money from the Arab oil states through subsidies, investment and remittances from Jordanians and Palestinians working in the Gulf and Saudi Arabia. But the United States remained the key power in moulding a settlement between Israel and the Palestinians, and hence with Jordan. And, together with Britain, it was still the main source of modern arms for Jordan, despite Jordanian efforts to diversify the supply. The Jordan air force acquired French-made Mirage fighter-bombers and negotiations were concluded for the supply of Soviet anti-aircraft weapons.

Jordan has also diversified its foreign trade. It now does increasing business with Western Europe, the Soviet Union and China. India is its biggest market for phosphates, its most lucrative export, and eventually China may take India's place as the best customer. There are plans for the development of Jordan's oil shale as a source of energy, with the help of Soviet experts.

Britain, Jordan's first Great Power partner and protector, still has substantial and expanding economic links with Jordan. British exports to Jordan more than doubled in value in the three years after 1977 reaching over £100 million in 1980. These figures do not include sizeable British arms sales. Exports to Jordan from the European Community as a whole almost trebled over the same period and are now worth over £300 million a year.

King Hussein sees his current policy as aimed at replacing the old special link with America – or with any other single Great Power – by a more balanced relationship between the main international power blocs: the United States, the Soviet Union and the European Community. His efforts in this direction have been encouraged by the launching by the EEC of the 'European initiative' for a Middle

East peace and by the coming to power in the United States of President Reagan. For Mr Reagan came to the White House with a strongly pro-Israel policy which treated Israel as the key point in a new anti-Soviet military system in the Middle East, a development he regarded as more important than the conclusion of peace between Israel and the Palestinians.

The Israeli invasion of the Lebanon and its attempted physical destruction of the PLO in June 1982 were evidence of the catastrophic effects of the Reagan–Begin policy. But they also illustrated the limits of either Soviet or European ability or willingness to play a decisive role in the Middle East.

The Lebanon crisis underlined the degree to which the fate of Jordan and of other moderate Arab regimes still depends on the attitude of the United States. Nor is this position likely to change except through a political revolt in the United States which compels the White House to put US national interests first in dealing with the Middle East. Or an internal political transformation of the Arab world which enables the Arabs to use their own resources more effectively to protect their own interests and to develop their independence from Great Power control.

Like most of the Arab states of the Middle East, Jordan was born from a combination of national aspirations, Great Power rivalries and some degree of historical accident. In the confusion following the collapse of the Ottoman Empire, Jordan, then known as Transjordan, was created, financed and legitimized by a Great Power so as to avoid a local armed collision which might have become international.

The historical accident which precipitated the creation of the Jordan state was the surprise march of the Hashemite prince, the Amir Abdullah, and an Arab military force northwards from the Hijaz towards Damascus in November 1920. The French army had just evicted Abdullah's brother, Faisal, from the throne of the shortlived independent Arab kingdom of Syria. Abdullah's intention was to demand 'the due which had been taken from him [Faisal]' in contradiction of British wartime promises.[1] The British, who had consoled Faisal with the throne of the new kingdom of Iraq, were alarmed at a possible clash between their two allies, Abdullah's force and the French army.

Abdullah was invited to Jerusalem in March 1922 to consult with Winston Churchill, then British Colonial Secretary.

According to Abdullah's memoirs, Churchill told him: 'France will not tolerate Faisal's return to Syria. If you remain here, behave well and pursue the right course in this matter both here and in the Hijaz, we hope that France may change its mind. Syria will then be yours again.'[2] The restoration of Syrian unity, sometimes called the 'Greater Syria' plan, remained Abdullah's dearest dream.

The 'here', where Abdullah was to remain and behave, was Transjordan, then a largely desert country with a cultivated fringe along the East Bank of the Jordan river. Traditionally it was regarded as part of what was then Syria. In the new partition of the defeated Ottoman Empire it had been included in the British mandate for Palestine.

Abdullah proposed to Churchill that he should, in effect, become King of Palestine and Transjordan in the same way as his brother Faisal had just become King of Iraq. 'It was explained,' says the British official record primly, 'that His Majesty's Government were already too far committed to a different system in Palestine for them to be able to adopt this proposal.'[3] Eventually Abdullah agreed, with obvious reluctance, to undertake responsibility for Transjordan for six months.[4]

Detached from Palestine and administered separately by the British mandatory power, Transjordan was excluded from key provisions of the Palestine mandate, including those providing for the official facilitation of Jewish immigration and settlement on the land.

Five years later, in 1928, the relationship of Transjordan and Britain was redefined in a treaty by which Britain recognized Transjordan as an independent state subject to British control of foreign affairs, defence and finance.

When the Amir Abdullah took over his principality, it had almost no government. The area had reverted to its secular condition of anarchic tribal rule. The foundations of a new administration were laid with modest British help – a few British officials, never more than seven or eight with some technical staff and, above all, the British-officered Arab Legion. The Arab Legion was originally responsible for internal security but under Glubb Pasha, who took over command in 1930 until his dismissal twenty-five years later, the Legion developed eventually into a small but fully-fledged national army. Indeed it became such an important element in the social and economic structure of the state that in the early years it sometimes made Jordan appear to be an example, like Prussia, of a state built round an army rather than an army built round a state.

The expanded Legion provided not only the main domestic support for the Hashemite regime but also served Britain's regional security interests. British strategists, such as General Glubb, saw it as potentially the vanguard, together with the Royal Air Force, of a kind of roving regional strike force or 'peace force', using the desert as navies use the sea, backing up diplomacy with armoured cars instead of gunboats. Available to show the flag or, if need be, to intervene in countries round the edge of the great desert spaces, the sand oceans, such a force would keep its main bases discreetly outside the populated areas to avoid political friction.

This role was exemplified on a small scale in the British intervention in Iraq in 1941 to overthrow the pro-German regime of Rashid Ali al-Gaylani. The Arab Legion then led an improvised British force known as Kingcol across five hundred miles of desert to break the Iraqi siege of the British air base at Habbaniyah and to capture Baghdad. This operation also served the Hashemite interest by restoring in Iraq the authority of the other Hashemite branch represented by the young King Faisal II and his uncle, the Regent, Prince Abd al-Ilah.

The Amir Abdullah's public commitment to the British alliance and his allocation of his forces to British command came during the darkest days of the war for Britain when, early in 1941, the British stood alone against the combined forces of Germany and Italy, and Vichy France controlled 100,000 troops in Syria. How far the people of Transjordan shared their ruler's loyal estimate of British prospects is a matter of opinion. General Glubb records a widespread feeling of support for the British based partly on years of friendly cooperation.[5] Sir Alec Kirkbride, the British Resident in Amman and chief adviser to the King for many years, was more sceptical. He wrote (in his book, *A Crackle of Thorns*) that 'the civil population of Jordan had decided that Great Britain had lost the war and that it was only a question of time before the German army would arrive and take over control. King Abdullah himself was in a state bordering on despair.'[6]

With the overthrow of the Iraqi rebel regime and the expulsion of the Vichy French from Syria and Lebanon, the position of both the

Amir Abdullah and the British in Jordan was assured. At the end of the war the Amir achieved his policital ambition. The Anglo–Jordan treaty was revised in 1946 to recognize Transjordan as an independent sovereign state with Abdullah taking officially the title of King. The new kingdom was born in troubled times, but this did not dim the celebrations of King Abdullah's coronation, which took place in the same year in Amman and which I had the pleasure of attending. The Jordanian capital, now a city of nearly a million people, was then a small market town of thirty thousand crouched amid the ruins of the Greco–Roman city of Philadelphia.

On paper at least the new treaty removed some of the military and financial restrictions on Jordanian sovereignty. But the new pattern of Anglo–Jordanian relations was still too paternalistic to satisfy a new generation of politically conscious Jordanians. Moreover the immediate postwar period faced the Jordanians with a more painful test of their relations with Britain. The armed conflict over the future of Palestine between the Palestinian Arabs – neighbours with many close personal and communal ties with Jordan – the Zionist Jewish immigrants and the British mandatory power had been largely in suspense during the Second World War. But by 1946 fighting had been resumed on a bigger scale. The British and their White Paper policy of restricting Jewish immigration were now the first target of a Jewish rebellion aimed at setting up a Jewish state. Under its impact and pressure from the United States, as well as from the Arabs in the opposite direction, the British announced their relinquishment of the mandate and their withdrawal from Palestine by May 1948. In 1947 the United Nations Assembly had approved (narrowly) a partition plan which was rejected by the Palestinians and most of the Arab states. The Zionists accepted the partition plan as the basis for the establishment of their new state of Israel on Palestinian territory.

Abdullah's policy towards Palestine was based on a mixture of ambition and realism. He recognized the limits of his power to realize his desires. During the Palestinian Arab rebellion which broke out in 1936, Abdullah had tried to keep Transjordan out of any conflict with the British, a clash he could not afford. In 1937 he had favoured Arab acceptance of the Peel Commission report on Palestine which recommended a form of partition confining the Jewish state to the fertile coastal strip from Tel Aviv to Haifa and uniting Arab Palestine with Transjordan under King Abdullah. He also endorsed the 1939 White Paper and the 1947 United Nations partition plan except for the proposed internationalization of Jerusalem. He strongly believed in the traditional duty and privilege of the Muslims to safeguard the Holy Places in Jerusalem.

When the Arab Legion together with small contingents from the Arab armies entered Palestine in 1948 to help the Palestinian Arabs, the official aim was to prevent the partition of the country and the creation of a Jewish state. However, the Legion concentrated on those areas which had been allocated to the Arabs under the partition plan. The big exception was Jerusalem where Abdullah ordered priority to be given to the battle for Arab control of the city.

Britain had officially dissociated itself from Abdullah's venture into the Palestine war. None the less the other Arab states, particularly Egypt and Syria with which Abdullah was scarcely on speaking terms, suspected that Abdullah was in collusion with the British to annex the territory his army controlled and unite the remains of Arab Palestine, including Jerusalem, in an expanded Jordanian kingdom. The British, it was believed, were using the Arab Legion to enforce the kind of partition they wanted. Having left Palestine by one door, they would come back through another.

The armistice signed in 1949 was followed by the incorporation of this area – the West Bank and the Old City of Jerusalem – along with its Palestinian inhabitants into the Kingdom of Jordan, a change not recognized by the Palestinians outside Jordan nor by most of Jordan's Arab neighbours.

After the armistice King Abdullah tried to reach an accommodation with the Israeli leaders in search of a more lasting peace and stable frontiers. His efforts produced no agreement but they led to Abdullah's assassination by Palestinian Arabs in the al-Aqsa Mosque in 1951. After a brief reign his successor, the Crown Prince Talal, who suffered from ill-health, abdicated in favour of his son and Abdullah's grandson, Hussein, the present ruler, who was then at school in England.

The death of King Abdullah marked the end of an era. The long partnership in Jordan between the Hashemites and the British had been based on the personality and historic role of Abdullah and on the still dominant position of Britain in the Middle East. Now Abdullah was gone and both the Hashemite monarchies and the British were being challenged by the new postwar forces of radical

Arab nationalism and by the increasing interest in the Middle East of America and Russia. The partnership still had a few years yet to run but its nature was changing. Abdullah believed seriously in the value of the Anglo–Arab connection to both parties. After a visit to Britain in 1946 he wrote that he found 'the greatest support for the idea of an Islamic front. This attitude was demanded by the interests of Great Britain who would be the friend of Islam everywhere if she could only find those who would understand her and profit by British advice, experience and strength.'[7]

'The character of the Arabs and the Muslim religion,' wrote Abdullah in his memoirs, 'is sufficiently broad to accommodate itself to the needs of the present day in the fields of economics, industry and national defence . . . It is the duty of Great Britain to comprehend this and reach an understanding in these matters after the bonds which have confined the Arab will in the Arab states have been loosened and an opportunity has been provided for the expression of suppressed desires and the exercise of rights that have been restricted and limited.'[8]

'Abdullah's wisdom,' observed a British writer, 'lay in using rather than fashionably abusing the mandatory Power that was thrust upon him.'[9]

When Hussein became king, the new forces and new Powers were already making themselves felt. Jordan itself had changed its modest, largely pastoral character with the incorporation in it of the politically more sophisticated and militant Palestinians who were now more numerous in the state than the original Transjordanians. The Palestinians saw themselves as victims of the West and especially the British whom they blamed for enabling the Zionists to establish a state in their country and drive most of the Arab inhabitants into exile. They felt themselves to be part of the new pan-Arab nationalist movement which was challenging the British military presence and political control in Egypt and most of Arab Asia.

The Arab nationalist drive was accelerated by the Egyptian military revolution in 1952 and the rise to power of Gamal Abdul Nasser. It soon collided with the Anglo–American attempt to replace the old and unpopular British bilateral treaties with a new regional defence alliance through the Baghdad Pact. The inclusion in the Pact of Iran, Turkey and Pakistan, with the United States as an active observer, was a sign of the increased American interest in the Middle East, an extension of Washington's policy of 'containment' of the Soviet Union.

The first and only Arab state to join the Baghdad Pact was Iraq. Nasser rejected Egyptian membership and strove to prevent the extension of the Pact to other Arab states, fearing Egypt's being left in isolation to face a more powerfully armed Israel. Jordan and Syria became the battlegrounds for a struggle for regional hegemony. Hussein's Hashemite cousins in Baghdad were urging him to bring Jordan into the pact, but he faced opposing pressures from all his other Arab neighbours and from their sympathizers inside Jordan. Nasser had great influence among the Palestinians who saw Egypt as their only hope for the recovery of their lost lands. Saudi Arabia was in league with Egypt because of its dispute with the British over the Buraimi Oases and its traditional hostility to the Hashemites. The Syrians were divided but there was endemic tension between Amman and Damascus over the Hashemite monarch's aspirations for 'Greater Syria'.

The tug of war was intensified when in September 1955 Nasser revolutionized the Great Power game in the Middle East by his arms deal with the Russians. A few weeks later Britain was told that Jordan was ready to join the Baghdad Pact. The British chief of imperial general staff, General Sir Gerald Templer, flew to Amman on 6 December 1955 bringing with him a tempting offer of weapons for a greatly expanded Arab Legion and Jordan air force. General Templer's arrival brought a cabinet crisis, strikes and riots. The government reversed its decision to join the Pact and Templer flew back to London empty-handed.

The Baghdad Pact and the Soviet arms deal internationalized the local struggle for power in the Middle East.[10] They brought America and Russia more actively into an area where hitherto the dominant Powers had been Britain and France. But the struggle was still being fought out in local terms and Britain was still the foreign Power most involved. Not for long, however. On 1 March 1956, the chief symbol of British influence in Jordan, General Glubb Pasha, the legendary commander of the Arab Legion, was suddenly dismissed from his post. The British Foreign Secretary, Selwyn Lloyd, was in Cairo dining with Nasser when the news came. Lloyd and Prime Minister Eden were enraged. They thought it was Nasser's doing, a deliberate act of humiliation. In fact it was a personal decision of King Hussein's prompted in part by the antagonisms between a twenty-one-year-old monarch and a foreign soldier more than twice his age.[11] It was also a sign that Hussein was now himself identifying with the nationalist tide.

The tide continued to rise over the coming year as Nasser's nationalization of the Suez Canal Company led to a world crisis and the joint attack on Egypt by Britain, France and Israel in the Suez–Sinai War. Jordan – at Nasser's request – stayed out of the war. But the newly elected radical nationalist government under Suleiman Nabulsi ended Jordan's alliance with Britain. It accepted from Egypt, Syria and Saudi Arabia a guarantee to replace the subsidies to the Jordan army that the British had hitherto paid. British forces were withdrawn from Jordan. Except for a dramatic postscript eighteen months later, this was the end of Jordan's partnership with Britain although friendly ties between the two countries continued.

Hussein's reliance on the nationalists and on Arab aid was short-lived. Only Saudi Arabia paid the promised instalments. But a new and stronger Great Power partner was on the horizon. The United States was concerned that the British withdrawal after Suez should not leave a power vacuum in the Middle East that the Russians or Nasser might fill. Through the 'Eisenhower Doctrine' the United States offered aid and support to any country, even one formally neutral, which declared its readiness to resist Communism. Hussein was already trying to check the radical trend of the Nabulsi government which he feared would increase Soviet influence in Jordan and might lead to the extension over his kingdom of the influence of one or more of his Arab allies. The Nabulsi government, following Nasser's line, was against the Eisenhower Doctrine and American aid.

By April 1957 relations between king and government had reached crisis point. The Jordan army was split politically. Its radical faction was said to be plotting a coup to overthrow Hussein who foiled it by rallying his own supporters in the army. He dismissed Nabulsi, dissolved the political parties and carried through a purge of Communists and dissidents.

The Jordan crisis had all the ingredients of the cold war which had begun to develop between Nasser with Soviet support on the one hand and the United States and its Middle East allies on the other. These American allies now included the three Arab kings – Hussein of Jordan, Faisal of Iraq, and Saud of Saudi Arabia who had taken fright and ended his alliance with Nasser. The struggle to fill the so-called vacuum in the Middle East reached its first climax in Jordan in 1957, and its second in the same year in Syria. Secretly but clumsily the United States planned the overthrow of the Syrian regime with the help of Turkey and Iraq. The Americans were prepared to go to the brink to prevent the Soviet takeover of Syria which they feared. But while Russia gave Syria arms and diplomatic support, it gave no military guarantees. The Syrian Government's own fears of increased dependence upon Russia and the local Communists led it to seek not American protection but union with Egypt under Nasser's leadership. The following year brought the struggle to a climax with the merger of Syria and Egypt in the United Arab Republic under Nasser's presidency, the outbreak of civil war in Lebanon because of differing views among the Lebanese on their links with the West, and the revolution in Iraq which overthrew Nuri Said and the monarchy.

President Chamoun of Lebanon asked for Western help against alleged UAR interference from across the Syrian border and the United States Sixth Fleet landed marines in Beirut. When the revolution erupted in Iraq, King Hussein also asked for help to check the spread of the revolutionary movement from Baghdad and Damascus to Amman. Two thousand British paratroopers flew to Jordan in July 1958. But stability was re-established through the formation of a Lebanese Government of national compromise and local security arrangements negotiated through the Arab League. The American and British forces were both withdrawn by the end of the year.

It was Britain's last imperial fling. From 1958 until 1973, when Jordan began to diversify its external relationships, Jordan's Great Power financier and armourer was the United States.

Jordan's relationship with Washington was complicated. The United States gave a higher priority to its support for Israel than to its interests in the Arab countries, and its relations with Nasser and the Arab radical regimes deteriorated sharply. Egypt's intervention in support of the Republicans in the Yemen civil war appeared to threaten the position in the Arabian peninsula of America's most important Arab ally, Saudi Arabia. For the 1960s were years of turmoil and revolution in the Arab world. By contrast, until the Six Day War in 1967, relative peace prevailed along the Arab–Israeli borders, although tension began to grow over Israel's plans to divert a large share of the Jordan waters to its own use.

In 1965 a new Palestinian guerrilla group, the nucleus of what later became, as al-Fatah, the main element of the Palestinian national resistance, began small-scale raids into Israel from Syria. The Palestinians were being wooed as never before by rival Arab camps. For the Arab League had split between the pro-Western monarchies and the Arab radical nationalists who had varying degrees of Soviet support. Jordan joined the camp of the West, and so became a choice political target for the radical regimes which surrounded it. Nasser tried to maintain his paramountcy in the Arab world and his claim to international non-alignment by keeping a certain distance from the Soviet Union, the Arab Communists, and the more radical Arab regimes such as the Syrian Ba'thists and the Algerians. Indeed the Syrian and Iraqi Ba'thists were not only Nasser's allies but also his chief revolutionary rivals.

Nasser also wanted to preserve peace along the Israeli borders, at least for a time. He believed the Arabs were not yet strong enough to win a war against Israel, especially as in the last resort Israel could count on American support to save it from defeat.

But he was being pushed towards war by the political auction between rival Arab regimes bidding for Palestinian support. The first and most spectacular bid was put in by Qassim who had led the revolution in Iraq and then quarrelled with Nasser. Qassim proposed the immediate creation of an independent Palestinian state or entity based on the West Bank and Gaza.

This is now the conventional wisdom of the Arab 'moderates' but then it seemed ingeniously designed to embarrass Nasser (for Egypt controlled the Gaza Strip) and to undermine Hussein by slicing off half the Hashemite patrimony in Jordan. Hussein had a ready answer: Palestinians were welcome as Jordan citizens. Nasser's response was to encourage the formation in 1964 of the PLO (Palestine Liberation Organization). The PLO was then a tame Palestinian political body without a territorial base, a popular mandate or any independent means of military action. Its official armed forces, the PLA (Palestine Liberation Army), which had fought courageously against the Israelis in 1956, consisted of Palestinian units attached to the Arab regular armies. The Chairman of the PLO, Ahmed Shuqairy, a Palestinian–Syrian lawyer and talented demagogue, suited Nasser's purpose of maintaining a bold

verbal front against Israel while ensuring that the Palestinians did
not get out of control and drag Egypt into war.

When this purpose failed for other reasons and Nasser was over-
whelmingly defeated, Jordan, perhaps unexpectedly, shared in the
disaster of the Six Day War.

Jordan's alliance with the United States was heavily strained but
not broken by the war and the defeat which left the West Bank and
Arab Jerusalem under Israeli occupation and over 300,000 more
Palestinian refugees in East Jordan. Jordan was the only one of the
Arab front-line states not to break off diplomatic relations with the
United States in protest against the military help which the
Americans were believed – mistakenly – to have given Israel in
the war.

The 1967 War had a double effect on Arab attitudes towards the
Soviet Union, including that of Jordan. The Arabs were grateful for
the support Russia had given them in supplying arms. But they
were aware that the Russians were not prepared to go as far in
support of their Arab friends as the United States was ready to go in
backing Israel. Moscow would not go to war for the Arabs, nor
could it secure from Israel the peace terms the Arabs wanted.

For a decade after the Second World War the Soviet Union had
made little headway in extending its influence in the Arab countries
of the Middle East. Perhaps Stalin was in no hurry to push the
British out of the area for fear that America, a stronger adversary,
should take its place. But when both America and Britain began
pressing the Arabs to join the Baghdad Pact, the Russians benefited
from the popular reaction. For many Arab nationalists suspected
that the new Pact was intended less to defend the area against Russia
than to prolong Western political and economic control of the Arab
countries and to protect Israel. The attitudes of Jordan and the
Soviet Union had hitherto been reciprocally hostile. The Russians
dismissed Jordan as a state still under British control, and the Soviet
veto kept it out of the United Nations until December 1955, by
which time Moscow had begun more actively to cultivate the Arab
states.

The wish of the Nabulsi government to establish normal diplomatic relations with the Soviet Union, and its countermanding by
Hussein, formed a major element in the 1957 political crisis in
Jordan. After years of mutual abuse, Jordan eventually established
diplomatic relations with Russia in 1961.

Jordan's maintenance of relations with the United States after the 1967 War was approved by the other Arab states. Having cut their own ties with the United States and so become dependent on Moscow for arms and diplomatic support, they found King Hussein a useful spokesman for them in Washington during the successive attempts to bring about an Arab–Israeli peace.

Dr Henry Kissinger, the chief architect of American foreign policy between 1969 and 1975, has given the most detailed version of American relations with Jordan and the attempts made at peace-making in the first four years of that period in the first volume of his monumental memoirs.[12] His book includes a blow by blow account of how the 1970 civil war in Jordan grew into a major international crisis involving a possible confrontation between the United States and the Soviet Union. Kissinger and President Nixon chose to treat the crisis as a dramatic test of American credibility as an ally in the Middle East, but its gravity went almost unnoticed elsewhere in the West at the time.

Kissinger was determined that the first aim of American diplomacy in the Middle East must be to reduce Soviet influence in the area. It must seek the expulsion of the Soviet military presence which, in the form of warships, combat troops, arms supplies and advisers, had grown enormously in the preceding fifteen years. Kissinger also wanted to make sure that Russia would not get the credit for any concessions the United States might wring out of Israel. In opposition to the line of the State Department under William Rogers, he was against American pressure for a general peace settlement until it could be seen more clearly what concessions the Arabs would make and 'until those who could benefit from it would be America's friends and not Soviet clients'. In the meantime Kissinger 'much preferred an Israeli–Jordanian negotiation which would involve just such a friend . . .'[13]

The United States and the Soviet Union had both voted for the United Nations Security Council resolution 242 of November 1967 which had become widely accepted as a basis for Middle East peace-making. Jordan's acquiescence in resolution 242 had been obtained in 1967 by the promise of the American ambassador to the United Nations, Arthur Goldberg, that the United States would work for the return of the West Bank to Jordan with minor boundary rectifications and that the United States was prepared to use its influence to obtain a role for Jordan in Jerusalem. Kissinger adds the comment that 'since there were no negotiations going on, the promise was meaningless'.[14]

Kissinger describes the visit to Washington in April 1969 of 'the doughty King Hussein of Jordan who had never bargained about his friendship with the United States'.[15] Hussein, speaking also for Nasser, told the Americans that both Jordan and Egypt were committed to resolution 242. He also recognized the need for some minor border rectifications.

In December 1969 the US State Department put forward proposals for peace between Israel and Jordan. They were based on Israeli withdrawal to the 1967 borders with the proviso that any change in the 1967 lines 'should not reflect the weight of conquest but should be insubstantial alterations needed for mutual security'. The plan was rejected outright by Israel. 'It was a misfortune,' observed Kissinger, 'that the strength of Hussein's bargaining position did not match his moderation and that his available options were not equal to his good will. He thus had the capacity neither for independent action nor for blackmail, which are the stuff of Middle East politics.'[16]

The peace-making was being overtaken by the growing 'war of attrition' between Israel and the Arab states, a smouldering and immensely destructive war of guerrilla raids, artillery bombardments and air attacks. Two new factors had emerged on the Arab side. Soviet combat personnel had arrived in Egypt in 1970 at Nasser's request to man new Soviet anti-aircraft missiles and fighters to help defend vital targets against Israeli 'deep penetration' raids with the American long-range Phantom fighter bombers.

The second new factor was the emergence of a substantial Palestinian national resistance movement. It was to make Jordan the arena for an American confrontation with the Soviet Union which was in part a retaliation for the increased Soviet military role in Egypt.

The Palestinians had put themselves back on the Middle East political map after the battle of Karameh in March 1968. Jordanian tanks joined by a small force of Palestinian guerrillas bravely and effectively resisted a large-scale Israeli attack on their base in the village of Karameh in the Jordan Valley.

The guerrilla movement rapidly gathered recruits, especially among the refugees, under the leadership of a reconstructed and revitalized PLO in which Yasser Arafat, the Fatah leader, had displaced Shuqairy as chairman. Guerrilla groups of different political persuasions were represented in the PLO. The main elements were the Fatah, the biggest group with a more purely nationalist commitment, and the two Marxist groups, the Popular Front for the Liberation of Palestine led by George Habash, and the Popular Democratic Front of Naif Hawatmeh.

Jordan became the main base for the guerrillas' operations inside Israel. But the guerrillas soon began to make more impact politically inside Jordan than militarily against Israel's strong border defences and retaliatory power. The left-wing guerrillas believed, in any case, that Palestine would be liberated only as part of a pan-Arab or world revolution. Most of the Fatah put the liberation of Palestine first and were prepared to cooperate with any country or regime that would help them reach this goal. So while in Jordan the left-wing groups concentrated on ideological evangelism, the Fatah wanted a *modus vivendi* with the Jordan government. The overbearing public behaviour of some of the guerrillas created popular resentment, especially among the original East Bankers. With their increasing weaponry the guerrillas began by the summer of 1970 to look like a state within a state. The king was urged by some of his advisers to smash the guerrillas before they grew strong enough to destroy him. At first it seemed as if talks between Hussein and the more moderate guerrilla leaders might lead to a compromise. Then the situation grew dramatically worse with the spectacular hijacking by the PFLP of three international airliners which they brought, full of hostage-passengers, to Dawson's Field, a desert landing ground thirty miles north of Amman. While negotiations continued for the release of the hostages, Hussein was preparing for a showdown with the guerrillas whose strongholds were in the refugee camps in and around Amman.

Hussein asked the United States to make a strong statement, if possible jointly with the Soviet Union, warning against any outside intervention in Jordan. He had in mind Syria and Iraq whose radical regimes supported the guerrillas. There were then 17,000 Iraqi troops in northern Jordan, left over from the 1967 War.

As the showdown approached, the United States made plans for possible military action by American forces or by Israel against any outside intervention. There were divided counsels in Washington. The State Department wanted to cool the crisis, while Kissinger advised 'implacability' in confronting the Russians. He wanted the military action to be taken by the Israeli air force with the United States standing by to deter any Soviet move to intervene. Nixon preferred the United States to act alone but later changed his mind to approve Israeli action. The United States Sixth Fleet in the Mediterranean was moved nearer to Lebanon and airborne units were ostentatiously put on alert. Israel began to mobilize and move troops to the Syrian border.

On 18 September, the day after Jordanian armed forces began their attack on the guerrillas in Amman, Moscow broke a long diplomatic silence and sent a conciliatory message to Washington. It said the Soviet Union had called on Jordan, Syria, Iraq and Egypt to end the civil war and asked the United States to urge restraint on Israel. The crisis seemed to be over. Two days later it flared up again with reports that Syrian tanks had invaded northern Jordan where the guerrillas were hard pressed by the Jordan army. By the end of the day it was reported that two Syrian armoured brigades with two hundred tanks had crossed the frontier and were attacking on a broad front. Moscow again contacted Washington with an assurance that attempts to restrain Syria were being made.[17] Before any of the military plans could be put into action, the Syrian tanks withdrew back across the border. The crisis now really was over.

Summing up, Kissinger claims: 'The forces of moderation in the Middle East had been preserved. The king had prevailed by his own courage and decisiveness. Yet these would have been in vain but for his friendship with the United States.'[18] It took almost another year for Jordan to complete the expulsion of the Palestinian guerrillas. The guerrillas established their bases in Lebanon leading to local friction and eventually the bloody Lebanese civil war (in which Syrian forces intervened massively, with apparent approval this time of the United States). Jordan entered a period of comparative calm at home and abroad during which its relations with the United States were intermittently strained by conflicting views of the terms of and tactics for a peace settlement with Israel.

Jordan was involved only partially in the 1973 October War, but after the war it, with Egypt and Israel, attended the abortive Geneva peace conference which was boycotted by Syria. During the following decade, with Israel still occupying the West Bank and Gaza, there was a growing feeling among the ruling establishment in Amman that priority should be given to preserving the original Hashemite state on the East Bank. In 1972 Hussein had offered the

West Bank a choice of autonomy within a Jordanian federation or 'United Kingdom' once the Israeli occupation had ended. It was rejected by the PLO.

Later, in 1974, Hussein accepted the decision of the Arab summit at Rabat that he give up responsibility for the Palestinians and to accept a declaration that the PLO was the sole, legitimate representative of the Palestinian people – an elevation of international status for the PLO symbolized shortly afterwards in the appearance before the United Nations Assembly of its chairman, Yasser Arafat.

The arrival of President Carter in the White House produced a switch in American Middle East policy, bringing Jordan back into play. In place of Kissinger's step-by-step peace-making – which had not yet tackled Jordan and the most difficult question of Jerusalem – there was to be an attempt at a comprehensive peace settlement. This would embrace all Israel's Arab neighbours and eventually – if a suitable formula could be found – the Palestinians through the PLO. It would also mean accepting Soviet participation. This new approach was just beginning to show some promise of results – in the remarkable Soviet–American joint declaration on peace in the Middle East and a possible formula for talks with the PLO – when it was suddenly thrown off track by the 'Jerusalem initiative', President Sadat's journey to Jerusalem to open peace talks with Israel.

Like the other Arab states Jordan had not been consulted by Sadat and joined in the Arab League's condemnation of the Egyptian president's separate peace moves. In addition to the separate peace treaty between Egypt and Israel, the Camp David agreements between Egypt, Israel and the United States called for Jordan's cooperation in talks on an interim period of autonomy for the Palestinians of the West Bank and in eventual negotiations about the West Bank's future status.

President Carter had begun by showing sympathy with the Palestinian claim to self-determination but he declared himself opposed, like the Israelis, to a separate Palestinian state on the West Bank. He saw the West Bank's future as linked with either Jordan or Israel or both.

As the Camp David autonomy talks made no progress, there was increasing discussion of the 'Jordanian option' as an alternative way of dealing with the Palestinian question. The Jordanian option

assumed that Israel could continue to block a settlement with the
PLO and the creation of a separate Palestinian state. As seen by the
Israelis, it envisaged an agreement between Israel and Jordan and
some Palestinians which would amount to a new partition leaving
substantial areas of the West Bank, including the whole of
Jerusalem, in Israeli hands. The areas returned to Jordan would be
demilitarized.

The Jordanian option might have had a limited value in at least
opening real bargaining over the West Bank, if the Israel Labour
Party had been in power, though their opening terms would
undoubtedly be unacceptable to both Jordan and the Palestinians.
But with Mr Begin as Prime Minister of Israel, such a deal was
impossible. For Mr Begin had made it clear that he would never
relinquish control of the West Bank which he regarded on historical
and religious grounds as part of Israel.

In the face of these Israeli attitudes King Hussein saw no interest
or incentive in opening a negotiation which was doomed to failure
and which could only make him unpopular with his Palestinian
subjects and the other Arab states. Jordan's relations with Syria and
Iraq and even the PLO had improved as a result of the Baghdad
summits which condemned and boycotted Sadat. But by the time
of the Amman summit in 1980 Arab unity was again wearing thin.
The union between the rival Ba'thist regimes in Syria and Iraq
broke down in bitter hostility as arbitrarily as it had begun. Jordan's
own *rapprochement* with Syria dissolved in a flood of propaganda
and a threatened Syrian invasion. At first it looked like a rerun of
1970 but the crisis faded out with the help of Saudi mediation. This
time neither the United States nor the Soviet Union showed any
signs of readiness to go to the brink in support of their respective
friends. The Arab confusion was further compounded when Iraq
suddenly launched a war against Iran, and King Hussein and other
conservative Arab regimes gave radical, Soviet-armed Iraq their
support.

By the beginning of the 1980s the character of the Jordan state had
begun to change and so had its relations with the Great Powers.
Beirut's decline meant Amman's rise, as some of the Lebanese
capital's financial and entrepreneurial functions were transferred to
Jordan. Jordan was also getting considerable aid from the Arab oil
states and from remittances from Jordanians and Palestinians working in Arabia and the Gulf. Jordan was no longer so dependent

financially on a Great Power subsidy. But it still needed American arms. When Washington showed reluctance to meet his demand for new weapons, Hussein turned ostentatiously to Russia.

Does Jordan still need a Great Power protector? Does the United States still need Jordan? Will Europe take its place?

So long as the United States treats Israel as its most favoured ally in the Middle East and is unable to bring about a settlement acceptable to the Arab moderates, the position of King Hussein and other moderate Arab rulers must become increasingly exposed. If the United States still needs Jordan now, it is not so much as a surrogate regional policeman – a role now being taken over, at least temporarily by Israel and Egypt. Jordan's value will be political – as the Arab state (with its large Palestinian population) most capable of being an effective model in the ideological struggle which will sharpen throughout the Middle East as oil money opens the door to the modern world for millions more people in the Arab lands. It is also in fostering Jordan's political and economic development and in sharing in military guarantees of a general Middle East settlement that the European Community and its members can make their most constructive contribution.

Notes

1. King Abdullah of Jordan, *My Memoirs Completed* (Longman, London, 1978), p. 30.
2. Ibid., p. 30.
3. Public Records Office, Cabinet Papers 24/122, quoted in Doreen Ingrams, *Palestine Papers 1917–22: Seeds of Conflict* (John Murray, London, 1972), pp. 116–17.
4. Ibid.
5. Sir John Bagot Glubb, *The Story of the Arab Legion* (Hodder and Stoughton, London, 1948), pp. 254 ff.
6. Sir Alec Seath Kirkbride, *A Crackle of Thorns* (John Murray, London, 1956), p. 130.
7. King Abdullah, op. cit., p. 60.
8. Ibid., p. 47.
9. Ann Dearden, *Jordan* (Robert Hale, London), p. 18.
10. Robert Stephens, *Nasser* (Allen Lane the Penguin Press, London, 1971), p. 177.
11. Ibid., p. 179.

12. Henry Kissinger, *The White House Years* (Little, Brown and Co.,
     Boston, 1979).
13. Ibid., p. 351.
14. Ibid., p. 345.
15. Ibid., p. 362.
16. Ibid., p. 362.
17. Ibid., p. 629.
18. Ibid., p. 631.

Jordan in the Middle East: The Art of Survival

Adeed Dawisha

In the early hours of 14 July 1958 some residents of Baghdad, the capital of Hashemite Iraq, were awakened to the clatter of moving armour on the capital's dusty roads. If they were somewhat bemused, Crown Prince Abd al-Ilah, prime Minister Nuri al-Said and other Iraqi leaders were not: these were two brigades that had been ordered to move into the other Hashemite kingdom, Jordan, in order to strengthen the defences of the smaller and more vulnerable ally from the revolutionary menace of the newly created United Arab Republic (UAR), and there certainly was no cause for concern. In fact, the two brigades made an unscheduled stop and occupied Baghdad, abolished the Hashemite monarchy and declared the birth of the Iraqi republic. The most powerful and seemingly most stable pro-Western regime in the Arab Middle East had been toppled in a matter of a few hours and had been replaced by a virulently nationalist, anti-Western group of young army officers.

If the stable and apparently well-in-control Iraqi Government could collapse so quickly and so dramatically, then, people surmised, the days of the Jordanian monarchy must be numbered. And, indeed, this seems to have been the view of Her Majesty's Government in London. For three days after the Iraqi coup British paratroops landed in Amman to bolster the Jordanian regime. Even so, the imminent demise of the one remaining Hashemite kingdom was confidently predicted.

Twenty years later, during which many new and fresh faces had exploded on to the Arab world as potential leading political figures only to disappear as quickly as they had arrived in the bewildering sandstorms of Arab politics, King Hussein arrived in Baghdad in November 1978 to attend the ninth Arab summit meeting, and emerged three days later as one of the most influential and respected Arab leaders. This does not signify that there has been a steady consolidation of Hussein's power during those twenty years. The events of July 1958 and November 1978 are simply two extreme episodes of the volatile history of Jordan exhibiting starkly the ups and downs in the fortunes of the country's monarch.

The Uncertain Years

The thirty years of Hussein's rule coincided with probably the most turbulent period of Middle Eastern history. In 1950, Hussein's grandfather, King Abdullah, united both banks of the Jordan in the wake of the Arab defeat against the new state of Israel. The Palestinian population was fired by the idea of a return to the original homeland and resented Arab leaders, who some Palestinians believed to have betrayed their cause for the sake of personal interest. Indeed, the assassination of Abdullah by a Palestinian a year later only served to emphasize to the young Hussein the dangerous and hostile environment in which he was to rule. Palestinian radicalism, moreover, became the focus of, and was itself reinforced by, the rising tide of militant Arab nationalism, as well as by the emergence of Gamal Abdul Nasser as its charismatic leader and keeper of its conscience. In a state facing difficult geo–strategic and demographic problems, the times ahead were bound to be testing for the young king.

He did not have to wait for his first clash with the forces of Arab nationalism. Britain and Turkey had tried in early 1955 to persuade Lebanon and Jordan to join the Baghdad Pact, a pro-Western alliance designed to link up to the West with the North Atlantic Treaty Organization (NATO), and to the East with the South East Asia Treaty Organization (SEATO) in order to contain the alleged spread of Soviet and Communist influence. Arab nationalism, however, at the helm of which stood Nasser of Egypt, considered the Pact simply as a new Western effort to maintain the dependence of the Arab world on the West. Perceiving the split in the Arab world over the Baghdad Pact, the Lebanese Government indicated that it wanted to know Jordan's decision before making its own. In fact, Jordan's Prime Minister, Haza al-Majali, had already declared his intention to join, and a formal request for membership was handed to the British ambassador on 16 November 1955. In December Sir Gerald Templer, the British Chief of Staff, arrived in Amman seemingly to discuss Baghdad Pact membership. Nasser's Egypt immediately unleashed a violent propaganda campaign against the Templer mission, in the wake of which Amman and other Jordanian cities witnessed, throughout the visit of the British Chief of Staff, a wave of disturbances, riots, demonstrations and strikes which was instrumental in bringing two governments down. The Templer mission failed, and both Jordan and Lebanon shied away from the Pact, never to contemplate joining it again.

This incident no doubt highlighted to the king Jordan's basic predicament: a small country, bounded by bigger Arab neighbours that it could not antagonize, bordering on a powerful enemy in Israel which it could not afford to befriend, containing a population many of whom extended their loyalty elsewhere, and boasting an economy almost totally dependent on the West, the current enemies of Arab nationalism. Not being able to confront all these dangers on its own, Jordan needed strong and reliable allies and, since in the 1950s few Arab countries were either strong or reliable, Jordan's dependence on Western support increased perceptibly. This dependence was demonstrated in 1957 when Hussein survived two coups engineered against him by nationalist, pro-Nasser officers. The Jordan Government declared martial law, arrested hundreds of opponents, severed diplomatic relations with Cairo, and asked for, and obtained, American military and economic aid. A year later, it was again the West, this time in the form of British paratroops, who helped Hussein overcome those few uncertain days following the Iraqi coup.

It was not that the king disagreed with the tenets and fundamental principles of Arab nationalism. On the contrary, as a direct descendant of the Prophet Muhammad through his daughter Fatima and cousin Ali, and as the great-grandchild of Sharif Hussein who led the Arab Revolt in 1916 against the Ottomans, the young

Jordanian king felt that his Arabness and his commitment to Arab nationalism were so self-evident that they needed no conscious and constant elaboration. However, as monarch of a small and vulnerable country, he was naturally suspicious of the revolutionary and expansionist Nasserite-type nationalism, which he saw as leading only 'to more disunity. The seeking of popular support for one point of view or one form of leadership in countries other than one's own has fostered factionalism to a dangerous degree, splitting countries to the point of revolution. It is nothing but a new form of imperialism, the domination of one state by another. It makes no difference if both are Arab states. Arab nationalism can survive only through complete equality.'[1] In the heady days of the late 1950s and early 1960s, however, Hussein's sombre perception of nationalist rules of conduct ran very much against the popular tide.

The emergence of a militant leftist republic in Iraq in addition to the Syrian decision to partner Egypt in the UAR under the leadership of President Nasser meant that Jordan was surrounded by antagonistic neighbours, except to the south where another monarchy, that of the House of Saud, shared the fear of Nasser and his brand of radical nationalism. Seeking strength and comfort in each other's company, Saudi–Jordanian relations improved considerably, and the king was one of the first statesmen to join with the Saudis in supporting Imam Ahmad and his conservative tribesmen in Yemen against the Egyptian-backed republican officers. But in the early 1960s, Saudi Arabia itself was a vulnerable state that could hardly give much support to its ally. At times under Nasser's heavy verbal gunfire, the disintegration of the Jordanian state seemed possible. In April 1963 violent demonstrations against the monarchy for its alleged 'anti-Arab unity stand' led to the imposition of strict military curfews throughout Jordan, to the dissolution of the lower house of parliament and the arrest of six deputies, and to the use of the army to suppress the mini-uprising.

In spite of all this, King Hussein managed to survive. The reason was simple; for while a large part of his population were Palestinian radicals, his army was drawn on the whole from Jordanians loyal to the crown. Even so, until 1967, Hussein's position was, to say the least, insecure, and the prospects for his survival were hardly very promising, for throughout the years of struggle against the radical nationalists, Hussein and his vulnerable country had had to confront an increasingly militant and belligerent Israel. Tel Aviv's hardest blows against the neighbouring Arab countries seemed to be reserved for Jordan, mainly because the latter could hardly mount an effective retaliatory operation. Thus Israel's reprisal raids for guerrilla action that was planned in, and emanated from, Syria, were directed at Jordan. There were, for example, massive raids on Qalqilya in 1965, on Irbid and Hebron in 1966, and a particularly heavy attack on Samu, supported by tanks and aircraft, in November 1966 which led to long and widespread disorder in a number of West Bank towns.

These encounters were all a prelude to the biggest military disaster in Jordan's history – the June 1967 defeat. Motivated both by a desire to assert and emphasize the Arab credentials and by a realistic appreciation of the domestic and external constraints on Jordan's policies in the Arab–Israeli sector, Hussein sealed Jordan's fate when, in an alarming atmosphere of rapidly rising tension between Israel and its Arab neighbours, he decided to sign a defence pact with Egypt on 30 May 1967. Five days later, the Israelis attacked and within less than a week had inflicted a devastating defeat on the Arabs. Yet paradoxically, it was this, Jordan's blackest week, during which the country lost to the Israelis its entire West Bank, including East Jerusalem, that freed King Hussein and his now dismembered country from the hostile attentions of Egypt's Gamal Abdul Nasser and other 'revolutionary' Arab leaders. And apart from the war with the Palestinian guerrillas in 1970, there has not been a serious challenge to the stability of the country or to the authority of its monarch since the defeat of 1967.

The Years of Consolidation

In the wake of June 1967, Jordan became considerably more vulnerable to an increasingly militaristic Israel. However, during the previous fifteen years, the real threats to the survival of Jordan's monarchy had come from the Arab radical republics which had implanted in the psyche of the Palestinian population in Jordan and of the Arab masses generally an image characterizing King Hussein as a force actively working to undermine radical Arab nationalist causes. After the 1967 War, no longer could any Arab leader level this kind of accusation at the Jordanian monarch. After all, it was he who flew to Cairo on 30 May 1967 and signed a defence pact with a country whose radio only hours earlier was inciting the Jordanian population to overthrow the Hashemite monarchy. He had accepted Egyptian overall command of his armed forces, and when the war did finally erupt on 5 June he and his forces fought valiantly and stubbornly but hopelessly against the quantatively and qualitatively superior Israelis. Hussein had lost disastrously. But now the Arab masses could only see a true Arab leader who had almost sacrificed his country on the altar of 'Arab nationalism'. Jordan's military defeat against Israel was Hussein's psychological victory over his Arab radical rivals, and after fifteen years of struggling against what sometimes looked like overwhelming odds, the king seemed finally to have secured the stability and survival of the monarchy.

In the aftermath of the 1967 defeat, Nasser had neither the will nor the capability to mount destabilizing, 'revolutionary' campaigns against other Arab leaders. With the whole of Sinai lost to the Jewish state and with Israeli soldiers camping on the bank of the Suez Canal able to march on to Cairo had they so wished, Nasser was bound to be occupied with the plight of Egypt rather than with revolutionary activity in the region. Nasser's need for immediate massive purchases of military and other equipment to rebuild not only his devastated army but also his structurally weak economy, made even weaker by the loss of revenues from the Suez Canal, forced him to seek financial help from the conservative oil-rich states. Becoming dependent on them for the economic well-being of Egypt, he could no longer depict them, or other monarchical orders, as reactionary.

Hussein's new confidence was clearly exhibited at the Khartoum summit of Arab heads of state which met to discuss the Arab response to the June 1967 defeat. It was Hussein and King Faisal of Saudi Arabia who, in the face of the radicals' obvious outrage, insisted on attaching to the militantly anti-Israeli resolution which the summit finally produced a clause stipulating that in the effort 'to eliminate the effects of aggression', all possible instruments needed to be utilized, 'including the political and diplomatic'.[2] Without his new stature and the weakness of his Arab radical adversaries, Hussein could not have fought for and won this important concession.

Freed from worries of domestic instability and encouraged by the increasing propensity of Arab states not to interfere in the affairs of each other, Hussein began to become more visible and more active in the Arab political theatre. But this role created its own constraints. To be an advocate of Arab causes carried responsibilities for that most central of Arab concerns: the question of Palestinian rights. Jordan's increasingly public pan-Arab posture coupled with the country's strategic proximity to Israel, gradually made it a haven for Palestinian guerrilla activities against the Jewish state. Hussein could stem neither the growth of the commandos' popularity and numbers nor the increased frequency of their operations against Israel which invited repeated heavy Israeli retaliation against Jordan itself. Much more worrying for the king was the guerrillas' anarchic behaviour in Jordan and their increasingly obvious contempt for the Jordanian authorities. The king could not allow this state of affairs to continue for very long. The Jordan army in particular had become restless and was demanding action against the unruly guerrillas. But at the same time, Hussein appreciated only too well Jordan's geo-strategic vulnerability. Israel's impatience with guerrilla incursions from Jordan was mounting dangerously; Syria threatened to support the Palestinians against 'imperialist plots'; and 15,000 pro-Palestinian Iraqi troops were stationed inside Jordan on the border with Iraq. The king had practically no allies, which meant that, alone, he faced considerable risks in his conflict with the guerrillas. On the other hand, a perhaps greater danger lay in the monarchy's gradual loss of authority to the 'Palestinian Resistance'. The time had thus come for the king and his troops to re-establish order in Jordan; it was a risky endeavour, but seeing no alternative, they decided to act.

Once the decision was taken, the Jordan army fought and defeated the guerrillas. In less than ten days in September 1970, later to be christened 'Black September' by the Palestinians, the Jordanian army not only succeeded in decimating the guerrilla fighting force, but also was able to repulse and beat back Syrian troops which had crossed the border in an effort to come to the rescue of the guerrillas. In a hastily arranged conference in Cairo at the end of September, the king reached an agreement with Yasser Arafat, the leader of the Palestine Liberation Organization (PLO) which considerably limited commando activity inside Jordan. Ten months later, in July 1971, the Jordan army used the agreement to end the guerrilla presence in Jordan altogether.

The Era of Confident Activism

The September 1970 Cairo conference was a turning-point in the history of inter-Arab relations no less important than the Arab defeat of June 1967. It marked the beginning of the gradual decline of the Palestinian movement as a potent radicalizing and destabilizing factor in Arab politics. The conference also led indirectly to the demise of two other radical Arab actors: President Nasser, less active after 1967 but still a symbol of revolutionary Arab nationalism, died from a heart attack at the end of the conference and was replaced by the conservative Anwar al-Sadat; and in Syria, the leftist Salah al-Jadid, who had been blamed for Syria's abortive intervention in Jordan's civil war, was overthrown by the pragmatic Hafiz al-Asad.

It was these two new leaders who successfully launched the Arabs' most successful military offensive against Israel in October 1973. For the first time since 1949, the Arabs could legitimately claim to have scored notable successes against the Israelis, and although the Israelis were finally to gain the upper hand, they did in the process suffer human casualties and losses in armaments that would have been unthinkable two years or even one year earlier. Not having been told of the timing of the Arab attack, Hussein could do no more than put his troops on the long Israeli border on alert, thus tying down a large number of Israeli troops and preventing them from participating in the war against Egypt and Syria. Later in the war when the Syrians began to feel the weight of the heavy Israeli counter-attack, the king sent two crack armoured brigades to the Syrian front which, along with Iraqi reinforcements, succeeded in halting the Israeli advance.

The October War did Hussein's prestige in the Middle East some good. He had played his part in a war about which he had no prior information. His limited participation in the conflict had been gratefully acknowledged by the Egyptian and Syrian presidents, and his people accepted that, faced with considerable constraints, Jordan had performed its part honourably. His authority inside Jordan was thus cemented even further. More significantly, the 1973 War was the culmination of a process of deradicalization in the region that had started with the June 1967 defeat and gathered momentum with the Palestinian defeat in Jordan in September 1970. The 1973 War was to show not only the primacy of 'states'

over 'revolutionary groups', but also the final ascendancy of pragmatic, even conservative, states over radical countries in the Arab
political theatre. By the mid-1970s, it was apparent that a significant
change in the mood and attitudes of the Arab population and leaders
alike had occurred. The rhetoric of revolutionary nationalism of the
1950s and 1960s began to sound peculiarly out of place in the more
pragmatic and businesslike atmosphere of the 1970s. Thus, while it
was Egypt's Nasser with his fiery brand of nationalist oratory who
dominated the Arab political theatre in the earlier period, the
principal actors in the post-1973 period were pro-Western, status-
quo leaders such as King Faisal and Prince Fahd of Saudi Arabia,
President Sadat of Egypt and, significantly, King Hussein himself.

As the 1970s drew to a close, therefore, the Jordanian monarch
had acquired an authority, not only in Jordan but outside the
country in the region as a whole, that would augur well for the
future stability of the Jordanian monarchy. No longer would
regional quarrels pose a threat to Hussein's survival. As the longest
surviving Arab leader, reigning over a stable polity and prosperous
economy, he could face up to political and military threats from
neighbouring states with a confidence that was lacking a decade or
two earlier. He would of course always need regional allies, for it
would be too risky for his small and strategically vulnerable country
to confront others alone, but in the status-quo milieu of the 1970s, it
was not too difficult to seek and receive support from like-minded
leaderships. Moreover, throughout the difficult years of the 1950s
and 1960s when he struggled to ensure Jordan's stability, Hussein
came to understand and accept the basic values and constraints that
influenced his country's regional and international orientations, and
learned to make decisions and devise policies in accordance with
these fundamental policy influences.

Factors Influencing Jordan's Policies

Throughout the three decades of King Hussein's rule, a number of
factors had influenced the direction and style of Jordan's regional
activities. In the first place, no Jordanian leader could formulate
policies without taking into consideration the country's geo-
strategic position. Of all the Arab countries, Jordan has the longest
border with Israel, across which the Jewish state regularly put into
practice its doctrine of 'massive retaliation'. As early as October

1953, the Jordanians experienced the ruthless military superiority of Israel, when in retaliation for an incursion into Israel by a handful of Palestinian guerrillas, a strong Israeli force attacked the small Jordanian village of Kibya, killing some fifty persons. Nor was Jordan able in the early 1960s to respond to Israel's decision to draw water from the Jordan valley for irrigation in the Negev. Indeed, with the growth of Palestinian guerrilla activity after 1964, the level of violence on the borders with Israel rose steadily, for although based in Syria, and encouraged and protected by the leftist Syrian regime, the guerrillas often crossed into Israel through northern Jordan thus inviting heavy Israeli reprisals against the villages of the West Bank. As pointed out earlier, one of these heavy Israeli operations occurred on 13 November 1966, when an Israeli armoured brigade, backed by the Israeli air force, demolished the Jordanian village of Samu, killing eighteen Jordanians and wounding fifty-four. Many analysts have pointed to this incident as the beginning of the chain of events that led eventually to the June 1967 War. The bloody expulsion of the guerrillas from Jordan in 1970 resulted in a much quieter border with Israel, but Jordanian strategic and military vulnerability to Israel remains undiminished.

A further factor that has contributed to instability on the Israeli frontier is Jordan's demographic structure. Particularly potent in the 1950s and 1960s, the Palestinian majority in Jordan meant that it was politically inopportune for the government to adopt anything less than an activist policy against Israel. Especially difficult was any effort to curtail the incursions by guerrillas into Israel, which rose steadily after the creation of the PLO in 1964. Only after September 1970 was full control over the border with Israel restored to Jordan.

The geo-strategic and demographic constraints have been equally potent in Jordan's relations with the Arab states. Being bounded on the north by the River Yarmouk and Syria, and on the east by Iraq, two radical Arab republics often at odds with the status-quo policies of Jordan, has left the Hashemite kingdom susceptible to the ever-changing moods and orientations of its two highly volatile neighbours. Thus, it was the 1958 Iraqi revolution which presented Jordan with its greatest peril in the 1950s, and then throughout the 1960s, it was one or the other or both of Jordan's 'revolutionary' neighbours that consistently worked to bring the Hashemite monarchy down. Indeed, even as late as the 1980s, President Asad of Syria was describing King Hussein as 'part of the imperialist conspiracy. He uses foreign forces against the Jordanian, Syrian and Palestinian people.'[3] With a much smaller population and armed forces than either of his two Arab neighbours, King Hussein needed always to be cautious when formulating and implementing his policies in the fertile crescent.

The roots of Jordan's insecurity *vis-à-vis* Iraq and Syria were as much ideological as they were strategic. This was exemplified by the Kingdom's seeming susceptibility to the radical nationalist symbolism used not only by Iraq and Syria, but also and more effectively by Egypt under Nasser. There was no quarrel over the tenets of Arab nationalism, since, to the king, nationalism meant 'the ultimate loyalty of the individual to the Arab world as a whole'.[4] The parting of the ways occurred over the prescriptions of Arab nationalism, particularly with regard to the realization of Arab unity. Whereas the Arab radicals and revolutionaries of the 1950s and 1960s demanded swift organic unity, Hussein preached the creation of loose and voluntary associations embracing 'only what the people of each country want to embrace – whether it be culture, economics or defence. Let political alliance, if it is desirable at all, be the last step.'[5] In that particular period of Arab historical development, where a rapid revolutionary transformation in the Arab world's political and economic institutions as well as in its social and cultural values, was taking place, the king's pragmatic and revolutionary strictures were out of tune with the impatient and rebellious moods of the Arab people.

Within this context, Jordan's demographic make-up with its sizeable radical Palestinian community made the country especially vulnerable to Arab nationalist rhetoric. It is this asymmetry between the maximalist goals held by the populace, which were fired by nationalist fervour, and minimalist objectives espoused by the leadership, which were formulated according to pragmatic interpretations of 'Arab nationalism' and realistic assessments of Jordan's geo-strategic and military vulnerability, that explains Jordan's instability during the 1950s and 1960s. It is significant that the contrasting stability and confidence of Jordan in the 1970s occurred only after the Arabs as a whole became disenchanted with revolutionary nationalism in the wake of the ignominious defeat of June 1967; after Jordan lost over 500,000 restless Palestinians to the Israelis; and after the army expelled the guerrillas in 1970. Nevertheless, even in the 1970s and 1980s, geo-strategic and demographic vulnerabilities continue to weigh heavily on the minds of Jordan's decision-makers, acting as effective constraints on Jordan's policy options in the Middle East.

Given these constraints, a major Jordanian policy has been to seek alliances and try not to act, or face threats, alone. In 1958 to counteract the dangers posed to the Kingdom by the Nasserite UAR, Jordan joined with Iraq in a federal structure called the 'Arab Union Federation'. Later, with the demise of the Iraqi monarchy and the ascendancy of radical republicanism, Jordan overcame the longstanding Hashemite–Saudi antipathy and endeavoured to establish an effective counteracting conservative alliance. Thus, both Jordan and Saudi Arabia in what seemed like a concerted move immediately recognized and supported the coup which took Syria out of the UAR in September 1961, and a year later, Jordan joined with the Saudis in backing the monarchical faction in the Yemen civil war. In the 1970s, when relations with the pro-Moscow Iraqi regime were strained, Jordanian–Syrian relations improved considerably. To President Asad, the Jordanians were 'close brothers who are the nearest kin to us',[6] and reciprocating this cordiality on an official visit to Damascus in May 1976, King Hussein expressed 'his full and absolute support for the Syrian initiative in Lebanon'.[7] Indeed, as Arab and international protest against the Syrian intervention in Lebanon gathered momentum, only Jordan remained a consistent and faithful ally and supporter of Syria's action in Lebanon. Yet, when relations with Syria began to deteriorate in the late 1970s, the Jordanians felt little threat, even when Syrian troops were moved to the Jordanian border, as they had already built an effective political and economic alliance with their other neighbour, Iraq, to say nothing of their ongoing *esprit de corps* with Saudi Arabia.

Moving beyond bilateral relations, the Jordanian king and his government have consistently supported and worked for the idea of Arab solidarity. This was to be expected of a prudent leadership, as inter-Arab conflict is bound to affect first and foremost the weaker states in the area, while at the other extreme, the all-engulfing idea of organic Arab unity is particularly destabilizing to geo-strategically vulnerable and demographically susceptible polities. Moreover, Arab solidarity, with its emphasis on cooperation between sovereign Arab states, has always genuinely been seen by the king as the best means of serving the interests of the Arab people. And in the process of proving this, he and Jordan have made great sacrifices, not least being Jordan's entry into the 1967 War. Other examples also show the king's eagerness for the concept of Arab solidarity and cooperation. For instance, after seven years of bitter hostility between him and President Nasser, King Hussein accepted without reservation an Egyptian invitation to attend a conference of Arab heads of state in Cairo in January 1964 because this signified a possible end to inter-Arab conflict. Furthermore, to exhibit his enthusiasm for the Egyptian initiative and encourage Cairo to maintain the process of Arab solidarity, the Jordanian king withdrew his support from the Yemeni Imam and recognized the republican government in Sanaa. Indeed, if one manifestation of Jordanian foreign policy has been consistent since January 1964, it is Amman's unquestionable faith in, and fervour for, multilateral Arab cooperative efforts. This is shown clearly in the leading role that King Hussein has played in the various Arab summits, such as the Khartoum summit of 1967 and more recently the Baghdad summit of 1978. Jordan's belief in multilateral Arab diplomacy was expressed by King Hussein after the collapse of the 1981 Fez summit: 'If any Arab leader has anything against his brother, he must air this at the summit meeting, motivated by eagerness to preserve Arab solidarity and by loyalty to our Arab nation, so that matters may be discussed with frankness, clarity and open-mindedness.'[8]

Jordan may at present have problems and disagreements with other Arab states, and may sometimes be the target of Israeli or Arab threats. But first, through gradual changes in the political environment of the Middle East which have occurred over the last two decades, and second through the skilful regional diplomacy of the Jordanian leadership which had come to terms with, and understood Jordan's geo-strategic and demographic vulnerabilities, and was thus able to utilize political action in the region that would not be hampered by Jordan's weaknesses, the Kingdom has emerged in the 1980s not only as a stable, but also a central, state in the area. Indeed, the onset of the 1980s has shown that the art of survival, the mysteries of which seem to be beyond the comprehension of many Arab leaders, has long been mastered by the Jordanian monarch and his government.

Adeed Dawisha

Notes

1. Quoted in Majid Khadduri, *Arab Personalities in Politics* (The Middle East Institute, Washington, DC, 1981), p. 106.
2. British Broadcasting Corporation (BBC), *Summary of World Broadcasts, Part IV, The Middle East,* hereinafter cited as *SWB*, ME/2559/A/2.
3. *Al-Thawra* (Damascus), 25 March 1981.
4. Quoted in Khadduri, op. cit., p. 106.
5. Ibid., p. 107.
6. President Hafiz al-Asad, *Speech Delivered before a General Plenum of Local Governments, 20 July 1976* (The Ba'th Arab Socialist Party, Damascus, 1976), p. 66.
7. *SWB*, ME/5206/A/3.
8. *SWB*, ME/6897/A/6-7.

Hashemite Rule
and the Emergence of the State

Suleiman Mousa

The State of Jordan was founded as a result of two main factors: the First World War and the Arab Revolt. During the Ottoman period, and in fact long before that, Jordan was an integral part of geographic Syria, never in modern times forming a separate entity within its present-day boundaries. When the Turks entered the war in 1914 on the side of Germany, the course of events in this part of the world underwent a drastic change. Great Britain, France and Tsarist Russia concluded an agreement to dismember the Ottoman Empire and divide it among themselves as the spoils of war. Unfortunately, geographic Syria and Iraq were targets for both the British and the French. Accordingly an agreement (the Sykes–Picot agreement) was concluded in May 1916 delimiting the sphere of control of each power. Thus Syria was split into four pieces to satisfy imperialist interests. Transjordan was to be given some sort of independence under British influence.

One month after the conclusion of the Sykes–Picot agreement, the Arab Revolt broke out in the Hijaz, led by Sharif Hussein, Grand Sharif of Mecca, the leader of Arab nationalism. The Arabs' aim was to establish an independent and united Arab kingdom comprising all Arab lands in Asia. An agreement was made (*vide* the Hussein–McMahon correspondence) by which Great Britain undertook to support the Arabs in their aim in return for Arab help against the Ottoman Turks. Arab forces fought their way from Mecca in the south to Aleppo in the north, under the command of the Sharif's four sons: Ali, Abdullah, Faisal and Zaid.

When the war ended an Arab state was established in present-day Syria and Jordan (East Bank) under the Amir Faisal. Iraq and Palestine came under direct British control, while on Lebanon direct French control was imposed. The Arabs had relied on Great Britain, their ally, to support them in realizing unity and independence, but Britain elected to be bound by the terms of the Sykes-Picot agreement rather than by her pledges to the Arabs, and allowed a French army to march in July 1920 from Lebanon, defeat the Arab army of Faisal, and enter Damascus.

Faisal was forced to leave his capital, Damascus, while the French consolidated their hold over Syria.

In accordance with the Sykes–Picot agreement, which placed Transjordan under British influence, the French did not advance southwards into this area. Consequently Transjordan remained virtually without a government. However, in the Hauran on Transjordan's north-eastern border, the French occupation led to serious disturbances, in the course of which the Syrian Prime Minister, collaborating with the invaders, was killed. The French took severe measures to stamp out all resistance and as a result some Syrian nationalist leaders fled for refuge to Transjordan. These leaders, together with a number of Jordanians, sent cables to Sharif Hussein in Mecca seeking his support and beseeching him to delegate one of his sons to lead a new national resistance movement against the French.

Sharif Hussein was very concerned about the turn of events in Syria. He had done everything possible to send military reinforcements to the Syrian army before the battle with the French. Now, learning of the Syrian resistance, his hopes revived. Receiving the telegrams from the Syrian and Jordanian leaders with enthusiasm, he hastened to instruct his second son, the Amir Abdullah, to proceed northwards to Syria. At the time Sharif Hussein was in a weak position, because his army had been defeated by the Saudis more than a year earlier (May 1919) and his British allies had stopped paying the subsidy he had been receiving since June 1916. But in spite of these problems he did not hesitate to come to the aid of the Syrians in their hour of need.

The Amir Abdullah was then Minister of Foreign Affairs for the Hijaz Kingdom. He left Mecca for Medina and from there proceeded by rail with a small force of regulars and beduin volunteers. After a difficult journey, because the line had been inadequately repaired after the damage sustained during the war, he arrived at Ma'an on 21 November 1920.

Ma'an was at the time a small town administered by the Hijaz. The Amir made it his headquarters, declared that he had come as a deputy of his brother Faisal, and called upon the Syrians to gather round him so that he might march at their head to attack the French and eject them from Syria. The response was much weaker than he had anticipated. Few Syrians ventured to undertake the long journey to Ma'an. But the response of the beduin tribes around Ma'an, who had fought the Turks for almost two years under the command of his brother Faisal, was positive and enthusiastic. Although the Syrians' response was disappointing, the sudden advent of the Amir created a stir in Transjordan and Syria. Exaggerated reports about the Arab army assembled at Ma'an – estimated by rumour at 7,000 men – reached the British and French authorities. Fearing an Arab assault timed to coincide with an internal uprising, the French mobilized a considerable force on the frontier with Transjordan and warned the British in Palestine that they would send a military column to attack the Amir, if the British did not take steps to arrange his withdrawal. Since the territory between Syria and Ma'an was under British mandate, the French considered it was Britain's responsibility to deal with the Amir and remove the threat he represented. As a result the British sent emissaries to Ma'an advising the Amir to return to Mecca and declaring publicly their disapproval of any movement favouring him. The Amir, however, would not be cowed. He was in Hijazi territory, he said, he had no dispute with the British, but neither had he any intention of going back to Mecca.

In fact the Amir was not happy spending the winter with inadequate facilities in Ma'an, but he felt he must remain there as long as there was any hope of something happening. Having few funds to sustain the needs of his followers, he was obliged to borrow £3,000 from Shaikh Audeh Abu Tayeh, the famous leader of the Howeitat tribe. During that winter (1920-21) a popular movement in favour of the Amir was maturing in Transjordan, whose leaders, in defiance of British warnings, invited him to go north to Amman. He was told that the country was in a state of chaos, due to the lack of a central government, and that his coming would unite it and save it from disorder. The Amir, intent on exploring all possible ways and means, delegated Sharif Ali al-Harith to travel north and study the situation. Sharif Ali was received with popular acclaim in Amman and Salt. The British, it was beginning to seem, had no definite policy towards the Amir and so did not interfere.

There was another factor which tended to influence the course of events. In certain quarters in England, there was a feeling that the British Government had treated its Arab allies very unfairly, especially in allowing the French to occupy Damascus. It was a shameful deal, many men of influence felt. This feeling was reinforced by the Iraqi revolution in the summer of 1920, which cost a lot to put down. It was public knowledge that the Iraqis were seeking independence and an Arab head of state who should be one of Sharif Hussein's sons. Hussein himself was raising the cry everywhere that the British had betrayed both him and the Arab cause once they no longer needed him and his people. He stubbornly refused to recognize the mandate or to accept the imperialist designs of Great Britain and France. In these circumstances the British Government felt itself bound in honour and self-interest to come to terms with Arab nationalism, represented at the time by Sharif Hussein, his sons and their adherents in Iraq and geographic Syria. Hence Faisal was invited to London.

The negotiations in London between the Foreign Office and the Amir Faisal aimed to reach a general settlement of outstanding questions in a way that would both meet Arab aspirations and safeguard British interests. An agreement was eventually arrived at, by which Iraq and Transjordan were to be recognized as independent entities under British mandate. It was tacitly agreed that Faisal would offer his candidature to the throne of Iraq.

While these negotiations were in progress in London, the Amir Abdullah decided to move northwards to Amman, where he arrived on 2 March 1921. He was welcomed by all the leaders of Transjordan, who offered him allegiance and loyalty. His arrival marked the end of the local administrations which were vainly attempting to bring law and order to the three districts of Irbid, Salt and Kerak.

The Middle East conference which Winston Churchill called in

Cairo early in March 1921 did not take a definite decision in regard to Transjordan except that it should be an Arab province attached to Palestine. When Churchill learned of Abdullah's arrival in Amman, he extended an invitation to him to a meeting in Jerusalem and towards the end of March the two men held four sessions to discuss the future of Transjordan. The Amir spoke of the Arabs' concern regarding British policy on Palestine and suggested that the best solution would be to unite Palestine and Transjordan in one state. When he was told that Great Britain was bound by its commitment to the national home of the Jews, the Amir proposed that some arrangement could be worked out to give expression to that policy within the proposed state. Churchill insisted that there was no possibility of changing Britain's policy on Palestine. He went on to propose that the Amir take charge of Transjordan, saying that the Amir's success in leading it to peace and order would encourage the French to follow a similar policy in Syria, and that there was a good chance of his being invited to rule in Damascus in six months' time. He promised that the British Government would use its good offices with the French in that respect.

The Amir consulted the Syrian, Transjordanian and Palestinian leaders accompanying him. All were of the opinion that, in the circumstances, it was imperative to accept Britain's proposal as a constructive and realistic step. It was considered that developments might convince the French and British to modify their policies on Syria and Palestine respectively, and that by wisdom and patience the Arabs would attain objectives they had no power to attain by force of arms.

The general lines of the agreement between Abdullah and Churchill were as follows:

1. The establishment in Transjordan of an Arab Government under the Amir Abdullah.

2. Transjordan would be independent under British mandate.

3. The British Government would assist Transjordan with an annual subsidy to maintain a force to keep order in the country.

4. The Transjordan Government would undertake to prevent hostile acts against Syria and Palestine.

5. The policy of the Jewish national home would not be applicable to Transjordan.

6. A British air force and some armoured cars would be stationed in Amman.

Thus we can see that the establishment of Transjordan was the result of combined factors: the Arab Revolt, British and French policy, and British and Arab mutual need for cooperation. Had the Amir Abdullah declined to accept Churchill's proposal, in all likelihood the country would have been subsequently amalgamated with Palestine and fallen prey to Zionist exploitation.

Early in April 1921 the Amir began working to establish the structure of a government. Amman, for various reasons, was chosen as the capital of the new Amirate which was officially named the Imarat (Principality) of Transjordan (but in English simply called Transjordan).

The Amir had to rely mainly on non-Jordanians to fill the posts in the new administration. Jordan's first cabinet included only one Jordanian, the other seven members being from Syria, Hijaz and Palestine. Two reasons lay behind this: first, there were simply not enough educated and experienced Jordanians to fill all the vacancies; and second, the Amir considered that Jordan was only a part of the state which the Arabs were endeavouring to create. Sharif Hussein and his sons saw the establishment of Iraq and Jordan as but one step on the path to the foundation of a great state that would include all Arab countries in Asia. True, the French and British had divided geographic Syria by force, but Hussein, his sons, and all nationalists had real hopes that the artificial partitions would soon disappear and their aim be realized.

Transjordan, cast as the launching-pad for this great nationalist enterprise, was – just after its birth as a state – scarcely well equipped for the role.

The country consisted of three districts: Irbid in the north, Belqa in the middle, and Kerak in the south. The population numbered about 300,000, two-thirds of whom were villagers and the other third beduin tribesmen living mainly to the east of the Hijaz railway. The villagers worked as farmers while the beduins raised camels and sheep. At that time a traditional animosity and mistrust existed between the two sections of the community. Beduin tribes did not content themselves with raiding each other, but raided nearby villages too and forced the inhabitants to pay a tribute called *khaweh*: brotherly fee!

During Ottoman times government control of the tribes was weak, and sometimes non-existent, due to the fact that the Ottoman military forces were inadequately equipped to penetrate the depths of the desert. Circumstances were such that the government had to pay yearly subsidies to tribes bordering the railway line in order to secure the safety of pilgrims on their way to the holy places of the Hijaz. Tribal traditions and values prevailed among both beduins and villagers. The economy depended on farm produce and stock-breeding. In most years cereals, such as corn and barley and animals, such as camels and sheep, were exported to Palestine. There was virtually no industry, so people obtained the manufactured goods they needed from the markets of Damascus and Palestine. Theirs was a simple modest life and domestic needs were few, consisting mainly of cloth and cooking utensils. There were no proper roads. Beasts of burden were the only means of transport. The Hijaz railway, completed in 1908 and linking Damascus and Medina, was the only mechanical device operating in the country. There were very few elementary schools and hardly more than one per cent of the population was literate. However, society was homogeneous. Islam was the religion of over ninety per cent of the people. The Christians, numbering about eight per cent, were descended from the original Arab inhabitants of the country and had lived for centuries in harmony and on equal terms with their Muslim fellow Arabs. In addition there was a small community of Circassians who had migrated from Russia towards the end of the nineteenth century to settle near water-springs in Amman, Jerash and other neighbouring places. The Jordanians were true to the cause of the Hashemites. Many of them had fought the battles of the Arab Revolt, and they were proud to have a descendant of the Prophet Muhammad and a son of Sharif Hussein as head of their new state.

This, in brief, was the community which the Amir Abdullah set himself to lead and guide. One of the most important challenges facing him was to gain the people's confidence in the government, a confidence which had been almost extinguished during centuries of tyranny and oppression.

But securing order was the immediate task. Formed in April 1921, the new government was faced in May with an insurrection in a hilly area in the north where the inhabitants refused to pay taxes and defeated the small force which attempted to subdue them. The Amir had to use his personal prestige to smooth matters over until a year later the government was able to muster an adequate number of troops to bring the rebels to heel. Then in June a group of Syrian émigrés residing in Jordan attacked the French High Commissioner for Syria, and, as a result, all troops were placed under the command of a British officer. There were also external threats to be met. Two major attacks were mounted by Wahhabi warriors from Nejd in 1922 and again in 1924. On both occasions the raiders came close to Amman, and on both occasions they were defeated by the combined efforts of tribesmen, military troops and British aeroplanes.

In 1923 the government had to deal with a serious internal threat, when several tribes combined and, to demonstrate their grievances, attacked Amman. They too were defeated.

On the question of sovereignty an important step was achieved on 23 September 1922 when the League of Nations approved a British memorandum excluding Jordan from the policy of the Jewish national home. Consequently on 25 May 1923 the British Government recognized Jordan as an independent state, and since then the independence of the country has been commemorated on this date.

Jordan enjoyed a good degree of internal independence until August 1924 when, to satisfy French demands, the British authorities in Palestine enforced tight control over the administration and the finances of the country and ordered a number of Syrian leaders to leave it. In 1925, as a result of the Saudi attack on the Hijaz, the southern district of Ma'an–Aqaba was incorporated into Transjordan which thereby acquired its dimensions of today.

However, the extent of Jordan's independence remained somewhat vague. Discussions to regulate relations with the Mandatory did not bear fruit until 1928 when a treaty was signed in Jerusalem. Its terms were almost dictated, but at least it defined each side's relations with the other and represented a legal recognition of Jordan's independence. Free elections for a Legislative Council followed which approved the treaty in due course.

Jordan forged forwards on the path of progress. It was a slow process but stable and sure. The country enjoyed a degree of peace and order not experienced for many centuries. New schools were established and roads constructed. People went about their business unmolested. An important advance was the establishment of the ownership of land which had formerly been common property. The state was Arab in character and in all internal aspects. Ruler and citizen were of the same nationality. British personnel in the country did not exceed ten who, with the exception of the commander-in-chief, worked as experts and advisers.

Britain needed Jordan to be quiet and safe for the security of Palestine and of the Iraqi pipeline, and gave a subsidy for this reason alone, to maintain a small force of police and gendarmes. In the final year 1925-26 the state budget amounted to £257,000, of which £101,000 was accounted for by the subsidy. For the first fifteen years of its existence Jordan had only one complete secondary school. In 1926 the first four students graduated from it, followed in 1927 by another five. During these early years educated Jordanians were not very welcome in high-level civil or military service. Preference was given to non-Jordanians, not only because they generally had better education or more experience, but also because they were more obedient and carried out orders without asking questions. It is true that most of these non-Jordanians served the country with dedication and loyalty, and with the passage of time settled for good in the country and aligned themselves with the original inhabitants. The first Jordanian to form a cabinet did so only in 1950 – thirty years after the establishment of the state.

In 1931 an important step was taken with the founding of the Desert Patrol, as a special branch of the army entrusted with the task of keeping order in the desert. The new force was founded and commanded by Captain Glubb who had ten years' experience in Iraq, but the novel aspect of it was that it enlisted tribesmen to keep order among the tribes. Glubb performed his task with singular dedication and achieved complete success. Although the force initially consisted of only about one hundred men, it established order, stopped raids and rounded up wrongdoers. Glubb's task was not only to maintain order in a wide area – roughly all the land to the east of the railway – but also to administer that area. This was achieved by goodwill and by dealing with the people according to their own traditions, habits and way of life. The greatest achievement was winning the confidence of the beduins and building a bridge of mutual understanding between them and the government. Gradually the beduins were led to realize the benefits of good order and to see the contribution they could make to the progress of the country. With their martial qualities, once exercised in raiding and tribal warfare, they found ready access to service in the armed forces.

The Second World War offered new possibilities to Jordan. The

policy of loyalty and steadfastness which the Amir pursued proved
to be to the country's advantage. Far-sightedly, Abdullah declared
himself and his country on the side of Britain, and, as a result, the
treaty was modified in Jordan's interests and the strength of the
army increased from a few hundred men in the early days of the war
to 8,000 towards its end. The Jordanian army, the famous Arab
Legion, performed an active and effective role, fought in Iraq and
Syria, and did essential duties in many countries of the Middle East,
from Iran in the north to Egypt in the south.

The Amir Abdullah expected that Britain would review its policy
towards the Arabs and make amends for the wrongs done to them
in the wake of the First World War. In 1941, as a result of France's
defeat, a great opportunity to revoke the Sykes-Picot agreement
presented itself. The Amir did all he could to unite Syria and
Transjordan, but the British continued to support the policy of
division.

Although the Amir Abdullah failed in his endeavours to unite
Syria and Jordan, he succeeded in gaining genuine independence for
his country. In March 1946 a new treaty was signed with Britain by
which the mandate came to an end and Jordan was recognized as a
fully independent state. This treaty stipulated that Britain could
station troops in Jordan, and that the Jordanian army would receive
a subsidy and be commanded by British officers. As a result,
on 25 May 1946, King Abdullah was proclaimed constitutional
monarch and the country named the Hashemite Kingdom of
Transjordan.

Thus King Abdullah steered the course of events in Jordan during
its twenty-five years under mandate. In spite of the smallness of the
British subsidy the country made remarkable progress and attained
a measure of maturity which entitled it to independence.

Government and Economy in Jordan: Progress, Problems and Prospects

Roger Owen

In an article published in 1967 H. Talal ('a pseudonym for one well acquainted with Jordanian affairs') asserted confidently that his country had taken 'large steps towards the achievement of self-sustained growth and economic self-sufficiency'. And, as evidence, he cited the progress which had been made towards achieving the aims of the government's 1964–71 development programme, notably a reduction in the chronic balance of payments deficit and an increase in the proportion of government expenditure financed out of domestic revenues.[1]

But no sooner had this article appeared, than the Six Day War of June 1967 provided a stark reminder of all the problems and outside pressures which the Kingdom continued to face. According to some estimates, the loss of the West Bank with its rich agricultural lands along the Jordan, reduced National Income by between a third and two fifths. There were some 300,000–400,000 new Palestinian refugees to absorb. Later continued tension along the border with Israel and between the government and the Palestinian *fedayeen* meant that confidence in the country's economic and political future remained low. Existing plans for development had to be abandoned or entirely recast.

Nevertheless, once these problems had been mastered in the early 1970s, the Jordanian economy bounced back to enjoy a long period of sustained growth. Both 1975 and 1976 were boom years. The real growth in national income during the 1976–80 plan has been estimated at just under 10 per cent per annum.[2] In large part Jordan was able to avoid most of the major stresses and strains to be found elsewhere within the intra-Arab environment and, once political stability had been restored, it was well placed to benefit economically from a whole variety of external events, whether as a haven for capital fleeing from the Lebanon, as an ally of Iraq in its war with Iran or as a provider of skilled labour to Saudi Arabia and the Gulf States during the oil boom of the later 1970s.

Some indices illustrating certain important areas of economic advance can be found in Tables 1 and 2. With the exception of agriculture, which suffered severely from a series of poor winter rains, the major sectors of the economy showed a substantial increase in income during the plan period 1976–80. There was a similar growth in money from external sources, including remittances from Jordanians abroad (sent through the banking system) which trebled between 1973–77 and 1980. The result was a large increase in imports, in consumption and in such major acts of private expenditure as the construction of new houses, some worth hundreds of thousands of pounds. Other statistics tell the same story. During the first three years of the last plan period, 1976 to 1978, capital formation rose from 25.9 per cent of GNP to 33.3 per cent.[3] Again, between 1973 and 1977 35 new industrial units were established, employing nearly 12,400 workers.[4] Finally, according to World Bank calculations, per capita income rose from $610 in 1976 to $1,180 in 1979.[5]

Official figures also provide a guide to some of the less happy features of Jordan's rapid economic advance. They show, for example, that the country remained just as dependent on foreign financial assistance as it had ever done, with export earnings continuing to provide no more than about a sixth of the money needed to pay for imports and with domestic revenues covering less than half of government expenditure, with the rest made up by foreign grants and loans (Tables 3 and 4). Meanwhile, politicians and planners began to inveigh against the fact that consumer goods provide such a large share of imports, a situation which may be even worse than it appears on paper because of the belief that a large quantity of private purchases enter the country unrecorded.[6] If to this is added the fact that Jordan depends heavily on the remittances sent home by its workers temporarily employed in its oil-rich neighbours and on official Arab aid, there is the same need as ever to try to reach a point where the country will be able to insulate itself against harmful external economic pressures by reducing its import bill and raising more of its income from domestic sources.

Second, the period of rapid economic advance has brought with it all the well-known stresses of modernization such as the acceleration of migration from country to town, increasing inequalities of income between rich and poor and between one region and another, shortages of cheap houses and demands for a very much higher level of government services. It was in recognition of the pressing need to pay attention to such problems that the government decided to lay great stress on social welfare in its 1981–85 development plan. It was thinking of the same kind which led to the appointment of the late Abd al-Hamid Sharaf as Prime Minister in December 1979. But before discussing government attempts to attend to some of the more pressing social problems and to find ways of improving the living conditions of the poorer sections of Jordanian society it would be useful to say something in general about the composition of Jordan's population, the structure of its economy and the role of government in its economic management.

According to the preliminary figures released for the census of November 1979 East Bank Jordan has a population of nearly 2.2 million. Of these, half live in five major concentrations of 40,000 or more, including one refugee camp.[7] Calculations based on earlier censuses reveal that Jordan has a young population (with nearly 50 per cent of its people under fifteen), that the rate of increase is high (over 3 per cent a year) and that something like 400,000 Jordanians are living and working outside the country.[8] Literacy rates are high compared with most Arab states, as is the degree of participation of women in the labour force (see Table 5). Nevertheless, given the fact that less than half the population are of working age and that the number of women in regular work is still relatively few, Jordan had a labour participation rate of only about 20 per cent – low by international (but not Middle Eastern) standards.

Turning to the structure of employment, the 1975 Manpower Survey revealed that something like 19 per cent of the labour force was engaged in agriculture, 15 per cent in government and other services, 10 per cent in construction, 5 per cent in industry and mining, with a further third in a category described as 'unidentified' but which, in fact, consisted largely of military personnel.[9] Another way of looking at these same figures is to say that, in the middle 1970s, nearly half of the total labour force of some 380,000 was employed by the government.[10] In 1979 there were also an estimated 50,000 to 75,000 non-Jordanians living and working inside Jordan, although this figure may well have excluded a large number of foreigners, mainly Egyptians and Syrians, who come in and out of the country on a seasonal basis.[11] By 1980 the remittances sent out of Jordan by these foreign workers had reached JD47million.[12]

Turning to the composition of the Gross Domestic Product, the Central Bank figures in Table 2 reveal that the government contributed 20.4 per cent of the total, with industry and mining providing 18.7 per cent, wholesale and retail trade 17.4 per cent and agriculture just over 7 per cent. This gives a clear enough indication of the type of economy to be found in a country with very few natural resources of its own and with the bulk of its income deriving directly or indirectly from the services which it is able to provide for its Arab neighbours. As far as its own domestic resources are concerned, the greater part of the government's efforts have been devoted to try to increase the output of irrigated agriculture in the Jordan Valley and to expand the production of phosphates and, in the future, potash from the Dead Sea. For the rest, productive activity depends largely on the contribution of a small but vital industrial sector, working up mostly imported goods (oil, chemicals, paper etc.) for sale in the Jordanian and local Arab markets.

The question of how such a country with so few natural resources and occupying such a central and such a sensitive position in the Arab world is properly managed from an economic point of view is clearly one of fundamental importance. Here it is necessary to draw attention to what at first sight may seem a major paradox: that of a government with considerable political and economic power at its disposal and yet choosing to run an open, *laissez-faire* system with a minimum of controls and a maximum emphasis on the need for cooperation between public and private enterprise. The power of the government's own economic position has already been underlined and rests on such important factors as its role as far and away the largest employer of labour, its control over local revenues through taxes and its access to foreign funds through its diplomatic alignments and the fact that, in so small a country, only the government will have the money and the determination to set up large projects like the establishment of the national airline (ALIA), the construction of the oil refinery at Zarqa and the development of phosphate mining. Given these assets it is also relatively easy for such a government to institute social security and welfare schemes directed mainly towards its own employees and to draw up development plans based largely on its own control over important national resources.

Nevertheless, in spite of these and other advantages, the government remains wedded to a *laissez-faire* economic philosophy based on the assumption that its main role is to create a proper climate for private enterprise to flourish. This philosophy is clearly and obviously expressed in the government's policies towards trade and payments, the banking and monetary system and the manipulation of tariffs and taxes. In all instances the basic aim is to encourage Jordanians, and also foreigners, to invest their money safely in productive enterprise. The same attitude can also be seen just as clearly in the scope which is allowed to private sector enterprises to influence and to criticize official policy whether through their representation on the board of public institutions like the Central Bank or through the presence of their members on the National Planning Council or the seventy-five-man National Consultative Council set up in 1978.

The reasons for the maintenance of such policies over thirty years remain more or less the same. On the one hand there is the government's – and especially the ruler's – perception of how Jordan can derive most economic advantage from its special position within the Arab state system. On the other, there is the fact that Jordan's political elite is itself deeply entrenched within the present system and actively supportive of it. In such a situation the limits of government intervention are widely understood and well defined. So too is the need for the government to gain the acceptance of new policies by persuasion and encouragement rather than by coercion and cajolery. Ideological support for the present system of economic management comes when necessary, from appeals to the special character of Jordanian society and to the harm which might be done to local capital and enterprise if Jordan introduced policies

involving a significantly higher degee of government control or a
very much higher rate of taxation than its oil-rich neighbours.

Economic policy is thus largely a matter of bargaining and
compromise. While the state is given free rein to set the country's
main economic targets, to identify growth sectors and to take the
lead in providing assistance for the larger projects, other goals have
to be pursued more circumspectly. A good example of this has been
the methods employed to try to control inflation and to make better
use of the remittances and other funds flooding into the country by
encouraging savings and by providing incentives for private and
institutional investors to put their money into productive enterprise. These included the opening of the Amman Stock Exchange in
January 1978, the creation of specialized credit institutions like the
Industrial Development Bank and the Housing Corporation, the
creation of industrial estates, the encouragement given to the
opening of private merchant banks and investment houses and
alterations in the rates of interest offered to deposit and current
accounts in the local banks. The result has certainly been a
significant increase in the amount of credit made available to
industrial enterprises even if this still remains only a small proportion of the total money lent at short term to the government and to
domestic and foreign borrowers.

Much the same type of procedure has been followed by the
government when it has turned its attention to measures to reduce
differences of income or to provide greater welfare support for the
poor. As elsewhere in the Middle East the major effort has gone into
those programmes for which there is a great popular demand and
from which all sections of society can benefit: notably health and
education. Figures from the World Bank show just how successful
the government has been in these areas with all of Jordan's school-
age children (both boys and girls) attending primary school from
six to twelve and nearly three-quarters of them completing
secondary school as well.[13] Again, of those who complete their
twelve years of schooling all but 8 per cent will have done so in
government or UNWRA schools which provide their teaching
completely free.[14] There is now a drive to develop institutions of
higher learning with nearly thirty, mostly private, community
colleges, and – as of December 1981 – two major universities with
over 20,000 students and a third one just starting construction.[15]
Meanwhile, as far as health is concerned, government programmes

have ensured that the national ratio of patients per doctor has fallen from 5,800 in 1960 to 1,960 in 1979 while life expectancy at birth has climbed from forty-seven to sixty-one years during the same period.[16]

Where progress has been more slow has been in the extension of social security and social insurance to more than a privileged stratum of the urban population, in providing the poor with cheap or subsidized food and housing or in developing a progressive tax system which could act as a proper instrument for redistributing income. It is these subjects which are now occupying the attention of Jordan's reformers, well aware that their country's new-found stability could be easily undermined by increasing social tensions, perhaps exacerbated by forces outside the country. There is also sound economic sense behind measures which might help to stop the drift from countryside to town and from the towns to the oil-rich states of the Gulf. For all these reasons Jordan's efforts to tackle these problems are of general interest, the more so as it seems to have been the first of the oil-poor states to recognize that the existence of the oil boom has produced a radical change in the Arab economic environment with effects which reach right through each Arab society.

As far as the tax system is concerned, Jordan, like the majority of its Arab neighbours, raises the great bulk of its revenues from indirect taxes, mainly customs dues. (Table 3). Only a small part of the revenue (15½ per cent in 1980) comes from direct taxes on the income of individuals and companies. This is a lower proportion than in Syria or Egypt but much higher than in the Gulf states to the east where income taxes are either very low or not levied at all.[17] In the case of both direct and indirect taxes the Jordanian Government has clearly been willing to sacrifice revenue in the interest of providing incentives to Jordanians and foreigners willing to invest in local industry. And in the case of the income tax there has been the additional administrative problem (again shared with its Arab neighbours) of finding out details of private earnings or dealing fairly with complicated systems of tax exemptions. In these circumstances, although the top rate of personal tax in 1981 was 50 per cent on incomes of over JD8,000 ($24,133), not many persons actually paid at this rate and thus the system's capacity to act as a machinery for redistributing wealth was low.[18] Given these constraints the best that governments have been able to do is to ensure that both

direct and indirect taxes are collected with greater efficiency – and
there is some evidence that this has actually been happening in the
last few years.[19] Recent governments have also been quite successful in raising duties on certain luxury imports like large cars. In
future, however, it will certainly be necessary to find some way of
taxing some part of the huge incomes which are accruing to the
growing group of businessmen, bankers and merchants making
high profits from present boom conditions. It may be that the
information about individual and corporate earnings now being
collected by the new Social Security Corporation could provide a
basis for a more rigorous system of assessment and collection.

The Social Security Corporation itself is part of a major effort to
extend and to improve the insurance cover provided for the
majority of Jordan's labour force. Its aim is to provide protection
against injuries at work and occupational diseases as well as
pensions for the retired, the permanently disabled and the
dependants of those who die.[20] The Corporation began its activities
in January 1980 and has been extending its cover in a number of
stages beginning with government officials and the employees of
large private organizations. As of January 1982 it was planning a
further extension to include university teachers, officials in the
municipalities and those either self-employed or working in small
private firms. In each case the inclusion of particular organizations is
the subject of negotiation. But once in, it covers all its employees
between the ages of sixteen and sixty. An unusual feature is that it
also applies to non-Jordanian workers, both Arab and foreign, all of
whom are entitled to the return of their accumulated contributions
in a lump sum if they want to leave the country. Altogether the
Corporation has made an excellent start. But, as in the case of Egypt
and other Middle Eastern countries which have tried to introduce
large schemes, the major problem comes when the attempt is made
to try to extend cover to workers outside the large towns and, in
particular, to those engaged in agriculture. The reasons for this are
obvious but will certainly have to be overcome if, among other
things, the Corporation is to make a contribution to the improve-
ment of rural conditions and the reduction of the flood of migrants
to Amman.

Government employees are also major beneficiaries of schemes
to provide low-cost housing and cheap food. In the case of the
former the main agency involved is the semi-independent Housing

Corporation, founded in 1967 and financed by loans from the Housing Bank (established in 1974), the Central Bank and the government. One of its main aims has been to provide accommodation for civil servants and other officials. Until 1980 the houses it constructed were allocated on the basis of a twenty-year mortgage with a low interest of 5 per cent. According to its Director it built some 10,000 housing units between 1970–71 and 1980 and planned to increase this to some 3,000 units a year beginning in 1982.[21] This should be seen in terms of an official estimate that Jordan would require an average of just over 16,000 new houses a year for the ten years from 1976. However, given the numbers of Jordanians who live in sub-standard shanty settlements round Amman and the other large towns it seems likely that this is something of an under-estimate and there is an obvious need for other organizations to help with the task. One such is the Amman Municipality itself which plans to launch a large-scale urban renewal scheme in 1982 designed to provide low-cost housing, services and community facilities for 56,000 of the city's poorest residents, with the aid of a loan from the World Bank.[22] Another avenue which is being explored is to encourage the private sector to make a greater contribution by concentrating more of its efforts at the lower end of the housing market.

Secondly, the main agencies for providing low-cost food and other products are the two consumer corporations, the military and the government, which, together cater to the needs of over half a million soldiers, officials and their families. In each case the corporations run special shops where prices are lower than elsewhere due to the fact that they are allowed to import their goods duty-free and are only concerned to make low profits.[23] For the remainder of the population the main support comes from the activities of the Ministry of Supply which sells certain imported goods, such as meat, at subsidized prices or sometimes acts to stabilize the price of essential food items.

In these circumstances undoubtedly the most significant government effort to improve the lives of the poor is the continuing programme (given great prominence in the 1981-85 development plan) of extending and improving the provision of health, educational and other government services for a larger and larger section of the population. One example of this is the scheme to bring electricity to nearly half of Jordan's villages – containing three-quarters of the rural population – by 1985.[24] Nevertheless, even if everything goes according to plan there will still remain significant disparities in terms of income and access to government services as between different regions and different groups. Figures to illustrate the present extent of such inequalities are difficult to find but one, taken from a study commissioned by the Economics Department of the Royal Jordanian Scientific Society, suggested that the average rural income in the Amman governorate was only 63 per cent of that in the city itself.[25]

These and other problems were given great attention by Sharaf in his speech outlining the policies to be pursued by his new ministry before the National Consultative Council on 24 December 1979.[26] The social dimension was essential to development, he asserted, and national wealth should be justly distributed as a result of fair legislation, the just application of taxation and the state's commitment – in economic and social planning and in the government's daily actions – to the people's welfare. He reaffirmed the government's resolve to provide jobs for Jordan's citizens as well as to satisfy such basic human needs as food, housing, medical treatment and education 'so far as this is reasonably possible'. But he also stressed the fact that it could offer these services efficiently only if it could obtain the cooperation of the people in quite a different way from the present. In particular the public should participate with the government in confronting 'runaway consumption' with the aim of directing the national economy towards the proper priorities: increased production, restrained consumption and a cutback on luxuries. Regionalism was another top priority. Administration should be decentralized to ensure that services were distributed throughout the Kingdom, as opposed to concentration in the cities, and as a way of halting further rural out-migration. Sharaf pursued these same themes in a number of other speeches, notably one before the Chamber of Industry in which he warned that the private sector would have to attune itself to 'the welfare society' and the need for 'social justice'. He also sought to publicize them more widely under the general slogan of the 'rationalization of consumption' which was intended to sum up his general belief in the need to reduce excessive consumption and to conserve the country's national resources.[27] Unfortunately, however, he did not live long enough to do more than make a small start towards the implementation of his programme but some of the steps he took indicate the general direction he wished to take. These included a very large rise in the import duty on what Americans call 'gas-guzzling' cars, a further rise in the price of petrol (the third in twelve months), the introduction of a new municipalities law and the establishment of a Ministry of Social Development headed by Jordan's first woman cabinet minister. It is also important to note that the opposition which part of his programme was quick to arouse would have made further progress difficult. Even with strong royal support his room to manoeuvre was narrowly limited.

Succeeding governments have attempted to pursue the same goals as Sharaf but with noticeably less drive. To do them justice they have obviously had to balance his emphasis on regional development and social justice with concern for a large number of other urgent problems such as the dangers posed by the easily predictable shortages of water and energy towards the end of this century, the need to push on with a whole variety of major projects like the completion of the new Amman airport and the rationalization of a government administrative structure in which the multiplication of semi-independent agencies has created new barriers to efficiency and orderly control. There are also many difficulties connected with the relationship between a public sector which has to plan in the national interest and the more sectional interests of private capital.

Some of these problems are particular to Jordan but others are shared by a number of other Arab states, notably those without oil like Tunisia which combine relatively open economy with large-scale labour migration and the need to absorb huge sums of money coming from the oil-rich states in the form of remittances, aid and investment. Once again the Jordanians, in the form of Crown Prince Hassan, have taken the lead in trying to find a constructive solution to a number of these difficulties, for example his plan to establish an International Labour Compensation Facility by which the richer Arab countries would help the poorer ones by paying towards the costs of training the labour which they import. As it is, a country like Jordan is committed to paying a significant proportion of its revenues towards professional and technical education only to see many of its brightest students leave for the Gulf almost as soon as they have completed their studies. Nevertheless, given the fact that neither Jordan nor any other Arab state in the same position could possibly contemplate imposing any workable limit-ation on labour migration, there is nothing to be done but to engage in a long process of argument and persuasion with their richer neighbours. This process continues.

In these difficult circumstances there are many influential Jordanians who assert that the best thing to do is to leave the whole subject alone on the assumption that the price which the country has had to pay for more expensive oil and for the loss of trained labour is more than compensated for by the general aid it has received from the Arab oil exporters, notably the sum of over a billion dollars a year for ten years agreed to at the Baghdad summit in 1978. But it would be wrong to leave it at that. Quite apart from the question of the immediate balance of financial advantage in the trade-off between money and labour, there is the more fundamental point that Jordan is undergoing a comprehensive and unstoppable process of structural transformation as a result of its role on the periphery of the Arab oil economy, a process which is surely destined to exacerbate present problems to a huge extent. It might be useful to try to list the most significant of these under four heads.

1. Agriculture: the flow of oil money into the towns will continue to increase the disparity between rural and urban wages. The rising price of energy will increase the cost of transport and irrigation. The present tendency to employ non-Jordanian agricultural labour, for example the many Egyptians now working in the Jordan Valley, will accelerate.

2. Industry: the import boom supported by the remittances of Jordanians abroad as well as the huge volume of remittances sent back in kind will act further to narrow the local market for Jordanian products. Industry will find difficulty in recruiting managers and technicians given the possibility of better-paid jobs abroad or in the Jordanian banking and service sector.

3. Banking: the multiplication of the number of banks in the late 1970s and the huge increase in the level of deposits due in large part to oil-related money will pose particular problems in terms of controlling credit and the supply of money. There will also be a significant leakage of funds abroad, attracted by the higher interest rates to be found in Europe and America.

4. The semi-independent government agencies: the temptation to use such agencies as a way of responding quickly to problems by getting round bureaucratic red tape and as a channel for the private investment of oil-related money will increase. But this will pose

serious problems of administrative control as well as acting to undermine the morale and efficiency of the regular civil service.

It would be wrong to suggest that the government is unaware of these problems. Apart from the emphasis on regional planning there have also been repeated efforts to try to make sure that remittances and other funds are directed towards investment in productive enterprise. What is not yet clear, however, is whether the sheer size of the problem has been properly grasped nor the inexorable way in which present trends will accelerate so long as the Arab oil producers continue to spend such huge sums of money on development. This is certainly the greatest challenge which those who direct Jordan's economic policy must face over the next decade.

Table 1
Major Economic Indicators   (in millions of JDs)

	Average 1973–77	1978	1979	1980	Change 80/79%
Gross National Product	405.9	725.5	880.3	1073.8	22.0
Remittances from Jordanians Working Abroad★	76.6	159.4	180.4	236.7	31.2
Income from Industry & Mining	53.2	84.3	102.0	142.7	39.9
Industrial Production Index of Principal Industries (1975 = 100)	—	159.2	188.0	232.0	23.4
Agricultural Income	30.6	58.6	43.6	58.5	34.2
Private Sector Deposits (residents)★★	147.7	327.6	411.2	512.4	24.6
Credit★★	130.4	271.6	383.6	460.8	20.1
Balance of Trade (net deficits)	–202.9	–368.0	–467.4	–544.5	16.2
Aqaba Port (in thousand tons)	2078.7	3659.1	5010.2	6598.6	31.7
Government Domestic Revenues	88.9	158.5	187.9	224.5	19.5
Government External Revenues	102.9	172.4	247.9	251.4	1.4
Government Current Expenditures	137.9	212.9	321.3	325.8	1.4
Government Capital Expenditures	76.4	148.6	194.3	191.8	–1.3
Cost of Living Index (1975 = 100)	—	136.9	156.0	173.3	11.1
Gold & Foreign Exchange Reserves & SDRs★★★	158.8	286.3	370.8	417.4	12.6
Balance of Payments Position: surplus (—); deficit (+)	–23.9	–36.9	–63.7	–106.4	67.0

★   This figure includes only those remittances sent back through the banking system. Some international agencies estimate the total at nearly $800m for 1980.

★★   Commercial banks only.

★★★   Central Bank only.

Source: Central Bank of Jordan, *Seventeenth Annual Report, 1980* 6.

Table 2 Gross National Product (At Market Prices)
(East Bank) (in millions of JDs)

	1975	1976	1977	1978	1979	1980*	Change 80/79%
1) Industries							
— Agriculture, Forestry & Fishing	26.0	37.3	41.7	58.6	43.6	58.5	34.2
— Mining & Quarrying	16.3	17.8	19.9	22.9	27.5	34.3	24.7
— Manufacturing	30.5	54.7	65.1	61.4	74.5	108.4	45.5
— Electricity & Water Supply	3.1	3.6	4.1	5.2	6.5	7.3	12.3
— Construction	16.1	23.3	27.0	35.0	60.5	75.6	25.0
— Wholesale & Retail Trade, Restaurants & Hotels	46.3	64.9	66.3	87.0	115.0	133.0	15.7
— Transport & Communication	24.9	32.5	35.9	67.3	71.9	75.3	4.7
— Financing, Real-estate & Business Services	29.7	33.4	43.6	53.1	90.3	103.8	15.0
— Community, Social & Personal Services	8.5	6.1	8.8	10.2	12.0	13.8	15.0
— Less: Imputed Bank Service Charges	2.9	3.0	3.4	12.4	16.5	20.4	23.6
2) Producers of Government Services	65.2	81.7	84.4	95.0	129.1	155.8	20.7
3) Non-Profit Institutions	5.0	5.5	9.1	10.5	11.2	15.5	38.4
4) Household Services	0.7	0.7	0.8	0.9	1.0	1.5	50.0
Total Gross Domestic Product at Factor Cost	269.4	358.5	403.3	494.7	626.6	762.4	21.7
+ Net Indirect Taxes	9.2	43.2	74.3	82.0	85.4	106.6	24.8
Total GDP at Market Prices	278.6	401.7	477.6	576.7	712.0	869.0	22.0
+ Net Factor Income from Abroad	63.9	140.8	145.9	148.8	168.3	204.8	21.7
= Total GNP at Market Prices	342.5	542.5	623.5	725.5	880.3	1073.8	22.0

Source : Department of Statistics, quoted in Central Bank, *Seventeenth Annual Report*, 8.

*: Estimates.

Table 3
Components of Public Revenues

(in millions of JDs)

			1979	1980*	Change 80/79%
Public Revenues			**435.82**	**475.93**	**9.2**
1)	**Domestic Revenues**		**187.89**	**224.50**	**19.5**
	a)	**Tax Revenues**	**151.09**	**173.16**	**14.6**
		Customs	72.06	82.80	14.9
		Excise	10.57	13.30	25.8
		Licences	15.59	18.24	17.0
		Fees	17.06	16.98	–0.5
		Additional Tax	8.01	8.88	10.9
		Income & Social Services Tax	22.38	27.00	20.6
		Other Taxes	5.42	5.96	10.0
	b)	**Non-Tax Revenues**	**36.80**	**51.34**	**39.5**
		Post, Telegraph, Telephones	8.87	14.10	59.0
		Interest & Profits	15.69	23.00	46.6
		Miscellaneous	12.24	14.24	16.3
2)	**External Revenues**		**247.93**	**251.43**	**1.4**
	a)	**Budget Support**	**210.30**	**208.80**	**–0.7**
		Arab	199.61	208.80	4.6
		USA	10.69	—	—
	b)	**Economic Assistance**	—	—	—
	c)	**External Loans**	**37.63**	**42.63**	**13.3**
		Arab	19.06	21.56	13.1
		Foreign	18.57	21.07	13.5
	d)	**Expected Loans & Technical Assistance**	—	—	—

* Preliminary.
Source: Central Bank, *Seventeenth Annual Report,* 47.

Table 4
External Trade by Economic Function

(in thousands of JDs)

	Average 1973–77		1978		1979		1980	
	Value	%	Value	%	Value	%	Value	%
Domestic Exports	**40,665**	**100.0**	**64,129**	**100.0**	**82,556**	**100.0**	**120,107**	**100.0**
Consumer Goods	18,853	46.4	32,630	50.9	41,994	50.8	54,233	45.1
Raw Materials	18,056	44.4	23,319	36.4	29,680	36.0	51,244	42.7
Capital Goods	3,744	9.2	8,179	12.7	10,875	13.2	14,630	12.2
Miscellaneous	12	—	1	—	7	—	—	—
Re-Exports	**14,044**		**26,781**		**38,360**		**51,188**	
Imports	**258,535**	**100.0**	**458,826**	**100.0**	**589,523**	**100.0**	**715,977**	**100.0**
Consumer Goods	98,251	38.0	175,669	38.3	215,211	36.5	240,154	33.5
Raw Materials	64,123	24.8	117,252	25.6	179,462	30.5	227,087	31.7
Capital Goods	88,551	34.3	161,232	35.1	193,575	32.8	246,743	34.5
Miscellaneous	7,610	2.9	4,673	1.0	1,275	0.2	1,993	0.3

Source: Department of Statistics, quoted in Central Bank, *Seventeenth Annual Report*, 62.

Table 5

Population, Income and Employment Data for Jordan as Compared with the OAPEC and and the World's Industrialized Countries

	Pop. 1977 in millions	Avg. annual pop. increase 1970-77 %	Avg. income/ capita 1977 $(US)	Urban pop. 1975 %	Pop. aged 15-64 mid-1970s %	Lab. partic. rate 1977 %
Jordan (OAPEC)	2.2 (1979)	3.4 (1970-9)	1,180	c50 (1979)	51	19.6 (1976)
Egypt	39.0	2.0	494	44	56.5	30.9
Syria	7.9	3.0	827	46	46.7	25.2
Algeria	17.1	3.1	1,151	54	46.8	19.6
Iraq	12.0	3.4	1,582	66	47.1	25.5
Saudi Arabia	7.6	3.0	8,248	44	49.5	23.6
Libya	2.6	4.2	7,340	59	51.7	24.9
Kuwait	1.1	7.0	11,671	89	53.1	30.3
Bahrain	0.3	5.2	5,366	80	52.9	29.1
Qatar	0.2	8.2	—	—	—	57.1
UAE	0.9	17.2	16,178	44	72.1	56.3
Total OAPEC	91.4	2.2	1,982	50		27.0
Average for industrialized countries			6,980	74	64.5	45*

* Figure for 1974.

Sources: (Jordan) IBRD, *World Development Report 1981*; Provisional census figures in *MEED*, Jordan Special Report (June 1980), 40–1 and labour participation rate in 1976 Employment Survey cited in J. S. Birks and C.A. Sinclair, International Migration Project, Country Case Study, *The Hashemite Kingdom of Jordan* (University of Durham, Nov. 1978), 6.
(OAPEC, Industrialized countries): National sources (some of which are very unreliable in *Ente Nazionale Idrocarburi* (ENI), *The Interdependence Model*, Vol. III, Annexe 1 (Rome, April 1981).

Notes

1. 'Growth and stability in the Jordanian economy', *Middle East Journal,* Vol XXI (1967), p. 98.
2. Bassam K. Saket and Bassam J. Asfour, *Jordan's Economy: 1980 and Beyond,* Economics Dept., Royal Jordanian Scientific Society, (Amman, June 1981), p. 37. The Central Bank of Jordan gives a slightly higher rate of 10.5 per cent based on 1975 prices, *Seventeenth Annual Report* (1980), p. 1.
3. Interview with Dr Hanna Odeh, President of National Planning Council, *Jordan Times,* 30 December 1979.
4. F. Rivier, *Croissance industrielle dans une économie assistée: Le cas Jordanien* (Beirut, 1980), p. 53.
5. IBRD, *World Development Reports* for 1976 and 1981, Tables 1.1.
6. Interviews with Crown Prince Hassan and Dr Bassam Saket, *Jordan Times,* 30 December 1979.
7. Quoted in *MEED, Special Report: Jordan,* June 1980, pp. 40-1.
8. J.S. Birks and C.A. Sinclair, *Country Case Study: The Hashemite Kingdom of Jordan* (International Migration Project, University of Durham, November 1978), pp. 3-9.
9. Foreign Area Studies, *Jordan: A Country Study* (Washington, 1980), p. 111.
10. Ibid., p. 112.
11. Ibid., p. 112. For the difficulties involved in giving estimates of the numbers of seasonal labourers see Birks and Sinclair, op. cit., pp. 25-6.
12. Saket and Asfour, op. cit., p. 19n.
13. *World Development Report 1981,* Table 23.
14. *Jordan: A Country Study,* p. 100.
15. Ibid., p. 100.
16. *World Development Report 1981,* Table 22.
17. For example figures in E. Tuma, 'The rich and the poor in the Middle East', *Middle East Journal,* No. 34 (Autumn 1980), pp. 424-25, and M. Abdel-Fadil, *The Political Economy of Nasserism: A Study of Employment and Income Distribution Policies in Urban Egypt, 1952-72* (Cambridge, 1980), ch. 5.
18. Details in *MEED,* 11-17 December 1981, p. 20.
19. For example, *MEED,* 7-13 August 1981, p. 12.
20. The Hashemite Kingdom of Jordan, The Social Security Law, Provisional Law Number 30 of 1978 and Social Security Corporation, Amman, 'Social Security Goals', mimeo (n.d.).
21. *MEED, Special Report: Jordan,* pp. 40-1.
22. *MEED,* 11-17 December 1981, p. 18.

23. Bassam J. Asfour and Mohammed A. Smadi, *The Economy of Jordan in 1978: A Review* (Royal Jordanian Scientific Society, Economics Dept., April 1979), p. 10.
24. 'Power plans transform Jordan', *Middle East,* No. 88, (February 1982), pp. 50-1.
25. Ahmad Malkawi, *Regional Development in Jordan – Some Aspects of the Urban Bias* (Royal Jordanian Scientific Society, Economics Dept., May 1978), pp. 18-19.
26. An English précis of the speech can be found in *Jordan Times*, 27 and 28 December 1979.
27. W. Lee, 'Jordan', in *Middle East Review 1981* (London, 1980), p. 189.

The Debate about Development

Umayya S. Tukan

When Mr Abd al-Hamid Sharaf became Prime Minister of Jordan in December 1979, our development efforts were faced with important problems, common to many developing countries, which classical prescriptions could not deal with adequately. The problems were not those of declining or slow economic growth rates. In fact a close examination of Jordan's economic growth over the past thirty years reveals an admirable performance overall. Considering the limited natural resources of the country, as well as the continuous pressures on those resources due to a perpetual state of war, the economic management of Jordan had clearly been working in the right direction. What then were the development problems facing Jordan towards the end of the 1970s and at the beginning of the 1980s? And why did they not lend themselves to classical treatment? These questions bring to mind two general issues, the first of which concerns growth.

The available evidence suggests that in any country, growth has been accompanied by undesirable consequences. The inequitable distribution of the benefits of growth, the pressures of industrialization and modernization, migration to urban centres with its associated stresses, and the neglect of the agricultural sector are a few of the unhappy effects to be observed in developing countries.[1] These effects have been blamed in the development literature on such factors as 'market distortions' and all sorts of 'structural rigidities' and 'structural gaps' in these countries.[2] Another category of undesirable effects resulting from economic growth relates to its impact on attitudes and values. In the sectors of the economy enjoying the highest growth rates and thus the highest incomes, a new pattern of consumption and new tastes and value systems tend to be acquired which are not compatible with the development aspirations of the country. It is not difficult to understand why increased incomes bring about increased consumption. It is far more difficult to explain why this pattern is not compatible with the country's development aspirations. The important point for debate, however, is the extent and method of government intervention in the situation.[3]

The second issue which seems relevant to the Jordanian experience relates to the debate distinguishing 'economic development' from 'economic growth'. Although for some time now these two concepts have been used interchangeably, as if they were synonymous, this practice is now becoming a source of confusion.[4] Traditional growth theories[5] concentrate on the increase in output and assume that this increase will automatically be distributed through the workings of the market mechanism to each and every member of society. Furthermore they assume that non-economic factors such as attitudes and institutions compatible with growth will automatically evolve. Development on the other hand addresses not only increased output but also non-economic factors that influence this growth. This approach maintains that factors such as human attitudes, social institutions, and the quality of life in general have a profound impact on raising output or gross national product. This may sound mere common sense. In development economics, however, it is considered a radical departure from neo-classical prescriptions, because of its very important policy implications. For instance, the outcome of a development plan with a given amount of investments greatly depends on what policies are pursued with regard to attitudes and institutions in conjunction with investment outlays. The distribution of growth is the outcome of deliberate policies which are not limited simply to subsidizing food, housing, health, education, etc. Improving the quality of life, especially for the poor, is no longer restricted to the area of 'welfare economics' but is a basic prerequisite of increased productivity and growth.

Needless to say, most of the development plans of developing countries during the 1950s and 1960s were based on traditional neo-classical theories, simply because this was the prevailing wisdom at the time. Advances in knowledge do not take place suddenly or overnight. New ideas need time to be tested against observation before they are added to the existing stock of wisdom. In 1966 Nobel Laureate Gunnar Myrdal of Sweden noted that both Germany and Japan had focused first on reforming attitudes and institutions, recognizing that these were the 'strategic' points and expecting the economy to follow the path of reform.[6] To differentiate structural and institutional inefficiencies from other sources of inefficiency, Professor Harvey Leibenstein of Harvard University gave them the rather technical name of 'X-inefficiency'.[7] This is not to say that such inefficiencies are the only obstacle to development. In the 1970s the developing countries came to feel that international arrangements in trade, finance, and other areas also constituted obstacles to their development and they called for a basic review of these arrangements in the hope of winning a remedy for the existing 'injustices', as they saw them.[8] The timing, intensity and content of the debates on the national and international levels underlined the need for *change*. The questions that remained unanswered were *how* and *in what direction?*

These were the sort of problems that Mr Sharaf faced.

The issues were not unique to Jordan. At the United Nations Mr Sharaf had closely followed the common experiences and frustrations of the developing countries, and had come to certain conclusions. His was one of the few Third World voices to say consistently that it served no purpose to put the blame for existing injustices on one country or group of countries. Equally, however, it was unacceptable to allow injustices to continue. If the essence of the relationship between the North and South was that of partnership, it followed that the rights and responsibilities of each partner should be honoured. *Balancing one's rights and responsibilities* lay at the heart of Mr Sharaf's thinking. It is interesting to note that this concept has historically been championed by the stronger party or 'donor'; rarely has the weaker party, or 'recipient', been outspoken on this concept. Instead the weaker party has traditionally struggled for its rights, feeling – and understandably so – that because it is weak or poor it has no responsibility. Later, as Prime Minister of Jordan, Mr Sharaf's view of government was that it too was a partnership, between the government or the public sector on the one hand and the non-governmental or private sector on the other.

Both in his view were equal partners under the supremacy of
the law.

   During his first weeks in office he invited representatives of the
private sector to meet him to discuss a common strategy. He told
them that their contribution to the public sector's efforts was
invaluable to the country as a whole. The government alone could
not carry the responsibilities entrusted to it without the care and
participation of the people. He stressed that the contribution he
expected from them was not limited to the orderly payment of taxes
but extended to an active involvement in public issues traditionally
considered the preserve of government. Public parks, public
libraries, academic scholarships, spiritual and recreational facilities
were some of the areas in which the private sector could make a
concrete contribution. Individual efforts on these lines were of
course being made all the time. What Mr Sharaf had in mind was to
synthesize the many dispersed efforts into an institutional process
which would assure the continuity of such activities and eliminate
the frustrations due to people working at cross purposes. He made it
clear that the government had neither the means nor the intention to
force the private sector to participate. It was a voluntary commitment he was seeking. A Milton Friedman, preoccupied with
'efficiency', would be delighted to note his emphasis on the private
sector's role, but Mr Sharaf's own preoccupation was rather with
'belonging' and 'participation'. He knew that the contribution of
non-governmental and voluntary activities, especially in a developing country and particularly in its rural communities, could not be
overemphasized, and he gave it the attention it deserved.

   The story of Mr Sharaf's handling of the economy is an interesting one. His university studies had been in areas not directly related
to economics and he never claimed to be an economist. Yet, having
listened to the 'experts', he would suggest a course of action which
in many ways displayed the soundest of economic thinking. It has
been said by distinguished economists, such as Paul Samuelson of
the MIT, that economics is really common sense. Whatever its
nature, Mr Sharaf believed it could not be isolated from other
human activity. His key economic concept was 'productivity',
which he was concerned to increase by addressing both the physical
and the human factors of production, and above all by maintaining
a healthy and stimulating environment in which the right to self-
expression was a basic ingredient. The theme of self-expression has

a special significance in Jordan where our parliamentary institution had to be suspended for well-known reasons following the Arab summit conference held in Rabat in 1974. As an interim measure and until such time as our full parliamentary life could be restored, a National Consultative Council was established with a membership representing all sectors of our society including women. This measure was intended to demonstrate the commitment of our leadership to self-expression and its recognition of the importance of having a forum where policy decisions could benefit from free discussion. Other measures aimed at maintaining a healthy environment concerned cultural and social activities. A new Ministry for Social Development was established headed, for the first time in the history of Jordan, by a woman.

A second area to which Mr Sharaf gave special importance was the agricultural sector. For him this was not just one economic sector among others, contributing at one point thirty per cent to gross national product and employing one-third of the labour force, but rather it had a role to play in achieving other policy objectives, such as countering the inflationary impact of food imports and the migration to urban areas and promoting self-reliance in food production. More significantly my feeling is that the agricultural sector represented values dear to Mr Sharaf, like simplicity, commitment, and an outlook on life which gave priority to the sense of belonging and to pride in one's country. Consequently he gave special weight to two ministries: the Ministry of Municipal and Rural Affairs and the Ministry of Supplies. It is interesting to note that the most recent thinking on industrialization in developing countries recommends the development of the agricultural sector as a prerequisite to industrial development.[9]

A third area that I would like to single out to reflect Mr Sharaf's thinking on development relates to attitudes, structures and institutions. As mentioned earlier, it has been observed in most Third World countries that the attitudes and value systems accompanying the growth process are not in line with these countries' development aspirations. Several explanations have been offered, most of which are not free of value-judgments.[10] For our purposes the important point is that the trend exists. In the case of Jordan and the Middle East region in general, additional financial resources from the adjustment of oil prices in the early 1970s seem to have had a further impact on attitudes. To meet the pressures and to foster an environment enabling us to proceed with our development efforts, Mr Sharaf urged two main themes. The first theme concerned the pattern of consumption resulting understandably enough from the increased economic activity in the region. He called for the 'rationalization' of our consumption and for the elimination of waste. The economic argument for more saving and less consumption is well established. Except for the possibility of foreign capital, savings constitute the only means to finance investments which will increase our productive capacity and thus provide our children with a higher standard of living than we ourselves have. More significant than any economic argument, however, are the implications of excessive consumerism in a society whose institutions are not yet developed enough to contain such a tendency in accordance with the laws of the country. The social fabric is more likely to be enduring if non-material achievements are given their proper place.

The second theme was embodied in Mr Sharaf's call for a basic evaluation of our educational system. On one occasion, in a highly moving and effective lecture to the Jordan University alumni club, he proposed the convening of a regional conference on education as a first step to tackling the irregularities of the development process in the Middle East as a whole. To him education did not mean only the syllabus – although that certainly needed revision to embody both the language and spirit of our age – but also the totality of issues relating to 'commitment' and 'belonging'. Young people were a special and cherished category. In them the forces of progress and change were to be found. It was essential that they be freed from misconceptions. Again, Mr Sharaf's emphasis on education was in line with established thinking which suggests that, unless the educational system responds to the challenges of development, it risks becoming in its turn a factor of under-development. 'Every serious commentator agrees that "major" reform within Third World education is long overdue.'[11]

Finally, Mr Sharaf was very aware of the importance of building institutions. As students in management sciences would be the first to confirm, unless people learn to think in terms of structures and process, the *development potential* of a high rate of economic growth may remain only a potential. Needless to say, institutions, including the government, consist of people. As Crown Prince Hassan has often said, 'Man is both the object and the instrument of development.' The circle is now complete.

Notes

1. Evidence of such patterns is abundant in development literature. The works of Hollis Chenery of the World Bank, Simon Kuznets of the MIT, I. Little of Oxford University, and D. Hirschman contain several case studies on these issues. At least one case of 'growth without development' has been observed by Robert Clower in *Growth without Development* (Northwestern University Press, Evanston, 1966).

2. This is a reference to the 'structuralists' school on development led by Raoul Prebisch and others. The traditional neo-classical school would emphasize factors *not* related to the 'market', such as 'inappropriate' policies or 'mismanagement'.

3. Most 'structuralists' advocate government intervention to balance the 'distortions' and assure social justice. Other economists, such as Keith Griffin of Oxford University and others, claim that government intervention itself produces the kind of distortions that the government is trying to avoid!

4. Charles Kindleberger and Bruce Herrick, *Economic Development,* (McGraw-Hill, Tokyo, 1977).

5. This reference is to neo-classical models of the 'Harrod-Domar' variety.

6. Gunnar Myrdal, *Asian Drama* (Penguin Books, London, 1968).

7. Richard Lipsey, *Positive Economics,* fifth edition (Harper and Row, London, 1978).

8. This is a general reference to the debate on the 'New International Economic Order' which characterized the 1970s and is still going on.

9. A strong argument was presented by Nobel Laureate W. Arthur Lewis in *The Evolution of the International Economic Order* (Princeton University, 1978). R. Sutcliffe in *Industry and Underdevelopment* and G.M. Meier, ed., in *Leading Issues in Economic Development* present similar sentiments.

10. This refers to a tendency in development literature which seems to blame most Third World problems on what is described as the 'Third World elite phenomenon', or on 'inefficient' governments of the Third World. I find this analysis rather too simplistic and superficial. Furthermore this approach underrates the tremendous responsibilities facing Third World policy-makers in coping with problems mostly originating in the period of colonization. One inherited problem relevant to this essay is the attitude of people towards the government which developed during the colonial era when the government was alien or from overseas.

11. Richard Jolly, Director, Institute of Development Studies, University of Sussex.

The Modern Record

Rami G Khouri

What does it mean to be a Jordanian today? Economic statistics can demonstrate the growth of Jordan's Gross National Product or money supply. Narratives of the past thirty years can point out the savvy political instincts of the child-king of the early 1950s who entered the 1980s as a time-hardened elder statesman of the Arab world. What may be less obvious to the outside observer – and probably more important for the long-term prospects of the Jordanian nation-state – is the symbiotic relationship that has developed between the state and the Jordanian individual over the past three decades. The remarkable achievement of the Jordanian leadership is that it has moulded and nurtured a Jordanian psyche where none existed, in an anonymous patch of earth appointed by the convergence of serendipity and twentieth-century Great Power politics to become the modern state of Jordan.

To be a Jordanian in the 1950s was a precarious business and, at times, a dubious distinction in the eyes of those who chronicled the comings and goings of ephemeral nation-states. To be a Jordanian in the 1980s is an altogether different matter. Jordan is now something of a model in the Arab world for balanced socio-economic development, coupled with a stable internal situation that compares well with the war- and dissent-racked societies all around it. If it is not exactly a definitive picture of the perfect society that the Arab national aspires to, it is nevertheless an attractive and widely respected example of what can be made of an Arab society, even one whose full developmental potential is constrained by the forces of regional conflict and warfare.

From the perspective of the Jordanian individual, the present internal situation offers enough to offset any anti-establishment stirrings which ideological frenzy or material deprivation might foster. While there are obvious economic imbalances, there is no unemployment to speak of. While there is obvious poverty in some parts of the urban landscape, with open sewage pits and mal-nutrition, there is to counter this the reality that any citizen of the land has the opportunity to study and work his way up the rungs of the economic ladder – and, in the meantime, has access to essential health, education and social services.

There are two routes to material security and satisfaction in Jordan today – through the dynamism, hard work and potentially lucrative returns of private sector work, or through the sheltered, subsidized apparatus of the civil service and the armed forces.

It is very possible for a Jordanian to be born in a government hospital, be treated as a baby in a Ministry of Health mother and child-care centre, be deposited in a government nursery or day-care centre during his mother's working hours, attend free government schools until the twelfth grade, go on from there to pursue free vocational training or to a Jordanian university at nominal cost, and – at the end of two decades of life largely courtesy of the govern-ment of the Hashemite Kingdom of Jordan – finally take up gainful employment. The new worker would immediately join the social security system and therefore be eligible for disability payments or compensation in the case of injury or death, as well as a retirement pension when the time came.

There are two parallel systems in Jordan that cater to the needs of almost the entire population – the free enterprise system of private houses, schools, hospitals, shops, clubs and jobs, and the public sector system of government schools, hospitals, housing, consumer cooperatives and jobs. Within the public sector is a third self-contained system – the armed forces – which is a world unto itself, with its own hospitals, food stores, communications systems, vocational training schemes, university, housing, recreational facilities and social security provisions. Within one of these three systems, the Jordanian national can find employment as well as the underlying support of the social services. Jordanian society also provides a third important element – access to the highest levels of decision-making, through one's family group, professional contacts or social circles. While this is obviously no substitute for a political system embodying the principle of the consent of the governed, it does provide a vitally important outlet for voicing routine grievances and requests which, if they were not dealt with, could cumulatively threaten the stability of the state.

Access, therefore, is the guiding principle of Jordanian society: access to jobs, schooling, health care, the ears of senior officials, better housing, telephones, drinking-water, cars, new clothing, nice furniture, low-cost foreign vacations, retirement income, disability payments, and a decent, honourable and reasonably priced burial at the end of it all. Access to all these is what makes Jordanian nationhood work as well as it does. But access in itself is insufficient to guide the state from the present stage of nation-building to the more demanding stage of nation-sustaining.

The single most important challenge for Jordan in the 1980s is to develop the political mechanisms and institutions for a greater degree of public participation in decision-making that Abd al-Hamid Sharaf had started to address. The last thirty years have shown clearly that the Arab world is incapable of replying coherently to the American–Israeli challenge – the most recent and extreme example of Arab paralysis was the shocking display of docility in the face of the Israeli invasion of Lebanon, launched in early June 1982, and the consequent siege of West Beirut. This paralysis stems from the fact that the domestic political structure of every Arab state precludes the genuine consensus-building which is required to involve people actively in political, economic or military mobilization. Deep commitment to true nationhood is lacking in most Arab countries, because the individual citizen is not involved in making the decisions that determine his or her daily life-patterns.

These broader themes of Arab failure and incoherence are acutely felt in Jordan, by both the leadership and the man in the street. There are indications that King Hussein would like to start moving down the road of democratization and direct public participation in decision-making. The formation of the National Consultative Council is one such sign. So is the decision giving women the right to vote and stand for public office. So too is the move to revitalize local government elections (with the enormous exception of

Amman municipality, where the mayor and city council are still appointed by the government). The lengthy public discussion of the details of the latest five-year plan, and the extensive debate about key legislation on such issues as labour, income tax and property rental are signs that while the law of the land is still passed down to the people from the government–establishment conglomerate above, there is an increasing amount of public participation which could, with time and a rational approach to political development, grow into a system where public officials are held accountable for their actions to the people they are supposed to serve. Such public accountability is often seen in Jordan today. It is generally the result of gross misconduct that is public knowledge and therefore considered by the political establishment as worthy of public trial and punishment.

During Jordan's sixty years of nationhood, however, such niceties of political punctilio have had to be pushed aside to make room for the hard, physical job of building a nation where none existed before. While this process has its intangible psychological-emotional side, it has been the more material aspects of the task that have kept the Hashemite leadership busy since the early 1920s. And this is where history shall probably record the Hashemites' most significant successes.

There are plenty of statistical indicators of the progress achieved under Hashemite leadership since the 1920s, and more particularly since the reign of King Hussein began in 1952. In the thirty years of King Hussein's rule, Jordan has been transformed from a charming little political and economic backwater of the Middle East into an increasingly self-reliant, self-generating nation-state that, for example, has a surplus of doctors and engineers and which exports skilled and educated workers to the rest of the Arab world, especially the oil-rich lands.

In those thirty years the country has become literate, with the latest statistics showing that over ninety-two per cent of males between the ages of fifteen and thirty are able to read and write (though the literacy rate for females in the same age bracket is lower, at some seventy-five per cent).

Thirty-five private and government hospitals with some three thousand beds offer full medical services throughout the country, with another dozen hospitals run by the armed forces and UNRWA.

The educational system has expanded steadily and now includes 2,750 schools with 28,641 teachers and 762,425 students. Of the total, 370 schools are privately run and 204 are run by UNRWA. Sixteen thousand students attend the country's three universities (University of Jordan, Yarmouk University and Mu'ta University), and no fewer than 66,000 Jordanians are pursuing higher education outside the country, with the largest contingents in Egypt (25,000), Lebanon (10,000), the United States (6,200), the Soviet Union (4,500), Romania (2,730) and Syria (2,260).

In the telecommunications field, Jordan now boasts over 75,000 telephone lines, with another 250,000 lines being installed during the current five-year plan.

Electricity generating capacity has risen steadily and now totals nearly 400 MW, most of which comes from the huge new Hussein Thermal Power Station at Zarqa. By 1985, the Jordan Electricity Authority's rural electrification scheme should have reached its target of providing electricity to all villages of over five hundred people.

The government's philosophical approach has been to concentrate on building large infrastructural works, such as airports, roads, ports and streets, while providing only those social services – basic health care, centres for the handicapped, schooling and vocational training – which cannot be provided more efficiently by a profit-motivated private sector. Yet even in these areas private enterprise has stepped in to shoulder some of the burden. Private hospitals have been set up. Recently there has been a surge in establishing private two-year community colleges, of which at least twenty have opened since 1976. Private charitable groups have assumed increasing responsibility for the funding and running of centres to treat the mentally and physically handicapped, as well as to meet the needs of other segments of society, such as the aged. By 1982 Jordan had a total of over 400 voluntary and charitable societies with some 50,000 volunteers and supporters, coordinated through the General Union of Voluntary Societies. Nevertheless, only about 3,000 handicapped Jordanians receive professional treatment or services, out of the estimated 40,000 handicapped in the population.

A more recent trend which has gained momentum since the late 1970s is the formation and development of sports clubs, alumni associations and community centres. While these would not appear to rank high on the list of nation-building institutions, in Jordan they take on an added dimension by providing opportunities for association, participation and community self-help that are otherwise not allowed for in the existing political order. They are institutional mechanisms that help add flesh to the skeleton of an increasingly self-reliant society. The community centres, for example, offer literacy courses to women in poor neighbourhoods of Amman who are deterred from attending similar government courses which lack the social cohesion and supporting psychological comfort of a neighbourhood centre staffed and funded by the community itself.

Similarly, children's centres have developed quickly since the mid-1970s. The Amman-based Haya Arts Centre, with its thirty field centres throughout the country, is the vanguard of this movement, but it is complemented by all-voluntary groups such as the Friends of the Children Club, which runs two children's centres in Amman and is opening a third one in 1983.

Very gradually over the past thirty years, the Jordanian psyche has started to make an important transition – from demanding that the government provide all services to the people on a silver platter to the realization that the government has resources to provide only essential and basic services, with many gaps left which the private sector and charitable/voluntary groups are required to fill. This process applies across the board, from mining and industry, through education, health and social services, to the more costly requirements of housing and agriculture. In some cases, such as in the Jordan Valley, all these forces are brought together in a concentrated and defined developmental effort that provides a precise picture of how Jordan functions as a nation-state.

The Jordan Valley, the 400-metres-below-sea-level depression that reaches its lowest point (and the lowest point on earth) at the Dead Sea, was long ago identified as the country's best hope for increased agricultural production. But it was only in the 1960s that the East Ghor Canal was built in the northern half of the 104-kilometre-long valley, allowing the start of a land redistribution programme based on family-owned and -operated farming units of four hectares each. The programme's momentum was halted by the 1967 War, and it was not until 1971 that the Jordanian Government once again turned its attention to harnessing the potential of the valley's land and water resources. After almost three years of drafting, the government produced a comprehensive development plan linking the valley's agricultural infrastructure (dams, canals, irrigation systems, farm roads, agricultural packing, grading and marketing centres) with the provision of social services for the population needed to make full use of the 36,000 hectares of prime farm land identified and surveyed as long ago as the 1920s. Fifty years later, in the early 1970s, the government started spending hundreds of millions of dollars on providing the agricultural/social services infrastructure to attract a population of up to 150,000 people to the valley which had been virtually depopulated by regional conflicts – the 1967 War, the subsequent war of attrition with Israel, and the internal Jordanian–Palestinian clashes. In the decade from 1973 the results of the government's expenditure have been gratifying. The population of the Jordan Valley has reached more than 100,000, all of whom are grouped into thirty-three well planned and fully serviced villages. More importantly, the private sector, according to government analyses, is spending about five dollars for every one dollar that the government has put into the valley, thereby pushing dramatically further the principle that the private sector in Jordan picks up where the government, having provided the basic social and infrastructural services, leaves off. The valley is now a year-round producer of high-value fresh fruits and vegetables, most of which are exported to the nearby Gulf states and help offset Jordan's food trade gap of some 370 million dollars.

Probably the single most important lesson of the Jordan Valley experience is that the Jordanian individual is willing to commit money and take risks in an erratic business such as agriculture, if he is convinced that the government is committed to providing him with what his family requires for a full and satisfying life. This citizen–government link, taken for granted by most Western nations, has had to be nurtured carefully in Jordan over the past sixty years of Hasehmite-led nationhood. In these first sixty years of Jordan's existence as a political entity, the symbiotic relationship between leaders and people has been based on a political trade-off: the government provided security, jobs, social services and a free enterprise system in which the individual had the opportunity to study, advance his prospects and make plenty of money, in return for which the citizen gave the government his allegiance. From the early 1980s, however, this trade-off has started to lose some of its lustre, as the gains of socio-economic development have been dulled by the lack of political development internally and the failure of Arab action regionally and internationally.

Apart from the close relationship between the Hashemite leadership and the armed forces, the single most important determinant of Jordanian prosperity today is the traditional stress placed on the development of human resources. Significantly – and despite the 1970 war between the Jordanian army and the Palestinian resistance – Jordan's emphasis on human development has included the education and training of an enormous number of young Palestinians, whether directly through the state schooling and vocational training system, or indirectly through the UNRWA institutions and the burgeoning private school network of the country.

This heavy stress on educational and vocational services has provided Jordan with the base of skilled workers and managers that is required to make the transition from an agriculture-services economy to one centred on manufacturing, industry and technological services. The decade 1973–83 has been the first decade of unbroken stability which the country has enjoyed, allowing it to capitalize on its long-dormant human/economic potential, within the broader context of an oil-fuelled Middle Eastern economic unit.

Thus Jordan and the Jordanians find themselves today in an anomalous and somewhat distressing situation – there is increasing prosperity, opportunity and security at home, but it is rendered virtually meaningless because of the Arab states' political inability to respond to the threats of hostile, highly motivated and well armed neighbours to the west (Israel) and to the east (Iran). To be a Jordanian today means to enjoy the fruits of a socio-economic system that is increasingly proficient at meeting basic human needs in education, health, transport, communications, water, housing, vocational training, recreation, culture and social welfare services, to mention only the most obvious. But the pace of economic development and the installation of an efficient infrastructure simply heighten the lack of parallel political development. Denied political participation, many Jordanians have tended to pull down the shutters and get on with the business of working and making money. This, in turn, has tended to aggravate the disparities in income and living standards which, although a normal feature of any society, Western or Eastern, could, if not checked, transform the existing frustration with insufficient means of political participation into a more overtly class-oriented struggle.

This distinction between rich and poor tends to be exaggerated in Amman where people of widely varying incomes and lifestyles live in close physical proximity. This proximity of rich and poor in the greater Amman area emphasizes class and income distinctions which are blurred in the capitals of the West, where rich and poor live in different areas separated by tens of kilometres. Recent statistical analyses indicate that, in fact, income distribution in Jordan has not changed in relative terms in the past two decades. While the rich get richer, the middle class gets richer and the lower class gets richer, keeping a proportionally static distribution of income throughout the spectrum of Jordanian society. The new analyses also indicate that about ten per cent of Jordanians could be classified as living below the poverty line, an altogether normal percentage for a developing country with a per capita GNP of slightly over $1,200.

Part II   Palestine

The Experience of Dispossession

Edward W. Said

By now the police car was leaving the city of Affulah on the
Bisan road, which led to my new residence. On both sides
refreshing water was being sprayed on to the green vegeta-
tion, fresh in the very heart of summer. Suddenly the big
man, cramped there with me and the driver in the front seat
of that dog-cart, was transformed into a poet.

While I sat there being my usual Pessoptimistic self, he
was ecstatic: 'Verdant fields! Green on your right and on
your left; green everywhere! We have given life to what was
dead. This is why we have named the borders of former
Israel the Green Belt. For beyond them lie barren mountains
and desert reaches, a wilderness calling out to us, "Come ye
hither, tractors of civilization!"'

Emile Habiby, *The Secret Life of Saeed,*
The Ill-Fated Pessoptimist

One of the two main characters in Michel Khleifi's remarkable film
The Fertile Memory is an elderly widow, Farah Hatoum, who has
remained living in Nazareth after 1948. We see her at work in an
Israeli bathing-suit factory, riding a bus, singing a lullaby to her
grandson, cooking and washing. Although the film also depicts
Sahar Khalifé's somewhat more impressive life on the West Bank –
she is a well-known young novelist and teacher from Nablus – it is

the old lady's presence that in the end haunts the viewer. Khleifi is careful to let her strength emerge slowly. He doesn't give in to the editorial sermonizing that her real situation, and his as her compatriot, might have provoked. Her daily existence, for example, is not portrayed as taking place directly against scenes of Israeli domination. And there is barely a glimpse of Israeli soldiers, none of Palestinian resistance fighters. Even the much more articulate, politicized Sahar Khalifé describes herself with some irony as a militant, and when she does so Khleifi again resists the temptation to italicize the significance of her claim, and therefore does not cut to scenes of Palestinian demonstrations, tyre-burning, rock-throwing and the like.

The central experience of the film is a dramatization of the old woman's relationship to the land. This is done in two connected scenes. She is first shown in discussion with her adult children, both of whom are seen trying to convince her to sell the land she owns but which has been in fact 'repossessed' by Israelis. She is still in possession of the title deed although, as she well knows, it is only a piece of paper. Now her children tell her that legal advice has convinced them that despite its expropriation by the Israelis, there is an opportunity for her to sell the land to its present tenants: apparently someone wants to legalize her dispossession by giving her money in return for final entitlement.

She'll have none of it. A large jowly woman, she sits rocklike at the kitchen table, unmoved by the logic of financial well-being and peace of mind being offered her. No, no, no, she says: I want to keep the land. But you don't actually have it, is the rejoinder: take the money and live a bit more comfortably. Ah, she says thoughtfully and feelingly – I don't have the land now, but who knows what will happen? We were here first, then the Jews came, and others will come after them. I own the land. I will die. But it will stay there, despite all the comings and goings. This is a logic that passes understanding on one level; on another it is deeply satisfying to her.

Later Farah is taken to see her land for the first time in her life. This is perhaps a curious thing but, as Khleifi explained to me, not so unusual for a woman of that generation whose late husband had owned the property, cared for it, and simply willed it to her when he died. When she came in to it, she had already been dispossessed. Miraculously Khleifi managed to record her first visit to it for his film and the result is stunning. We see Farah step tentatively on to a field; then she turns around slowly with her arms outstretched. A look of puzzled serenity comes over her face. There is no hint on it of pride in ownership. The film unobtrusively registers the fact that she is there on her land, which is also there; as for the circumstances intervening between these two facts, we remember the useless title deed and Israeli possession, neither of which is actually visible. Immediately then we realize that what we see on the screen is only that, an image making possible a connection between Palestinian individual and Palestinian land. Then the scene fades.

Sahar's presence in the film is by no means nostalgic or inarticulate. Although at odds with her immediate context as a divorced working woman would be in the predominantly Muslim and traditional town of Nablus, she is securely in place nevertheless. True the Israeli occupation is just evident enough in the film to recall its reality to us, but her life is led where she has always led it. Yet she not only belongs to a younger generation than Farah's, she is more self-aware as a woman and as a Palestinian. Her language is analytical as well as ironic. Nevertheless she too is dispossessed, since her work as a novelist and as a nationalist is enfolded within, and aborted by, the structure of Israeli power holding the West Bank. She expresses alienation from political and of course sexual fulfilment; both have been denied her, the first because she is a Palestinian, the second because she is an Arab woman.

The aesthetic juxtaposition of the two Palestinian women is made possible by Khleifi, the film-maker himself. His is the third form of dispossession. He lives in Brussels and carries an Israeli passport although he is an Arab. Like that of every exiled Palestinian, his story is complex in its unhappy details, easy to grasp in its essence: no country, no formally recognized national identity, no very bright political future to look forward to. Because he is never seen in the film and because one is aware of his intelligence in the process of making and guiding the film, he is not so much an implicit presence as an exterior (if invisible) consciousness. It is his particular achievement to have embodied certain aspects of the Palestinian actuality in film, an internationally current medium; moreover he has given the women's lives an aesthetic form which, to a Palestinian viewer, connects directly with a corresponding personal experience of dispossession.[1]

Yet the Palestinian alienation from Palestine *out there* continues none the less, and the catastrophic events of 1982 have scarcely reduced, much less stopped, the force of a process whose efficacy and uni-directional power seem to have acquired an almost epochal, trans-historical resonance. Aesthetic objects such as *The Fertile Memory* highlight the detailed quotidian misery of dispossession; they set it somewhere for viewers to observe, they allude to and quote from it, all in order to break the ongoing course of Israeli colonization, like a stone breaking the flow of a running stream. None of this, however, actually lessens dispossession. It makes it easier to see. But along with that there comes a deeper apprehension of a reality which gives the unique Palestinian experience – from the preposterous Balfour Declaration, to the trauma of 1948, through the additional losses of 1967, to the appalling devastation of Beirut, Sidon, Tyre, the massacres of Sabra and Shatila, the increased dispersal, the sudden, uncounted anonymity of 400,000 Palestinians in Lebanon: one ghastly line trailing millions of lost, maimed, distorted, deformed lives along with it – a universality of considerable importance, which it is my purpose here to map.

The loss of Palestine, like Palestine itself, has two dimensions: one, an irreducibly real domain, the other, the domain of ideology, imagination, projection, art, religion. In the first, Palestine is the land on which native Arab Palestinians lived, a land they lost, a land now ruled over by others, *from* which Palestinians have been dispossessed and *on* which many of them live in a state of internal colonialism. In the second, Palestine is the place written about, dreamed of, planned for. As a public realm then, it belongs by a kind of transcendental entitlement to anyone laying some sort of claim to it. If Palestine for the Palestinians has a special, grounded interiority to it – it was the natally implicit origin of their history, and its *telos* – the other Palestine exists historically as exteriority. It is there for the Crusader, the colonizer, the pilgrim by virtue of its existence outside, exterior to, the lived actuality of its inhabitants. Few other places have this compellingly intertwined double dimension to them. Today, as Khleifi's film demonstrates, the exterior dimension is almost as available to Palestinians as their own: this is both a measure of their dispossession as it is also of their new access to what has been denied them historically. Thus Palestinians are enabled to read their own history *elsewhere,* exorbitantly, as I shall be doing here. A paranoid history has emerged, creating in Palestinians that sustained hermeneutic of suspicion which is both permanently at work and permanently unsatisfied.

Still, this is a new moment in Palestinian history, as laced with problems as with a difficult but on the whole positive political and cultural opportunity, which the production of cultural documents such as Khleifi's *The Fertile Memory* adumbrates. What I shall be describing first are the contours of a public, ideological history of Palestine occurring away from Palestine, a history grounded in the elimination, absence, silence of the native Palestinian. This great curve of history culminates in the actual dispossession of the Palestinians in 1948 and thereafter. Then I shall attempt to show how because of the very nature of that ideological dynamic, a contrary, antithetical force, taking for its point of departure the latent but lived historical reality of the native Palestinians, develops, gathering strength over time. This force is directly connected to the setting, the medium, the successes of the dispossessing ideology. This antithetical current emerges in force at the very moment when Palestinian dispossession creates a historical community of suffering; it matures paradoxically at moments like this, in the aftermath of the evacuation from Beirut, when for the first time in our history we can see ourselves acting on the same world-historical stage as our oppressors, suppressed but not in fact eliminated by them. At such a moment – which is the moment this whole essay is trying to make concrete – 'another way of telling' (John Berger's suggestive notion) is demonstrably available. Dispossession is no longer an inert fact but both culturally and ideologically a contestable experience.

Where it is contestable deserves some specification. Doubtless it is fought over in Palestine, as succeeding generations of Palestinians battle eviction, censorship, land expropriation, detention, torture and death. But that is only one arena of struggle. Another, no less pertinent to any resolution of the Palestinian–Israeli struggle, is at the intersection between ideas, ideologies, values, and visions on the one hand, and, on the other, real people and territories. This is what I shall be discussing here in a limited, highly selective way and I intend these reflections as part of the struggle I refer to above, not as their passive catalogue.

An important (but not the only) aspect of Zionism of importance to Palestinians is that the 'national liberation movement of the Jews' (as it has been called) was first conducted in colonial terms, on a territory already inhabited by another people. The dispossession of that people is completely overlooked as a result. The residual force of this fact continues today when, for example, people applaud Israel for setting up an impartial inquiry to investigate the Sabra-Shatila massacre and celebrate the consequent return of Zionism's original idealism. For decades such rhetoric went by unchallenged. That it is eminently debatable today, that many non-Palestinians refuse to accept it supinely is an indication of how far the effort for Palestinian self-determination has come. No longer can it be assumed that Palestinians will acquiesce in their own suppression. And so it has become possible to reassess the Palestinian experience not only in terms of its concrete gains and losses, but also in the terms formerly reserved for Europeans, European Jews and Zionist supporters. It is this latter assessment that will be undertaken here. I am fully aware that its transgressions, its crossing over into domains not often accustomed to seeing natives there, its heightened consciousness of an aggressive Other, are all unthinkable without that collective will to resist which the Palestinian people has infused into what was for so long someone else's eminent domain.

Let us work our way backwards from some recent events. Consider the international furore over the massacre in Sabra and Shatila. In the United States, for example, there was some effort made to connect this massacre to a longstanding history of Israeli and pre-Israeli Zionist terror attacks on Palestinian civilians. On the whole, however, that effort was small-scaled and suffered from the absence of detailed information. A much more successful effort derived from a view that the occasion could be interpreted as a confirmation of Israel's democratic character; thus the large-scaled demonstrations against the massacre that took place in Tel Aviv and Jerusalem revealed 'Israel's soul'. Commentators vied with each other in trying to 'praise Israel's shame', (*New Republic,* 11 October 1982). In time the massacre itself was shown to be an event entirely located within the Israeli-Jewish consciousness. Retrospectively, the genuine anguish about Israel's Lebanese adventure was transformed not into a general historical examination of Israel's policy towards the Palestinians, but rather a public self-confirming display of Israeli 'humanity', the object of that humanity not necessarily being anyone who did not happen to be Israeli or Jewish.

There is no point in trying to minimize the importance of the stirrings of conscience that are taking place among Jews in Israel and in the West. My point, however, is that even when remorse is expressed over an atrocity for which Israel was manifestly to blame, one senses the almost total absence of any Palestinian content in that remorse. Palestinians are a collectivity without any particular distinction, except that they oppose Israel in an ahistorical, abstract, and clear way; when a few of them die quite horribly, there is first a faltering awareness of abused humanity among Jews and Westerners, then when no specifically concrete image of a Palestinian comes to mind, that awareness gives way to a renewed confidence in what is after all familiar and trusted, Israel's moral virtue; this then replaces the first, disorienting impression of something very wrong and very awful. Even when regular criticisms of Israel's Palestinian policy are published by important journalists and commentators, the evidence used is uniformly Israeli and/or Jewish. Almost never is there a quotation from an Arab source, or a statement cited as fact in support of a credible argument ascribed to a named Palestinian. Dissident Israelis are interviewed at great length, and the work of oppositional journalists regularly published as further testimony of Israel's fundamental rightness (the recent 'Reflections (Lebanon)' by Jacopo Timerman being a noteworthy case).[2] Implicit in all this is the notion that the Palestinian, whose very fate and present circumstances are at issue, is less credible, less apprehendible, less quotable and reliable, in short, less real than the Israeli, the Westerner, the Jew.

This would be a curious, almost incomprehensibly persistent contemporary phenomenon were it not for the knowledge we now have of how generations of Europeans viewed the non-European world. Fundamental to depictions of 'the Other' was, as the anthropologist Johannes Fabian has so convincingly demonstrated, in his *Time and the Other: How Anthropology Makes its Object,* the denial of the coeval status of the Other; indeed Fabian goes further than that by showing that scholarly disciplines like anthropology were premised for their existence on this denial.[3] And indeed this coincidence between knowledge of the Other and, during the period of immense European colonial expansion, the actual elimination of the Other by suppression, subjugation, or mute incorporation, is constitutive of what we have come to call the modern ethos of inquiry into objective reality, from journalism to the social sciences. Tzvetan Todorov's *La conquête de l'Amerique,* Partha Mitter's *Much Maligned Monsters,* Jablow and Hammond's *The Africa that Never Was*: these works illuminate this coincidence in different ways, as well as how knowledge of the Other, far from consequently being mere fiction (because tautologically constitutive of the very Other supposedly being investigated) acquires the solidity, status and efficacy of a genuine socio-cultural praxis.[4]

But we must not forget that in the meantime, millions of natives suffered and perished. Their voices, much less their ideas, were never heard or felt. Their presence, in a word, was not so much attenuated as it was pressed into service for other purposes than theirs, with little more than an infrequent trace of interference from them. And so Palestine was historically not the place of residence for native Palestinians, but for Europeans the place of salutary pilgrimage. Thus Shakespeare treats it. His sequence of English history plays, *Richard II* and *Henry IV* Parts One and Two, deal with the illegal accession to the throne of Bolingbroke, later to become Henry IV, and the subsequent consolidation of his dynasty when his son, Prince Hal, takes the throne as Henry V. The competition between Hal and Hotspur, who is one of the challengers to Hal's father, forms the main political struggle at the centre of the First and Second Parts of *Henry IV*; the other struggle is between Hal and the idling, carousing, and unrestrained corruption and pleasure offered him by Sir John Falstaff. The last two plays are punctuated with scenes in which the former usurper but now king, Henry IV, expresses his concern about the troubles besetting his kingdom and his family. At a number of places he pauses to reflect that once his troubles are over and his kingdom is set right, he will go on a pilgrimage to the Holy Land. When, after much war and civil unrest, he dies, Prince Hal is coincidentally mature and strong enough to take the crown from his dying father: England is put right. Ironically, however, Henry IV dies in the Jerusalem chamber, which of course is in England, and this is a further sign that his reign, flawed in the origin, cannot be fully sanctified by a pilgrimage to Palestine.

On the other hand, Hal, who has come to the throne more properly than his father, can perhaps look forward to a more satisfactory end. The dying king's last words are:

It has been prophesied to me many years,
I should not die but in Jerusalem;
Which vainly I supposed the Holy Land.
But bear me to that chamber; there I'll lie;
In that Jerusalem shall Harry die.

This is a small motif in three of Shakespeare's plays. I point to it only as an index of how much Shakespeare's vision of consecrated English royalty depended on Palestine as a sort of final seal of approval, and of how naturally and easily he could rely on a place whose Christian significance completely overrode Palestine's inhabitants. It doesn't matter in the slightest who or what they were. Anyone seeing the *Henry* plays appropriates Palestine – as Shakespeare did – to the tensions, struggles and fulfilments of the play; this is as true, I think, of an audience today as it was of Shakespeare's audiences almost four hundred years ago. Palestine was a place inert and empty except for what a European Christian wished to accord to it by way of religious, cultural, historical, or political endowment.

Three centuries after Shakespeare George Eliot writes *Daniel Deronda,* her last novel. Relatively late in life its central character discovers his Jewish birth, although he has been raised as a young English aristocrat. When he discovers that new fact he throws his spiritual lot in with a nascent Zionist movement, a group of Jews who plan to emigrate to Palestine. Once again, in European Christian imagination, Palestine is a place to be given over to essentially non-Palestinian uses: it falls completely within the proprietary range of the English aristocracy and of European Jews. Nothing at all is said about native inhabitants. When they are spoken about – for example in Lamartine's *Voyage en Orient* or in Mark Twain's *Innocents Abroad* – they are negligible, much reduced figures, to be patronized or ridiculed. At any rate they do not amount to impediments in anyone's future calculations for Palestine. Nor did they count for very much in the extended political and ecclesiastical manoeuvring between Britain and Prussia over the highly symbolic question of establishing a Prostestant Bishopric in Jerusalem. When one was established in 1841, it was entirely a matter of European, and not of local, interest.[5]

No matter how economically such representations of Palestine functioned, no matter how much imaginative dispossession of the natives took place, no matter how much reality was fixed within a prevailing orthodoxy and an alien, as well as displacing, knowledge, the natives remained present. If in most nineteenth-century photographs of the Holy Places, Frith's especially, natives were usually not seen (the better to appreciate those venerable sites without human intrusion) they might on other occasions be permitted a special role. Then they would be cast as replicas of biblical figures – Mother and Child, A Samaritan Woman at the Well, Shepherds Abiding in the Field, etc. – the easier for a European to observe a millennial continuity between ancient and modern dwellers in Palestine: Bonfils's photographs (collected and commented upon by Sarah Graham-Brown in her *Palestinians and Their Society, 1880-1946*) are an excellent case in point.[6] The natives could no longer be ignored: they were to be figured in if the full reality of Palestine was to be incorporated by a European sensibility. To look at those photographs today is to be wounded equally by the poses and by the captions. The former bend unwitting bodies into unfamiliar, demeaning service, the latter curtain off their identities, history, communal attachments, even their names, with a tag from the Bible.

At a time when the European imperial project was at its height, geography acquired a fundamental importance. Curzon called it 'the most cosmopolitan of all sciences' since it rationalized the extraordinary urge for territorial discovery as a necessary prelude to territorial acquisition, what Conrad in another connection called an 'unappeasable desire'. Insofar as territories contained people then they too were acquired, although it is symptomatic that the importance of geographical knowledge during the period of high imperialism elevated the importance of land to supremacy over the presence of people on it. Note the valences accorded the elements of geography by Lord Curzon in a speech made in 1912 to the Geographical Society. Everything here indicates that 'knowledge' includes, but by no means gives a privilege to, residents of a territory considered suitable for geographical knowledge (i.e., for territorial appropriation by a great imperial power). Curzon speaks in the position of one for whom geography is not entirely an academic subject:

An absolute revolution has occurred, not merely in the manner and methods of teaching geography, but in the estimation in which it is held by public opinion. Nowadays we regard geographical knowledge as an essential part of knowledge in general. By the aid of geography, and in no other way, do we understand the action of great natural forces, the distribution of population, the growth of commerce, the expansion of frontiers, the development of States, the splendid achievements of human energy in its various manifestations. We recognize geography as the handmaid of history . . . Geography, too, is a sister science to economics and politics; and the moment you diverge from the geographical field you find yourself crossing the frontiers of geology, zoology, ethnology, chemistry, physics, and almost all the kindred sciences: that it is part of the equipment that is necessary for a proper conception of citizenship, and is an indispensable adjunct to the production of a public man.[7]

Geography figuratively redisposes people into new components (geology, zoology, chemistry, physics: Curzon has little use for sociology) much as a nation bent on geographical knowledge spills across frontiers in order to create new ones. Gerard Leclerc puts it as follows: '. . . la constitution de l'espace lointain comme objet de savoir a été le plus souvent liée à la constitution de cet espace comme dominé et, en même temps, inconnu et à connaître'.[8]

Geography and the spatial sense consequently reorganize societies and the temporal sense. This is an imaginative and a political activity of fundamental importance to the modern actuality of the peripheral, colonial world. A new element was being appealed to, land, whose role in the mind, Gaston Bachelard has argued provocatively, is to supply the will with resistance by giving it something solid to be against, *contre*.[9] Once one's own territory was conquered, it became a matter of extension to look away from the metropolis to the outlying territories whose availability to geographical (i.e., imperial) appropriation was enhanced by diminishing the human status of their inhabitants. Bachelard does not link the imaginative status of the triad of land–resistance–*contre* to the historical enterprise of colonialism, but the connection seems to me inescapable.

Now I would not wish to be understood as saying that colonialism was essentially or even principally a matter of reordering the status of history and geography in the priorities of thought: the supervening processes of economics, political competition between various European nationalisms, and the pressure of expanding industrialist societies are of major importance too. What I am saying, however, is that in order to understand the curious essentialization, even disappearance of the resident natives of Palestine – a mode of negation which, I have argued, continues into the present with a persistence that is positively overwhelming for those Palestinians able to observe it together with their own totally discrepant reality – we must by way of explanation have recourse to the notion of a particularly strong imaginative will. This imaginative will sees land as a resistance to be overcome, and natives as either to be overlooked or transmuted into subject races, slaves, 'the distribution of population', a demographic problem, and the like.

Certainly the evolution of this fact of late nineteenth- and early twentieth-century history out of antecedent European cultural visions of Palestine is an important component of the recordable experience of Palestine dispossession, even though one hesitates to reduce Shakespeare, Mark Twain, Lamartine and George Eliot to each other and, by extension, to European imperialism. But one could have mentioned more names, from Chaucer and the *Song of Roland* to Nerval, Blake, Chateaubriand, Melville and a whole host of European and American statesmen, for all of whom Palestine is a geographical idea quite distinct from its people and their geography, to say nothing of its lived history and the wishes of its residents. But to these residents, while distinctions have to be made say between Shakespeare and Balfour, the outcome in the late twentieth century has been the same, so far as their lives have been concerned. No one consulted them, no one cared to think of them as consultable, let alone competent to decide on matters having to do with the destiny of a place considered quintessentially as much more important than the human beings concretely resident in it. Palestine was imagined, it was planned for, it was promised, it was pronounced over from Shakespeare to Camp David as a central idea of Euramerican life, with results that recent events concerning Palestine illuminate luridly. Balfour spoke for this idea in 1915 when he said in connection with Zionism (although he might have spoken with equal force about any of the European ideas of Palestine then current) that such an idea, 'be it wrong, good or bad, is rooted in age-long tradition, in present needs, in future hopes, of far profounder import than the desires and prejudices of the 700,000 Arabs who now inhabit that ancient land'.[10]

A cold view to take, this apparent veneration of an idea over and above the wishes of inhabitants whose lives were to be changed irreversibly for generations. I quote it here not to resurrect an unchangeable history, but to note that the attitude making it possible is still influential today. There is something far more pernicious here than an ordinary disregard of inferior beings. Natives are not just being robbed or beaten or dispossessed: they are not considered something worth being robbed. They cannot even violate the idea of their land held by major, albeit foreign, personalities.

A not so difficult transition can be made from the Western Christian view of Palestine as a geographical entity to the Zionist one. I obviously cannot enter here into a detailed history of Zionism, but I can generalize about it by noting that debates about Palestine that take place in Zionist circles now, as well as in the past, most infrequently deal with the embarrassing truth that there was (and still is) a large population of Palestinians already resident in Palestine when the idea of 'a land without people for a people without land' became the motto of the Zionist movement early in this century. We can very easily be impressed with the quality of thought and rhetoric that exists in classical Zionist writing – so well anthologized by Arthur Hertzberg in his compilation of extracts in *The Zionist Idea* – and still be aghast that scarcely any time is given to those other people there in Palestine, whose opinions, lives, and bodies must have furnished the incoming settlers with some momentary doubts. In fact Hertzberg's collection reflects this perfectly: in its 637 pages, his anthology mentions, but nowhere discusses, the Arabs no more than half a dozen times. And this given that all of the 637 pages concern a territory on which an Arab Palestinian society already existed.

The symbolism of this curious omission in Hertzberg's work is persistent. I cite it here as a symptom of something else, and not as invidious criticism of an eminent historian and, most recently, independent thinker within the organized Jewish world. When in response to the Reagan initiative and the Sabra-Shatila massacres he wrote a major attack on Begin's policy (in the *New York Review of Books*) it was disheartening to note that Hertzberg accorded the Palestinians no more than the choice of federation with Jordan, and that before any negotiations could take place: no self-determination,

no state, no PLO, and nothing but 'dispersion' for the non-residents
of the West Bank and Gaza. This, he said, was a 'classical Zionist'
solution, by which he meant that if accepted by the Palestinians it
would represent a Zionist-type acceptance of a 'half-a-loaf-reality'
by them; he did not see instead the irony of what he was in fact
doing, proposing a 'classical Zionist' *refusal* to treat the Palestinians
as a people with any national rights in Palestine.[12] On a smaller
scale, there is another less impressive example of American Zionist
'anguish' in a piece for the *New York Times Sunday Magazine* by
Mark Helperin, which although critical of Begin, manages to
discuss Israel and its problems (with an eye to solving them)
without once mentioning the Palestinians by name.[13]

Edmund Burke was certainly right to say that it is both wrong
and impossible to indict an entire people, and even though the
recent spectacle of Palestinian suffering at the hands of Israeli
soldiers tempts one to such indictments, we must honour the
injunction. For indeed there were many Jews – Judah Magnes
principal among them – who opposed the idea of a Jewish state in
Palestine on the grounds that it would incur Arab hostility for
perfectly understandable reasons. There were and are many other
Jews for whom Jewish nationalism as represented in Israel's
expansionist and discriminatory policies towards non-Jews is
something about which to be very critical. But what strikes one
more and more forcefully is the tendency present within the
movement from its modern inception a) to ignore the Arabs as
human beings, b) not to connect Zionist policy directly with the
continuing suppression of an exiled, occupied, and colonized
population of Palestinians on the ruins of whose society Israel was
created as a state in 1948 and c) to accept the epochal, millenarian
and fundamentalist premises of a movement whose rhetoric – as it is
delivered by the Revisionist leadership of Israel – is invulnerable to
criticism, common humanity, and to doubts about its infallibility
and absolute righteouness. Acting in compliance with many Jews,
Menachem Begin has transmuted politics from the realm of the
everyday, in which even Palestinians can love, suffer, die and hope,
to the fixed, sterile and frigid realm of the apocalyptic, in which the
world exists for him to defend against the onset of another
Holocaust, which he imagines in the future as vividly as he
remembers it in the past.

There is a particularly acute and complex analysis of Zionism's epistemological structure by Uri Eisenzweig, in his book *Territoires Occupés de l'imaginaire juif.* The Western European Zionists who longed for a utopia in Palestine – and, although Eisenzweig does not say so, depended somewhat on other European ideas of Palestine as the Holy Land of Europe, rather than of Palestine's actual inhabitants – these people imagined an essentially indeterminate locale in Palestine, where all historical contingency might be eliminated in order for them to realize their hopes there. On the other hand, the Eastern European Zionists inscribed Palestine with, he says, their unconscious desire to reconstitute the closed space of a *shtettl,* in which the hated outsider–oppressor would be definitively absent. In both instances Palestinians were discursively and ontologically eliminated from Palestine and, Eisenzweig asserts, reality, in the form of real people and real objects was subverted by the powers of the imagination.[14]

Eisenzweig's thesis is plausible enough in explaining what might have been at the origin of the Zionist idea of Palestine, at least so far as it concerned the natives and how they were to be treated. My only quarrel with Eisenzweig is that he does not spend enough time looking at how the structures of the imagination were always being translated into institutions and practices, in which collective myths of Palestine were metamorphosed into ideology and ideology into detailed practices, both of them assuming that Palestinians would remain without humanity, full identity or allowable resistance, and hence primed for dispossession.

Consider, for example, Israeli official justification of the invasion of Lebanon and one immediately sees how it flows from these earlier tendencies. Take the argument about terrorism and security on Israel's northern border. Here human beings, Palestinians, are stripped of everything but an anonymous quantity entitled 'terrorism'; that they are in Lebanon because they were displaced there from Palestine by Israel, is dropped from the argument and not mentioned. More crucially, all of their efforts at trying to create a national identity, from military defence to social and health services, vocational training and the like, all these are reduced to the clinical word *infrastructure,* which, as Generals Sharon and Eytan never tire of repeating, should be destroyed. In other words, the dense fabric of Palestinian life is reduced not because it is a military threat – the entire number of Israeli casualties caused by Palestinian actions from Lebanon between 1967 and 1982 was 282 (calculated from Israeli sources: see B. Michael, 'A Reminder about Numbers and Victims', *Ha'aretz,* 16 July 1982) whereas in one day during the August 1982 bombing of Beirut Israel was responsible for the death of at least twice the number, to say nothing of Israeli devastation of Lebanon as a country – but because the existence of real, actual, breathing and willing Palestinians in and of itself threatens to violate the almost transcendental countervailing idea of Palestine held by many Zionists, that Palestine is *Eretz Israel* and only that.

A more advanced application of the same notion was demonstrated during the Israeli army's entry into West Beirut in mid-September 1982, after the PLO evacuation and immediately following Bashir Gemayel's assassination. Aside from an excremental orgy of looting and vandalism, reported graphically by Loren Jenkins of the *Washington Post* (29 September 1982), the Israelis made it a point to destroy the Palestine Research Centre systematically after first removing its archives and cultural artefacts for transport to Israel. Quite literally then the Israeli military believed itself to be completing the material erasure of the Palestinian people by attempting to destroy or capture the records that document their history. As even those Israeli doves who oppose annexation put it habitually, the Palestinians pose a demographic problem for Israel, whose Jewish character would be threatened; this, far more than the political aspirations of the dispossessed Palestinians, is the way we are regarded.

Carl Schorske describes the effect of a performance of Wagner on Theodor Herzl as follows:

> No fanatical Wagnerite, or even an opera-goer beyond the Viennese norm, Herzl was this time [1897] electrified by *Tannhäuser.* He came home exalted and sat down to sketch out in a fever of enthusiasm akin to possession his dream of the Jewish secession from Europe. That it was Wagner who should have triggered the release of Herzl's energies into a torrent of creation: how ironic, yet how psychologically appropriate! . . . *Tannhäuser,* the romantic pilgrim who, having sought in vain the help of the Pope in his crisis of Christian conscience, reaffirmed his own integrity by affirming the profane love which he had tried in vain to shake off. Could Herzl have felt in

Tannhäuser's morally liberating return to the grotto a parallel to
his own return to the ghetto? We cannot know . . . Herzl now
plunged toward his break with the liberal world and the secession
of the Jews from Europe. The Zionist movement would be a
kind of *Gesamstkunstwerk* of the new politics. Herzl sensed this
when he said, 'Moses' exodus would compare [to mine] like a
Shrove Tuesday *Singspiel* of Hans Sachs to a Wagnerian opera.[15]

This combination of totalistic theatricalism and ecstatic self-
absorption is also to be found in Zionism, the movement Herzl
founded. From the vantage point of the late twentieth century to
Palestinians, Zionism carried on a good part of its work in the West,
where the glories of a pioneering culture in backward Palestine,
'making the desert bloom', bore little relation to the gradual dispossession that culminated in the disasters of the period from 1948 to
1982. We were left out almost completely. When we appeared
intermittently as 'Arabs', natives or terrorists we were also made
aware of how far we had to go, how much we had to do before our
reality would receive acknowledgement, to say nothing of applause
and affection. Wherever we turned or looked, the stage managers
seemed to have the *Gesamstkunstwerk* well under control. It spoke
the language, partook of the same discourse as, even contributed to
the history of the West, of which it declared itself to be an integral
part – the West, that is, as it saw itself barring Asiatic (later
Communist) barbarians from disrupting its serene civilized
contentment. The violent conflation of history with time, a matter
about which John Berger has written with great insight, was
accomplished.[16]

Until the middle 1970s very little disturbed the spectacle of Israel.
As the military occupation grew more repressive, and as Palestinian
nationalism increased in magnitude and authority, the edges of the
picture started slowly to appear contrived, not to say unreal. The
very same techniques by which Israel represented itself to itself and
to the world – images in the mass media, rhetorical brilliance and
universality, the stated incarnation of 'Western' values such as
humanism and democracy – inevitably started to gather in such
interferences as Israeli soldiers brutalizing civilians, the horren-
dously unattractive zealots of Gush Emunim, the disproportion-
ately destructive practices of the Israeli military, the unremitting
expansionism of Begin and company, Israeli disregard for inter-

national opinion. Despite the meretricious US claims that Camp David brought peace, it became apparent after 1979 that Israel's view of peace with Sadat was, on the one hand, contempt for Egypt and, on the other, a willingness to employ a scorched earth policy everywhere else in the Arab world.

This is not the place to itemize the steps by which Israel lost the security of her ideological dominance on the world stage. That the loss was inevitable should be emphasized however, and it might very well furnish a classic case of the law that representation based on an unambiguous suppression of a good half of the reality being represented cannot be sustained for long. For years Israel's claim had been that it was 'the Arabs' who refused Israel (true), and that was the whole problem (untrue). Nothing was ever said about the Palestinians, without whose *absence* Israel's self-portrayal as Western, humane, democratic would have been impossible. The mere continued existence of the Palestinians therefore menaced the Israeli claim, and in time – as Begin and Sharon realized when they invaded Lebanon in 1982 – that existence had to be destroyed.

No other of Israel's wars was *preceded,* as this latest one was, by a concerted effort to discredit the means of representation, i.e., the public media. For precisely those means that had formerly trained their sights on Israel's brilliantly convincing surface achievements, all of which ignored the hidden reality of Israel's dispossessing Palestinian policy, were now inevitably looking at Israel in brutal action against the Palestinians, who were now visibly opposite (if not completely equal) antagonists. The essence of the Zionist anti-media campaign was exactly the opposite of what the Zionist pro–media campaign had been: in the past one was told, see what we do, ignore what you can't see. Now it was: ignore what you see, focus on what you can't see, the terrorist international, the bombing of northern Israel, etc. Even if all the evidence and such facts as were accessible suggested the opposite, it was the negation of the senses that Israel and its supporters now demanded so peremptorily. Otherwise, as the embarrassingly strident hysterics of American fanatics such as Martin Peretz and Norman Podhoretz proclaimed, you were anti–Semitic. Podhoretz, ever the unashamed violator of known canons of argument, went further: to criticize Israel is to demonstrate a failure of Western nerve.

The well–coordinated chorus of Israeli apologists tried in 1982 to reduce the significance of Israel's actions against the Palestinians, which culminated in the Sabra and Shatila massacres. Many more people were killed in East Timor, in the Iran–Iraq war, in Hama, in the Lebanese Civil War: why, Israeli apologists asked, does everyone concentrate on Israel's victims? A disingenuous question, which is not by any means to say that the Western media were honest and unhypocritical. They aren't and weren't. But what the Palestinian understands instinctively now is that a large part of Israel's project was premised on its theatrical presence before the world's attention. Look here, see what we do, how pioneering we are, how Western, humane, democratic. That very spectacular intensity is not suddenly going to be turned off, just at the moment when ideological self-representation was actually seen to be in discrepant congruence with its own claims. The images of Israeli soldiers literally causing civilian death and havoc occurred in the same confined place where previous images of Israeli pioneers once held centre stage. Something had changed profoundly.

The change was very far from benefiting the Palestinians, who remain dispossessed, but this is another story, neither theoretical, nor ideological. Certainly it needs to be told but, I would argue, on a different ideological-cultural terrain than the reactive one now vacated by Israel's retreat. We exist, I would claim, not only by dint of what Israel has done to us, but by virtue of the only current Arab vision that is both radically pluricommunal and radically secular. Nevertheless the ideological closure provided by the cataclysmic events of 1982 requires a brief conclusion here. Once again this history, as distended and over-pronounced as it is, gives evidence of how the ideological dimension anticipates and long prefigures the real. For three decades preceding 1948 major ideological currents in Zionism dispossessed the Palestinians; in 1948 the reality caught up with its prefiguration. Three decades later, Israeli ideological representations in a sense deconstruct themselves as they grate against images they indict for being mere images. As I write in late 1982, we are now at a moment when for the first time in the history of the struggle between Zionism and the Palestinians two things have emerged, and together they will surely alter the face of things irrecusably; together they must determine the future course of Palestinian history, otherwise there can be no Palestinian history to speak of. One new thing is that a constituency of disaffected Jews, Zionist supporters, Israeli nationalists, as well as fully aware Palestinians has emerged. The second new thing is that an unusual ideological–cultural–political space has opened up, making it possible for the first time to discuss and act on the question of Palestine in its own terms, not simply as a function of superpower rivalry or of the so-called Arab-Israeli conflict.

The defence and the fall of Beirut swept away a great deal, including a lingering faith in the US which did not even abide by its commitment to guarantee the safety of Palestinians left behind after the PLO evacuation. But, as I have been saying, the aftermath has created new political formations in a new political territory. The limits to which Israel can go in its ethnocide against the Palestinians for the moment are defined internationally and regionally; the PLO remained intact as the actual political expression of Palestinian nationalism, Sharon's murderous actions and the Village League quislings notwithstanding. Yet on all sides the problems continue to accumulate. Dispersal and dispossession are accentuated in the post-Beirut period. The imminent likelihood of a credible military option, to say nothing of a credible Arab deterrent, is not very high. Yet everywhere that Palestinians are to be found – Lebanon and the Occupied Territories especially – the political pressure to achieve a solution to the question of Palestine is exerted in ways designed to reduce Palestinians to uncountable statistics, the better to absorb them mutely and anonymously to someone else's scheme. Thus Ronald Reagan wishes them associated with Jordan, Israel sees them as uncomplaining resident natives, some Arabs want them as the spearhead for the wars they either cannot or will not fight.

It is of the essence therefore that much of the residual force that went into the defence of Beirut should now go into formulating a clear Palestinian political programme. Historically, our formulations of where we are going also included such detritus as laments about an unacceptable past, attacks on our enemies, ideological pronouncements aimed at a complex web of interlocking, sometimes contradictory Arab (and even Palestinian) constituencies. There can be no return to this impure style. Our constituency, given the Arab non-response to what happened in Lebanon, is neither the old one, nor a collection of salvaged remnants. There is first a Palestinian constituency that emerged from outside the barren avenues of official routines, positions and structures. This constituency can only be nurtured by a leadership sensitive to its make-up, to the innovative claims it makes, to the novel manoeuvres it can allow. The other important, indeed crucial constituency, is that of

Israeli and non-Israeli Jews who find Israel's present course
unacceptable and disastrous.

Moreover, the loss of Beirut as a substitute for Palestine and the
gain of many new places of exile accentuates the focus on the
Occupied Territories, those last bits of Palestine still inhabited by
Palestinians. The urgent issue now becomes the problem of keeping
Palestinians there – despite, and because of, Israeli desires to expel
them all – and expanding the juridical, political and cultural framework in which they live. Here too the old formulae do not apply
any more, as the disasters that overtook Camp David amply prove.
The conflict in Palestine is not simply a territorial one: this fact
cannot be strategized, Sadatized, or Kissingerized. There is a radical
conflict between a view stating that Jews have more rights than
non-Jews, and a view – as yet to be formulated with the cogency
and power it deserves – stating that all present communities and
individuals have civil rights in Palestine that are posited as equal in
principle. Every departure from this second view has brought
sustained disaster to opponent and proponent alike. The need for a
new politics on the Occupied Territories is the need for a new
effective theory for combating tyrannical exceptionalism, by which
one community's claim is given divine status, the other's reduced to
an occasional appearance from time to time.

None of what is being said here can minimize the unimaginable
complexity of the tasks ahead. No Palestinian is ever afraid to admit
that the struggle we face may be far bigger than we are. Certainly
any political theatre that incorporates the swirl of Arab nationalism,
Zionism, the history of anti-Semitism, anti-colonialism, Islamic,
Jewish and Christian apocalyptic millenarianism, de-colonization,
imperialism, the threat of nuclear annihilation to say nothing of
every variety of human degradation and exaltation, is an epochal
stage indeed. To be a Palestinian is then to stand at the nexus of these
forces, either to be swept away by them or in some way to comprehend and employ their force constructively. If an Israeli military
solution, no less than a cosmetic American or Arab solution, will
not serve, this is the exact moment for Palestinians collectively,
using all the means at their disposal, to state what will serve. Rarely
in human history has the articulation of a programme acquired so
much revolutionary and far-reaching significance. But rarely too
has so much of a people's political identity depended on the collective art of counting, rendering, projecting and re-possessing them-

selves – beyond the armies, the states, the lamentable stabilities of the present.

Notes

1. Michel Khleifi, *La mémoire fertile,* Marisa Films, Brussels, 1980.
2. Jacopo Timerman, 'Reflections (Lebanon)', *New Yorker,* 18 October and 25 October 1982.
3. Johannes Fabian, *Time and the Other: How Anthropology Makes its Object* (Columbia University Press, New York, 1983).
4. Tzvetan Todorov, *La conquête de l'Amerique: la question de l'autre* (Seuil, Paris, 1982); Partha Mitter, *Much Maligned Monsters: History of European Reaction to Indian Art* (Clarendon Press, Oxford, 1977); Dorothy Hammond and Atla Jablow, *The Africa that Never Was: Four Centuries of British Writing about Africa* (Twayne, New York, 1970). See also S.H. Alatas, *The Myth of the Lazy Native* (Frank Cass, London, 1977) and Edward W. Said, *Orientalism* (Pantheon, New York, 1978).
5. A.L. Tibawi, *British Interests in Palestine, 1800–1901* (Oxford University Press, Oxford, 1961), pp. 37 and following.
6. Sarah Graham-Brown, *Palestinians and Their Society, 1880-1946: A Photographic Essay* (Quartet Books, London, 1980).
7. Quoted in Edward W. Said, op. cit., p. 214.
8. Gerard Leclerc, *L'Observation de l'homme: Une Histoire des enquêtes sociales* (Seuil, Paris, 1979), p. 31.
9. Gaston Bachelard, *La Terre et les rêveries de la volonté* (Jose Corti, Paris, 1948).
10. Quoted in Christopher Sykes, *Crossroads to Israel, 1917-1945* (Indiana University Press, Bloomington, 1971), p. 5.
11. Arthur Hertzberg, ed., *The Zionist Idea,* Atheneum, New York, 1976.
12. Arthur Hertzberg, 'The Tragedy and the Hope', *New York Review of Books,* 21 October 1982.
13. Mark Helperin, 'American Jews and Israel: Seizing a New Opportunity', *New York Times Sunday Magazine,* 7 November 1982.
14. Uri Eisenzweig, *Territoires Occupés de l'imaginaire juif: Essai sur l'espace sioniste* (Christian Bourgeois, Paris, 1980), pp. 14–15.
15. Carl Schorske, *Fin-de-siècle Vienna: Politics and Culture* (Knopf, New York, 1980), p. 163.
16. John Berger and Jean Mohr, *Another Way of Telling* (Pantheon, New York, 1982), p. 105.

An Arab Perspective of Jerusalem

Prince Hassan bin Talal

'The problem of Jerusalem is one of the most emotional and explosive issues in the world . . .'[1] Jerusalem '. . . is the spiritual and religious heritage to one half of humanity'.[2] It is 'the Arab sitting at noonday in the shaded edge of his tent, or walking at eventide in the fields where it is pitched' who 'is the true son of Abraham . . .'[3]

Yet sadly today if monotheism is the sacred ground we share, prejudice and hatred have made our struggle for Jerusalem a conflict of extremes. For it is the Zionist movement of today which combines historical and religious claims with the hard facts of continuous control and annexation of the Holy City.

The reality of the State of Israel and the Arab perception of it are reflected in the words of Count Folke Bernadotte: 'It was clear that the Jews in Palestine could not hope to live permanently among millions of hostile Arabs. They would therefore probably be willing to join a Confederation of States in the *Middle East, provided* the basis of such a Confederation were *geographical factors and not racial considerations.*'

In 1948 he said '. . . *the Jews would agree to that* in order to counter Arabs' fear that the Jews in the Middle East served as a tool in the hands of foreign interests, as an instrument for imperialists, be they British, American or Soviet Russian'. The United States at the time was, in the popular perception of the Arabs, not regarded with the same suspicion as the Imperial Powers. Woodrow Wilson's reference to 'the whole disgusting scramble' for the Near East was indirect criticism of his Allies. Furthermore, the concept of self-determination which he expounded gave hope to the Arabs of 'Greater Syria', affected, as they were, by the Skyes-Picot partition between the British and the French.

Over thirty years later we can sadly reflect that morality and power politics seldom match. Demography and racial superiority in numbers mean more to the adversaries in Palestine or their foreign champions than coexistence and peace. Israel argues that it cannot relinquish its security to the Arabs, whom it describes as radical. The United States of today sees Israel as a 'strategic asset' facing its paramount concern of the Soviet threat to world peace. For us, as Arabs, the question is: what has brought about this radicalism, and what justification is left today for moderation or centrism?

'The fact' is 'that what we are dealing with in the Middle East is not an ordinary conflict of interests among nations . . . It is, rather, a peculiar phenomenon of relentless territorial aggrandizement by a *territorially undefined state,* driven by fanatical obsessions, and enjoying the almost blind and inexplicable backing of the most technologically advanced group of nations in the world.'[4]

The predominant inhabitants of Jerusalem have for at least 8,000 years been the Arabs, under various ancient tribal names. The indigenous inhabitants of Jerusalem 'were descended from the original Carmel of Man of Palestine and from the Semitic Arab tribes of Amorites, Canaanites and others who had entered the region from Arabia in migratory waves'.[5]

Jerusalem was built by the Jebusites, a sub-group of the Canaanites in about 3,000 BC. The Jebusites made Jerusalem a Holy City and built a temple for their God Shalim or Salem, and it was the Jebusites who gave it its name – Uashalem or Uasalem. The City was dominated by a succession of peoples: the Persians (538-332 BC), the Greeks (332-164 BC), the Jews during the Maccabean revolt (164-63 BC), the Pagan Romans (63 BC–323 AD), the Christian Romans (324-614 AD), the Persians (614-628 AD) and the Christians again (628-637 AD). Jerusalem was captured by the Caliph Umar ('The Commander of the Faithful') in 638 AD. He made the City the capital of the Arab territory. The content of the covenant with the Patriarch Sophorius '. . . granted them safety for

Abd al-Hamid Sharaf with Wasfi Tal, Amman 1966

Abd al-Hamid Sharaf with King Faisal of Saudi Arabia, 1966

With President Johnson at the White House, 1967

With Pope Paul VI, 1977

With King Hussein at the Arab Summit, 1978

Abd al-Hamid Sharaf with King Hussein and President Tito, 1978

With President Asad of Syria, Damascus 1978

Abd al-Hamid Sharaf with King Fahd of Saudi Arabia, 1979

With President Saddam Hussein of Iraq, 1979

Abd al-Hamid Sharaf with President Ben Jedid of Algeria, 1979

With President Castro, Cuba 1979

With Brzezinski and Dobrinin, Washington D C 1980

Abd al-Hamid Sharaf with Sultan Qabus of Oman, 1980

With Secretary of State Muskie, Leila Sharaf and President Carter, 1980

their lives, their possessions, their churches . . .' in the Holy City
'. . . nor shall any of them be molested'.[6]

Arab rule in Palestine continued until the arrival of the Crusaders
who captured Jerusalem in 1099. They established the Kingdom of
Outremer, ruled from Jerusalem. By contrast, the Caliph Umar
had shown humanitarian compassion. He disproved that Islam is
'. . . supposed to have been the "Ishmaelite in church history",
with hand against every man from the first. Really, when it was
Arabian, as it remained for four centuries, it was very tolerant, and
the Christian pilgrims, priests, and monks were little disturbed.'[7]

It was the history of the Crusades, by contrast, that shook the
Muslims and Christians of the Arab East. 'It was truly a war of the
worlds: the world of western Christendom, which was emerging
painfully from the barbarism of the Dark Ages, came into collision
with the immensely civilized world of Byzantium, which had
passed its political prime; and both were opposed by the world of
Islam . . . These two momentous centuries were also notable for
internal religious divisions on both the Christian and Muslim sides,
for as the years passed the Christian participants in the events of
the time were divided into two bitterly hostile camps; western
Catholics distrusted and despised the Byzantine Christians of the
Orthodox Church, and were heartily detested in return by their
Greek-speaking brothers and sisters in Christ; while the world of
Islam was also split between Sunnites, who acknowledged the
authority of the Abbasid Caliphs in Baghdad, and Shi'ites, who
gave their allegiance to the Fatimid Caliphs in Cairo.'[8]

The Christian Kingdom lasted until 1187 when the Crusaders
were defeated by Saladin, the Saracen ruler, and Jerusalem was
restored to Arab rule. In 1190 Saladin invited the Jews to return to
Palestine.

Palestine played little part in history for the ensuing two
centuries. In 1517 the country, including Jerusalem, was conquered
by the Ottoman Turks under Sultan Selim I. It remained under
Ottoman rule until 1917 except for a brief period between 1831 and
1840 when it was subject to Egyptian rule.

The Arabs fought with the British during the First World War in
their search for national identity. The closing years of the Muslim
Ottoman Empire could only have invited balkanization of the Near
East and left the Arabs no choice. 'The aim of the Arab nationalist
movements,' wrote Amir Faisal, who represented the newly

emerging Arab political identity at Versailles, 'should be remembered today.' His father, Sharif Hussein bin Ali, became the leader
of the Arab Revolt after appeals from the Syrian and Mesopotamian
branches. 'His goal was to unite the Arabs eventually into one
nation.'[9] This movement was 'to restore the supremacy of Mecca
and Medina'.[10] Yet he was forced to die in exile and chose to be
buried in Jerusalem.

Though the history of Jerusalem transcends the politics of conflict
in our region, it is also a history of rebuttal of human aspirations.
Sharif Hussein bin Ali '. . . embodied, above all, the essence of the
Arab national spirit which prevails until today. To the Arabs his
was the first voice to seek the right to exercise self-determination in
Palestine. *"Tarku Ikhitiyari masiriha li ahaliha"*.'[11]

Nevertheless, Jerusalem and Palestine were occupied and mandated by the British from 1917 to 1948. The Balfour Declaration, by
which the correspondence of 1917 between Lord Balfour, Foreign
Secretary, and Lord Rothschild is well known, was indeed a
declaration where 'one nation solemnly promised to a second
nation the country of a third'.[12] The partition of Jerusalem was
effectively to be an indirect product of this generous promise. So
were the provincial capitals and principal towns in Palestine sacred
to the believers of the three monotheistic religions included in the
Declaration. To Muslims, the 'greatest of all honour was accorded
by Islam to Jerusalem as the city of the Prophets of God which
served as Qiblah (orientation in prayer) during the first fourteen
years of the prophethood of Muhammad (SAAW) in Makkah and
Madinah. Moreover, the ascent of Muhammad (SAAW) to heaven
had to come through Jerusalem, whose prophets made a tradition of
which he was the last exponent. Islam saw itself as another moment,
final and culminating of the tradition of Jewish prophets . . . Thus
Islam was a continuation of that same tradition of the one true
religion revealed by God to Man.'[13] We, as Arabs and Muslims, live
the spiritual humiliation of the twentieth century's disregard of this
historical reality. Religion is politicized and many of the followers
of the three great Abrahamic faiths are polarized by the status quo.

The Arab sense of injustice is legitimate and is heightened by the
fact that the Israelis used force in the creation of their state in
Palestine in 1948. The United Nations, to whom the British, with
apparent helplessness, ceded this explosive problem, was ignored in
its appeal for the recognition of both Arab and Israeli rights in

self-determination and statehood in Palestine. In the immediate aftermath of the first war, there was no apparent quarrel between Arabs and Jews in Palestine. The founder of contemporary Jordan, the late King Abdullah, had in 1938 proposed the establishment of a united kingdom. His proposal provided for an elected administration involving Jews and Arabs. His appeal for democracy in Palestine was turned down by, *inter alia,* the British Parliament. His words ring true today. 'The pillars of Zionism are three: the Balfour Declaration, the European nations which have decided to expel the Jews from the territories and direct them to Palestine, and those partisans of the Arabs *who will accept no* solution but are content with weeping and wailing and calling for help to those who cannot aid them.'[14] In this last statement was the Arab self-criticism of a great Arab patriot, a quality much in demand today.

The Arab Army had, under his command, fought in Jerusalem in 1948. This force had entered Palestine in response to the call of her Palestine Arab inhabitants.

In the historical perspective the late king maintained that Jerusalem could be shared between all believers. This sharing could include sovereignty, municipal rights and inter-religious agreements for Arabs and Israelis. 'Abdullah was asking Israel to cede the Jerusalem–Bethlehem road and the former Arab quarters of West Jerusalem. Israel was offering to make these concessions in exchange for the Jewish quarter of the Walled City.'[15] The late King gave his life for Palestine. His realism was the cause of his assassination and for him the following dictum applied: 'Jerusalem is the centre of the Universe.'[16] '. . . to die in Jerusalem is as good as dying in heaven'.[17]

Reason and a willingness to talk have continually led the extremes to violence. 'Without Bernadotte there would [also] be no Bernadotte plan, no prospect of the Israeli Government yielding to international pressure, and no possibility of a federation-type settlement imposed by distant powers.'[18] The utter revulsion one feels at these individual assassinations is only compounded by the massacres in Palestine where terror invited counter-terror. It was in these fraught conditions that peace was so hard to obtain. War has subsequently bred war until the present day.

'One particular terrorist outrage must be mentioned not only by reason of its revolting nature, but also because of its disastrous effect on the Arab population and its influence on the course of events.

This was the massacre by troops of the Irgun Zvai Leumi on 9 April 1948 of the inhabitants of Deir Yassin, a small peaceful village which lies one and a half miles to the west of Jerusalem and is located in the *corpus separatum*. An authentic account of this savage and cold-blooded massacre was given by Jacques de Reynier, the Chief Delegate of the International Red Cross who, at the risk of his life, was able to reach the village and witness the aftermath of the tragedy.

> Three hundred persons, were massacred . . . without any military reason or provocation of any kind, old men, women, children, newly-born, were savagely assassinated with grenades and knives by Jewish troops of the Irgun, perfectly under the control and direction of their chiefs.

'Moreover, to make sure that the massacre had its intended effect on the Arab population, the few survivors, including some women, were paraded by Irgun forces in three trucks in the streets of Jerusalem to be shown as the prize of their "military victory", and on the same night the Jewish terrorist leaders who planned and executed the outrage held a press conference and boasted of their deed.

'Dr Stephen Penrose, President of the American University of Beirut, explained the connection between the Deir Yassin massacre and the exodus of the Palestinian Arabs in 1948 in these terms:

> On both sides dreadful deeds were committed, but, in the main, the Zionists made better use of terrorist tactics which they learned only too well at the hands of Nazi taskmasters. There is no question but that frightful massacres such as that which took place at Deir Yassin in April 1948 were perpetrated for the major purpose of frightening the Arab population and causing them to take flight. The Zionist radio repeated incessantly for the benefit of Arab listeners "Remember Deir Yassin". It is a small wonder that many Arab families began a hasty exodus from the battle area and from sectors which might soon become battlegrounds. Terror is contagious, and it built up the tremendous migration which has led to the results which may be witnessed in the refugee camps.'[19]

As an Arab I note with interest the recent comment of Arthur Hertzberg so relevant to that period of violence and crisis, which undermined the period of rapprochement and peace, as it does now. 'When the King David Hotel was blown up by the Irgun in 1946 the Zionist leaders presented it not as a great act in the cause of liberation, but as the deed of a small faction – led by Begin – which stood against the main principles of Zionism. The notion that it was the destiny of a "Jewish liberation movement" to regain the biblical borders of Israel and to assert its might in the world, thus recapturing Judaism's ancient dignity, was not the basis of the United Jewish Appeal, which asked American Jews to contribute to draining swamps and making the desert bloom, or of the Jewish lobby in Washington, which has traditionally argued that Israel is a moral cause, consonant with America's highest ideals – helping people to rebuild their lives and creative communities to flourish.'[20]

It is the same violence which is eroding tolerance from all parties to the Jerusalem question and the Arab/Israeli conflict. Let us compare, for a moment, the attitude of Muslims to the fire in the Omayyad Mosque in Damascus in 1893[21] where 'great numbers of Muslims threw themselves into the flames in the attempt to rescue the head of John the Baptist; while a copy of the Koran – one of the original four copies – which lay below the relic, was forgotten and destroyed'.[22] Yet when the Aqsa Mosque was burnt in August of 1969, the Israeli authorities stood idly by to watch this heinous crime which shocked the world. For those who lived through World War II the significance of the burning of the Reichstag was only too well-known.

Israel today reminds the world of Article 9 of the Palestinian National Charter: 'The armed struggle is the only way to liberate Palestine.'[23] Yet the Herut Party, central to Israel's government promotes the following: 'The right of the Jewish people to the land of Israel in its historical completeness is an eternal and inalienable right.'[24] Confrontation of these two extremes cannot be ignored through selective disregard for the rhetoric of one side.

In the words of Bertrand Russell, 'We are frequently told that we must sympathize with Israel because of the suffering of the Jews in Europe at the hands of the Nazis. I see in this suggestion no reason to perpetuate any suffering. What Israel is doing today cannot be condoned, and to invoke the horrors of the past to justify those of the present is gross hypocrisy. Not only does Israel condemn a vast number of refugees to misery; not only are many Arabs under occupation condemned to military rule; but also Israel condemns the Arab nations, only recently emerging from colonial status, to continuing impoverishment as military demands take precedence over national development.'[25]

We must understand the need to develop political middle ground. Today, it is clear that the definition of UN Resolution 242 has been subjected to distortion as a result of changes made by Israel to the West Bank and Gaza Strip. Clear examples are the biblical terms 'Judaea and Samaria', used by Israel to describe these areas (Begin retained this usage for the West Bank after the Camp David Accords). This terminology leaves open to interpretation the question of Jerusalem, which is, in a sense, the core of the problem. The nationalization of the City of Jerusalem as well as a projected metropolitan region, constitutes a glaring Israeli disregard of the rights of Arab Christians and Muslims alike, in the peace hitherto envisaged. It is clear that no political settlement can be divorced from the political and legal future of the City of Jerusalem and the status of the Holy Places in general. The thesis advanced that these issues can await resolution until after the controversial Camp David Accords have run their course may be disproved by violent changes in the City of Jerusalem.

In addressing the psychological issues, where people matter, it should be remembered that Palestine was a Class A Mandate in 1922. The Zionists implemented self-determination by use of force in 1948. The establishment of the State of Israel did not constitute a right to regard Palestinian Arabs as subject people to be gradually decolonized. Jordan's position, in common with several Arab governments, is clear, and emanates from the twin principles of justice for peoples and security for states, where free self-determination should be distinguished from limited autonomy. These principles gained open support in the European Venice Declaration of 1980. The process of 'creeping annexation' and the attempted change in terminology through Israeli attribution, from President Reagan's reference to the settlements as illegal, which has been the consistent US position, to merely an impediment to peace, is highly provocative. If settlement suburbs built by Arab labour and Arab taxes were inhabited by Arabs, freedom and peace could be achieved.

Physical changes, *per se,* will not contribute to the quality of life in Jerusalem. The Israeli search for national identity cannot take the form of nationalizing Jerusalem. 'We must seek for Israel in the human life of the land,' stated one historian.[26] Will time permit such a hope to be realized?

The World Zionist Organization's Five Year Plan[27] stated that 'the disposition of the Israeli settlements must be carried out not only around the settlements of the minorities, but also in between them. This is in accordance with the settlement policy adopted in Galilee and other parts of the country.'

The obstinacy of the Israeli leadership in continuing and expanding the settlements is all the more surprising if one takes into account the fact that the majority of Israelis have, from the beginning, been against this policy. Israelis take pride in a democratic spirit and in fact use democracy as an important selling point when seeking aid from the West; yet, according to reports on Israeli polls from 1978 and 1979, almost seventy per cent of Israelis believe that the right to settle in the so-called Judaea and Samaria areas was less important than peace within secure and recognized boundaries. Some sixty-four per cent reportedly opposed the new settlements on the West Bank as an obstacle to peace. Israel's claim on the occupied territories is based on biblical grounds that make little sense in the context of international law, practice and contemporary history. If one were to take centuries' old claims to land seriously, no national boundary of any nation would escape scrutiny today. If force were to be used to occupy lands which supposedly belonged to a people thousands of years ago, the whole world would end up in a state of utter chaos.

Israel's commitment to the principles of withdrawal from the occupied Arab territories as specified in Resolutions 242 and 338, is seen by the Arabs as the key to a 'comprehensive' settlement of the dispute with Israel. In a speech on 1 May 1974, King Hussein said: '. . . I must make it clear that our demand for the disengagement of forces is only the beginning of the application of the principles of complete Israeli withdrawal from the Occupied Territories. We have repeatedly said that if Israel wants peace it must abandon the territory. Under no circumstances at all will Israel be able to do both.'

The Arabs', and hence Jordan's, determination to achieve peace before and since the Camp David Accords has been real and not tactical. The strategic consensus that Jordan contributed to in the Baghdad and Tunis conferences, in which the late Sharif Abd al-Hamid played an active role, kept the peace option alive,[28] so did the Amman summit conference, a process which should continue if reason is to prevail.

What is also clearly sought today is an American commitment to preserving centrism in the region and achieving credible peace. The psychological bitterness of confrontation involving Muslims, Christians and Jews, promoted by nationalism and religious and ethnic extremes of one form or another, can only cause centrism to be engulfed by the tide of nationalism it should be diverting. Full peace, it is believed, is possible when its fullness hinges on Israel's readiness to coexist on a basis of mutual respect for the other parties' legitimate rights.

In concluding, let us remember that Jerusalem is a city where Arabs live today. It may be the objective of certain Zionist leaders obsessed with the demographic imperative to reduce the numbers of these Arabs drastically in the years to come. Arab Christians constituted 3 per cent of the population in 1973 and 4.1 per cent in 1967.[29] We would thus face a situation where these same leaders would assume the role of 'Self-Determinists' when there are no Arabs left to self-determine.

When Pope Paul VI received President Sadat at the Vatican on 8 April 1976, he said: 'With deep concern for this generation and for generations to come, we extend our sincere encouragement to continue to seek a peaceful and just solution to the Arab/Israeli conflict which must include an equitable solution to the problem of the Palestinian people, for whose dignity and rights we have repeatedly expressed humanitarian and friendly interest. And the question of Jerusalem and the Holy Places must be resolved with due regard for the millions of followers of the three great mono-theistic religions, for whom these represent such exalted values.'[30] Recent events have shown us, yet again, that only comprehensive peace can endure.

However, though Arabs are divided in their approach to many issues, it is noteworthy that the Israelis are not united over Jerusalem either. In the words of Israel's former Deputy Mayor of Jerusalem, Meron Benvenisti, 'Jerusalem represents for Israeli and Arab alike certain basic interests: *identity,* a sense of belonging to one's home town and motherland; *control* over their destiny; *recognition* and self-esteem; *security* and *welfare*. The political expression of these basic interests is national sovereignty and the symbols of sovereignty are flags, army, capital city, national institutions. Therefore, sovereignty and its symbols are "non-negotiable", as one cannot give up or compromise on basic human needs.'[31]

He further states that the 'three components of the Jerusalem problem (political) sovereignty, religious (holy places, religious organizations), and ethnic-municipal matters are interrelated, but not identical, and a solution for one is not necessarily a step towards a solution for the others . . . The mediator or the objective onlooker can see how the seeds of long-term solutions are sown in practical arrangements. The problem lies in devising a process in which the parties are brought gradually and slowly to the point where they could conceivably agree on a specific settlement. Each step in this process should be devised so that the parties can perceive it as not contradictory to their stated principles. If successful, the process will gradually become more manageable and the decisions with which the leaders and the people are faced will seem reasonable. The risks of compromise will seem tolerable to each side and the two governments will move towards a final agreement.'[32]

Such an objective onlooker is Lord Caradon who stated in August 1979: 'Was East Jerusalem occupied by Israel in the 1967 War? Of course it was. Was the United Nations Resolution 242 intended to apply to occupied East Jerusalem? Of course it was. Nor is this issue of East Jerusalem academic, remote or unreal. It is, as I say, fundamental, immediate, overriding.' He continues, in his 'proposed draft resolution to the UN General Assembly', to say: 'There should be an Arab Jerusalem and an Israeli Jerusalem each exercising full sovereignty within its own territory, (i.e., Israel and the new Arab State of Palestine), but with no barriers between them and no impediment in freedom of movement between them.'[33]

More recently, Crown Prince Fahd of Saudi Arabia has introduced a plan which restates the essential elements of a comprehensive, just and durable peace and could serve as a good beginning for a new peace process involving all concerned.

In brief, the plan consists of eight points:

(1) Israeli evacuation of all Arab territories seized during the 1967 War, including the Arab sector of Jerusalem;

(2) dismantling the settlements set up by Israel in the occupied lands after the 1967 War;

(3) guaranteeing freedom of religious practices for all religions in the Jerusalem Holy Shrines;

(4) asserting the rights of the Palestinian people and compensating those Palestinians who do not wish to return to their homeland;

(5) commencing a transitional period in the West Bank of Jordan and the Gaza Strip under United Nations supervision for a duration not exceeding a few months;

(6) setting up a Palestinian State with East Jerusalem as its capital;

(7) affirming the right of all countries of the region to live in peace;

(8) guaranteeing the implementation of these principles by the United Nations or some of its members.

Crown Prince Fahd is reported to have declared that if a 'comprehensive settlement was reached with Israel then it would be possible to discuss the issue of recognizing Israel within the same framework of a united Arab stance with the agreement of the Arab states'.[34]

The Saudi Plan and Jordan's position address all the basic issues and represent a sound basis for peace negotiations. What is clear, however, is that there is no exclusive peace process. The hope may be that overriding needs inherent in both regional and international interdependency may achieve comprehensive peace and well-being in the Middle East. The alternative of ethnic and religious dismemberment reminiscent of the dark days of the Crusades, with a mosaic of Christian against Christian and Muslim against Muslim, and possibly Jew against Jew, would commit us to further dreadful exploitation. The believers in the three Abrahamic faiths must coexist if their very identity and values are to be preserved.

In the words of the late Dag Hammarskjold, it is truly 'a work of reconciliation and realistic construction'. Jerusalem is both the City of and the Key to peace. 'All sides have both a role and a stake in the just and durable peace that can ensue.'

Notes

1. Henry Cattan, *Jerusalem* (Croom Helm, London, 1981), p. 11.
2. Ibid., p. 11.

3. John Kelman, *The Holy Land* (Adam and Charles Black, London, 1902), p. 100.

4. The late Sharif Abd al-Hamid Sharaf's address at Chatham House, 3 July 1979.

5. M.A. Aadmiry, *Jerusalem, Arab Origin and Heritage* (Longman, London, 1978).

6. A.L. Tibawi, *Jerusalem, Its Place in Islam and Arab History* (Institute for Palestine Studies, Beirut, 1969), p. 7.

7. John Kelman, op. cit., p. 164.

8. Anthony Bridge, *The Crusades* (Granada, London, 1980), p. 9.

9. Zeine N. Zeine, *Arab Turkish Relations and the Emergence of Arab Nationalism* (Khayat's, Beirut, 1958), p. 125.

10. Bassam Tibi, *Arab Nationalism – A Critical Enquiry* (Macmillan, London, 1981), p. 88.

11. Foreign Office Archives, FO 676/764, pp. 242, 255.

12. Arthur Koestler.

13. Isma'il Raji al Faruqi, *Islam and the Problem of Israel p. 75.*

14. King Abdullah of Jordan, *My Memoirs Completed* (Longman, London, 1978).

15. H. Eugene Bovis, *The Jerusalem Question, 1971-1968* (Hoover Institution Press, Stanford, California, 1971), p. 74.

16. The saying of Abu Hurayrah, a companion of the Prophet.

17. Count Folke Bernadotte, *Till Jerusalem* (Hodder and Stoughton, London, 1951), p. 9.

18. J. Bowyer Bell, *Terror out of Zion* (St Martins Press, New York, 1977), p. 336.

19. Henry Cattan, op. cit., pp. 44-5.

20. Arthur Hertzberg, 'Begin and the Jews', *New York Review,* 18 February 1982.

21. Mohammad Kurd Ali, Al-Shams Plans, 5th edition (Al Taraqi Press, Damascus, 1927).

22. John Kelman, op. cit., pp. 166-67.

23. Palestinian National Charter; first adopted at the founding congress of the Palestine National Council (PNC) held in Jerusalem in May 1964; amended in July 1968 and reaffirmed by the Thirteenth Congress of the PNC held in Cairo, March 1977.

24. 'Herut Party Principles and Ways of Action' (platform for election to the Fifth Knesset).

25. 'Memorandum by Bertrand Russell', 31 January 1970; written two hours before his death, in John Bagot Glubb, *Peace and the Holy Land* (Hodder and Stoughton, London, 1971), pp. 363-64.

26. John Kelman, op. cit., p. 96.

27. Drawn up by Mattiyahu Drobles, head of the Jewish Agency's Land

Settlement Department and head of the Rural Settlement Department of the World Zionist Organization. The Plan was drawn up in 1978 and updated in 1980.

28. Were it not, *inter alia,* for the role of Jordan at these conferences, Arab reaction to the Camp David Accords and the resulting process could have been a lot more violent.
29. Stavro Danilov, 'Dilemmas of Jerusalem's Christians', *Middle East Review,* Spring/Summer 1981.
30. *L'Osservatore Romano,* 15 April 1976.
31. Meron Benvenisti, 'Some Guidelines for Positive Thinking on Jerusalem', *Middle East Review,* Spring/Summer 1981.
32. Ibid.
33. *Guardian,* 27 August 1979.
34. Crown Prince Fahd in an interview with the Kuwaiti daily *Al-Rai Al-Aam,* 9 March 1978.

The Development of PLO Peace Policy*

Hisham Sharabi

National liberation movements, the product of waning colonialism in the twentieth century, are not constituted the way political parties are formed; they are rather the outcome of armed revolt and its vicissitudes. At first the movement is diffuse and inchoate; it reaches maturity only when a unified leadership emerges, putting an end to factionalism and creating the umbrella under which a unified national front is formed. Setting up political, military and administrative structures constitutes the next step.

From the moment it is formed, the national liberation movement is a *de facto* government and exercises all the functions and responsibilities of a provisional government. It alone has legitimacy to end the war and to negotiate peace.

But in practically every instance, at precisely the moment the revolt is transformed into a unified national force, i.e., into a liberation movement, it is denounced by its colonial adversary as lawless rebellion, and subjected to attempts at its destruction. Failure to do this invariably leads to attempts at setting up quisling leadership (one which is 'moderate', willing to cooperate). This occured in Algeria, Vietnam, Angola and Zimbabwe until the real leadership was recognized. With respect to the Palestine Liberation

*This essay was written before the Israeli invasion of Lebanon in June 1982 and therefore does not cover events since then – Ed.

Organization, Israel (along with the United States) is now (1982) at
the mere cognition stage, that of seeking a substitute interlocuter to
the PLO. Israel refuses to recognize the PLO unconditionally until
the PLO recognizes Israel's 'right to exist'. When this phase is
completed the stage will be set for a change of attitude. Sooner or
later, the PLO will be recognized as the only legitimate authority
with whom alone negotiations can be held and an end to the conflict
be brought about. The classic example of this pattern is Algeria, and
its most recent application is the Rhodesian–Zimbabwe experience.

No national liberation movement in the world has enjoyed the
recognition and support which the Palestine Liberation Organization has received. Nor has any revolutionary cause occupied so
much attention and for so long a time as has the Palestinian issue,
despite systematic efforts to obscure and mystify it.

For anyone who is familiar with the facts, the uniqueness of the
PLO lies not in its 'terrorism' but in the kind of democracy it
practises. The Palestinians, despite their dispossession and dispersion, exercise today probably one of the few functioning democ-
racies in the Third World. The real power of the PLO derives not
only from its growing military capability but also from its political
strength, and its capacity to bring ever more strongly Arab and
international opinion to its support.

The National Charter (Covenant) of the Palestine Liberation
Organization, promulgated in 1964 and amended in 1968, expressed
a radical, maximalist position.[1] It called for the liberation of *all* of
Palestine and for the dismantling of the Zionist establishment. Seen
in historical perspective and in the light of subsequent resolutions of
the Palestine National Council over the last decade, this position is
much less extreme than it appears at first blush. By the mid-1970s
the maximalism of the 1960s had undergone significant change; a
policy of realism and moderation began to evolve: armed struggle,
which was viewed in 1968 as the *only* means of liberation, now
became *one* of the methods of struggle, along with political and
diplomatic struggle, which was now emphasized. Israel, which
until the early 1970s had been viewed as a single monolithic entity,
was now seen as a politically varied structure open to influence and
change.[2] A Palestinian–Israeli accommodation now appeared
possible. This change of outlook can be seen in the modification of
the PLO's central goal from the 'dismantling' of the Zionist state

(Article 19) and the establishment of a 'secular democratic state', to that of erecting an independent Palestinian state in the West Bank and Gaza, *alongside Israel*. Thus within a few years PLO policy shifted from an extreme, maximalist position to one of realism and moderation supported by a broad international consensus.

The Palestine National Charter vests all power in a national assembly (The Palestine National Council), which is composed of representatives of all segments of the Palestinian people, including, after 1967, the guerrilla organizations. The policy guidelines for its executive body, the Executive Committee, are set forth at the regular yearly sessions of the PNC. The Executive Committee itself is composed of a broad cross-section of the PNC and is responsible directly to it. This is why the PLO has not broken up into warring factions or deteriorated into dictatorship, and preserved its practice of collective leadership.

The PLO represents an advanced example of the non-territorial state. Since its establishment in 1964, and particularly since its reorganization after 1967, it has developed into a full-fledged government-in-exile, in fact if not in name, with extensive administrative machinery alongside its military and political structures. Some of the health, educational, and social services it provides for the Palestinian people rival those of many states in the region. According to a study commissioned by the *Journal of Palestine Studies* in 1972, the number of Palestinian university graduates had by 1971 exceeded per capita that of any Arab country.

The PLO enjoys a special status in the Arab world, and disposes of privileges which few national liberation movements have known. It has observer status at the United Nations and participates in some capacity or other in practically all international bodies. Most countries of the world, including several European countries, have accorded it recognition and have invited it to open information and political offices in their territories. It is a full member of the League of Arab States and is formally recognized as the 'sole, legitimate representative of the Palestinian people'. It has received similar recognition from Islamic and non-aligned states.

The enormous strength which the PLO has in the Arab world derives from the fact that the Palestinian cause is a pan-Arab cause and not merely a Palestinian one. For nearly three and a half decades the question of Palestine has been the central issue in Arab political life and a major factor in the internal politics of Arab countries. Arab commitment to the Palestine cause has provided the PLO with considerable political and material support, which is not likely suddenly to dry up. Today, the Palestinian question occupies a special place in the Muslim world, with political and military implications – particularly where it affects Jerusalem – little understood in the West.

For the PLO, as for all national liberation movements, the means of struggle, as well as the goals of the successive stages of struggle, are largely determined by its perception of the character of its adversary and its intentions. PLO perceptions of Israel's character and its goals may be summarized as follows:

(1) Israel is the product of colonization and illegal expropriation of Palestinian and Arab land.

(2) It is in the nature of Zionist colonization to refuse recognition of Palestinian rights and to annex all the territories it can occupy.

(3) Israel will continue its policy of dispersal of the Palestinian people and the destruction of Palestinian society in the West Bank and Gaza.

Obviously, the alternative to a zero-sum solution is some form of Arab-Jewish coexistence. The PLO has moved toward such a solution since 1969, when it first put forth the idea of a democratic secular state in Palestine. It from the start made clear that a just and lasting solution cannot be achieved by a *separate deal* or on the basis of the established facts and that a comprehensive settlement can only be based on international agreement and legality. The international community has spelled out the basic principles of such a settlement, central among which are *the Palestinians' right of return, the inadmissibility of the acquisition of territory by conquest,* and *the right of the Palestinian people to self-determination.*

For the Palestinians the right of return is an *inalienable* right. Whether in practice all Palestinians or only a small minority can or will choose to return to their homes and property in Palestine (rather than receive compensation) is not the issue. The issue is recognition of their inalienable right to make the choice, a right which cannot be surrendered or taken away. Arguments against repatriation based on lack of space and resources, or on social and political considerations, do not affect the principle of right. The argument that the Palestinians' return to their homes would change the 'Jewish character' of the state is morally and legally untenable. The term 'Jewish character' is a Zionist term which reflects the discriminatory character of Israeli perception and law, which is in violation of human rights. As a distinguished international lawyer put it, 'The United States is under no more legal obligation to maintain Zionism in Israel than it is to maintain apartheid in the Republic of South Africa.'³

The inadmissibility of the acquisition of territory by force is another basic consideration. This applies to Israel's *faits accomplis* in the West Bank, Gaza Strip, Jerusalem, and the Syrian Golan Heights. The Zionist position on Jerusalem epitomizes Israel's attitude towards all the other issues: its refusal to see the world in terms other than its own; its blindness to the rights of others; its suicidal tendency to shut off external reality.

Finally, regarding the principle of self-determination, PLO policy has based itself on Article 51 of the UN Charter, which states that where a people has been denied its right to self-determination by armed force it has the right to regain it by all means *including* armed struggle. The PLO has taken up arms against Israel to end Israel's illegal occupation, to put a stop to its expropriation of Arab land, and regain for the Palestinian people freedom and the right to self-determination.

It is important to note that this policy has not been fashioned by any one faction or group within the PLO. It does not express a moderate or an extremist position. It is, rather, the outcome of long debates within the leadership circles and of gradual evolution expressed in the resolutions of the Palestinian National Council. In 1964, the aim of the PLO, as put forth by the National Charter, was simply 'the Liberation of Palestine'.⁴ In this unqualified formulation the National Charter reflected the condition of the Palestinians at that time – their sense of abandonment and despair.

The emergence of the guerrilla movement to dominance after the 1967 War and the formation of a National Liberation Front by the major guerrilla organizations under the PLO umbrella, restored Palestinian confidence and brought about new political attitudes.

The goal of liberation was now transformed: 'the establishment of a free democratic society in Palestine composed of Palestinian Muslims, Christians, and Jews'.[5] The Jews, for the first time in fifty years of conflict, were formally included in a solution that acknowledged their equal rights in Palestine.

Unattainable as the goal of a democratic binational state may now appear, it then represented perhaps the first genuine possibility of settlement based on reconciliation between the two communities, rather than on displacement of one by the other. Psychologically – as well as politically – the concept of the democratic state brought about a qualitative change in Palestinian thinking about eventual settlement, and the idea of Arab–Jewish coexistence has become a basic element in it ever since.

Unfortunately, the cynicism with which the Israeli leaders received the idea of a democratic state eliminated the possibility of exploring it in depth, and as a result it has remained a largely opaque, undeveloped concept. The Zionists, now militarily a regional superpower and ruling over an area three to four times the size of Israel in 1948, were in no mood for talk about coexistence and peace. They, more than anyone else, must be held responsible for scuttling an historic opportunity, one providing a just and humane solution of the Arab–Israeli conflict.

The next major development of PLO policy took place shortly after the 1973 War. It was a move away from the idea of the democratic state (without formally abandoning it) and towards the concept of a separate independent Palestinian state side by side with Israel. This was the result of much debate in Palestinian circles, particularly at the twelfth PNC session held in Cairo in June 1974. The new policy was now phrased in such a way as to make the shift acceptable to the broadest possible constituency: 'to use all means, above all armed struggle, to liberate Palestinian soil and to set up on any part of it which is liberated the militant national authority of the people . . .'[6] (For national authority, read 'state'.) In 1977 this was further clarified as signifying 'self-determination'[7] and 'the right to establish an independent Palestinian State'.[8]

Opposition to the new policy, however, was strong. It later became embodied in a minority 'rejection front'. But the PNC approval of the political programme made the Palestinian state concept official policy. And when Chairman Arafat addressed the United Nations General Assembly later that year, he referred to the secular democratic state as a 'dream', and opened the door for a solution based on the establishment of an independent Palestinian state in part of Palestine. This was the maximum compromise the Palestinian mainstream leadership could achieve without under-mining Palestinian unity. 'Today,' Arafat concluded, 'I have come bearing an olive branch and a freedom fighter's gun. Do not let the olive branch fall from my hand.'[9]

As the formulation of PLO policy gained clarity and precision, it also gained strength and support and enhanced the prestige of the PLO internationally. At the Baghdad Arab summit in 1978, the Arab states backed the PLO position and, for the first time in thirty years, reached collective agreement on a principle for settling the Palestine problem.

From the start the PLO's position regarding the Camp David agreements was clear: it rejected these agreements because they ignored Palestinian rights and sought settlement outside the UN framework and without the participation of the Palestinians. It regarded any agreement arrived at within the Camp David frame-work as aiming to take Egypt out of the Arab–Israeli conflict and to extend Israeli control over the West Bank and Gaza indefinitely. The PLO has called for genuine negotiations in which all the parties concerned would participate and where a comprehensive settle-ment based on UN resolutions and international consensus could be reached. Chairman Arafat called upon the Arab governments to take a more determined stand on this issue and to use all means at their disposal, including those of energy and finance, to defend the rights of the Palestinian people and to bring about a just and comprehensive peace.

Unfortunately, not only have the hopes for such a peace not been fulfilled, but a dangerous turning-point has now been reached. Failure to find an avenue to peace in the short term is likely to affect the stability of the status quo in the Middle East and to lead to a situation of severe international crisis. What makes the situation still more dangerous is Israel's insistence on imposing its military supremacy as a way of achieving an Israeli peace, forgetting that the possession of nuclear and biological weapons cannot remain the exclusive monopoly of any one country in the region.

Structurally, both the central error of Zionist thinking and the
disaster to which it is leading in the Middle East have always derived
from one basic misconception: that it is possible to fulfil Zionist
ambitions in the area at the expense of another people's rights and to
bring about lasting settlement by force.

To be sure, there are those in Israel and within the American
Jewish community who oppose this position and call for a political
solution based on a fair sense of justice; but they constitute only a
small (and, so far, ineffectual) minority. The Labour coalition also
speaks of a political solution, but in terms of a partition of the West
Bank and Gaza with Jordan; it rejects altogether the idea of an
independent Palestinian entity. Labour's position on the Palestinians
is essentially the same as Mr Begin's, except for language and style.

King Hussein has repeatedly said that he will not replace the
Palestinians in any negotiations on their behalf and has maintained
that a lasting solution depends on the Palestinians exercising the
right of self-determination. The King of Jordan has formally
recognized the PLO as the Palestinians' 'sole legitimate spokesman'.
And in the West Bank and Gaza support for the PLO has been
almost total; not a single significant Palestinian leader or group has
come out in favour of autonomy. It is rare under conditions of
occupation to see such unanimity.

Only with difficulty was Arafat able, at the PNC meeting in April
1981, to stem the rising opposition against his moderate line of
policy. This time his attackers came not only from the left, but also
from the mainstream; their point was that the policy of conciliation
had proved ineffective, since neither the Israelis nor the Americans
had responded positively to any of Arafat's advances.

Outside the Council some of Arafat's opponents talked of curb-
ing further 'moderate' moves and called for withdrawing the
Council's 1977 recommendations which called for encouraging
'progressive and democratic forces' in Israel. When Arafat, in *al-
Hawadith* (December 1980), defended the dialogue conducted with
members of the Israeli peace movement by one of his advisers,
Issam Sartawi, these opponents strongly criticized the PLO leader.

The general feeling of frustration was reinforced by the attitude of the Labour Party (then considered the likely winner of the Israeli elections in June) and that of the new Reagan administration, which persisted in denouncing the PLO and in refusing all dealings with it.

The Labour Party's platform of December 1980 had made clear three crucial points: that full Israeli withdrawal from the occupied territories was out of the question; that no Palestinian state in Palestine would be allowed to emerge; and that no negotiations with the PLO would be undertaken under any circumstances.

It now became clear that what Shimon Peres, the leader of the Labour coalition, meant by the 'Jordanian option' – an option categorically rejected by Jordan – was simply a proposal to form a Jordanian-Israeli condominium over the West Bank, in which Jordan would get back nearly half of the occupied territory and Israel would control or annex the other half, including presumably Gaza. Significantly, under this proposal Israel's share would include 90 per cent of the area's arable land with almost all the water, and Jerusalem would remain the undivided capital of Israel.

It may be recalled that under the UN Partition Plan of 1947, 54 per cent of the mandate of Palestine had been assigned to 35 per cent of the population (Jews) and the remaining 46 per cent to 65 per cent of the population (Arabs). In the 1948 War Israel expanded its share to 78 per cent of the total area of Palestine (Gaza and the West Bank constituted the remaining 22 per cent). Now, the Labour Party proposed partitioning the remaining 22 per cent by returning the equivalent of 10 per cent of the total area of Palestine. Thus the Palestinians were to be denied not only the right to self-determination but also of any title to their national territory.

The Reagan administration's position on the Palestine problem, as expressed by Mr Reagan himself soon after taking office, had the effect of reinforcing opposition to Arafat's policy of conciliation. Mr Reagan, in an interview in the *Christian Science Monitor*[10] shortly after taking office, made three damaging points. Asked whether he had any 'moral feelings' towards the Palestinians and their aspirations as he did towards the Israelis, he answered 'No,' indicating that he considered the Palestinians as merely 'refugees' without the claim accruing to the survivors of the holocaust. When questioned about the PLO, he associated it with 'terrorism' and expressed doubt that it was 'the representative of the Palestinians'. And concerning Jewish settlement in the West Bank and Gaza, he frankly sided with the Zionist position: 'I disagree with the previous administration . . .' he said. 'They [the settlements] are not illegal.'

The administration's military approach to the Middle East crisis, of viewing the area in terms of a 'Soviet threat' rather than seeking a comprehensive peace settlement, further discouraged those who still hoped for an international settlement involving the various parties and the two superpowers. Such a possibility now seemed remote; only the European initiative seemed to hold some hope. But in his report to the PNC (in April 1981) Arafat was not very optimistic and referred to the European effort in critical terms – as lukewarm, as slow in coming, as insufficient. Still there was general agreement that the European effort should not be opposed, and Arafat was given full mandate to further it. Though Arafat finally succeeded in gaining renewed backing for his policies, he was keenly aware that this time there was far less warmth in the support given him. It was also clear that if he failed to achieve positive results during this phase, crucial in determining the Palestinian future, this policy was likely to lose all support in the next Council meeting. As one Council member put it, 'We have waited long enough. We have been asked to be patient and to be moderate – to wait until the next American elections, to wait until the next Israeli elections, to wait until the next UN session, to wait for the European initiative. What has been the result? The Israelis have annexed Jerusalem, the Americans have accepted the settlements as not illegal, the Europeans have failed to put their initiative together, and the UN General Assembly will soon pass another resolution in our favour . . .'

Even if the Reagan administration were to ignore the centrality of the Palestinian problem, the Arab states, including those most friendly to the United States will have to oppose this trend, for even if they wished to extricate themselves from the Palestine problem, the forces in the region are bound to pull them back to it. It is always necessary to remember that Arab support of the Palestinian cause is based as much on state interest as it is on considerations of justice and right for the Palestinians. It is generally agreed that burying the Palestine problem was simply impossible for the Arab governments, and relegating it to a lower place on the agenda would alleviate little of present difficulties and would probably create many more. The threat Israel posed to the Palestinians was basically the same kind of threat it presented to all the surrounding Arab states. This realization was firmly embedded in the Arab perception, thanks to Israel's agressiveness and inflexibility.

My point is that the Arab regimes must strive to achieve an acceptable solution of the Palestine problem as an act of self-defence. If achieved, the goal of a Palestinian solution will not only serve to stabilize the area but also to put a limit to Israeli expansion and, on another level, to remove justification for unlimited American military support for Israel. In this light, the PLO is not a burden or a liability to the Arab states, but rather an indispensable factor in achieving a just and lasting peace to preserve the established state system in the Arab world.

It is fair to assume, that under certain conditions (such as conditions of war, as in 1948 and 1967) mass expulsion of Palestinians from the West Bank and Gaza by Israel may become possible. An Israeli general, speculating before a British television crew in 1978, spoke of Israeli bombing, in the event of another Arab–Israeli war, of Arab urban centres in the West Bank and Gaza, to cause mass exodus of people. Economic pressure and selective expulsion would continue in times of peace; so that in five years or so, not only the economic and political character but also the demographic structure of the occupied territories would be transformed.

On the other hand, it may be that even extreme measures may not be sufficient to uproot the Arab population – witness the tenacity of the Palestinian population of 150,000 left behind in 1948, which now numbers over 600,000 and constitutes an increasingly cohesive force within Israel. In Lebanon a large-scale invasion, involving Syria in all-out war, would probably bring about Soviet intervention. But even if carried out, such an invasion is by no means certain to achieve its strategic and political goals. The Litani campaign of 1978 demonstrated the limitations of sophisticated warfare against guerrilla forces rooted in civilian populated areas.

Clearly, there is no moral or legal right for Israel to continue the occupation of Arab lands, yet arguments about Israel's security and claims about historic rights are still put forth, preventing a just settlement. Israel's torture of Palestinian political prisoners, its expropriation of Palestinian propety and annexation of Arab lands, are routinely ignored or rationalized by the Western media. In retrospect it becomes clear that since 1967 the Zionist goal has all along been not so much to achieve peace as to preserve the status quo created by war.

From this point of view, peace may be seen only as a bonus added to a settlement that recognized the established facts, including the annexation of Arab Jerusalem and the Golan Heights. Zionists, both in the United States and in Israel, still seem to think that giving back the Sinai is sufficient price for keeping the West Bank, Gaza, and the Golan Heights. Their problem – at least for the moment – is not so much the two million 'Palestinian natives' in their midst, but how not to give up the occupied territories despite almost total international opposition (and mounting opposition in the United States). Begin believed that the best policy, so often successful in the past, was to confront the United States and the world with accomplished facts; so long as he had US support he felt he could ignore the rest of the world with impunity.

This illustrates a point I made earlier, namely, that so long as the settler power has material superiority it will have little interest in solutions that do not meet its territorial and political demands.

Thus Israel is not likely to negotiate with the PLO in the near future, not because the PLO refuses to recognize its right to exist or for any such abstract reason, but because Israel is not interested in a settlement that recognizes Palestinian rights and calls for giving up territory. For Israel the only acceptable Palestinian interlocuter is one who will not make national demands and will accept limited administrative autonomy and submit to Israel's diktat concerning land and sovereignty.

We are told that it is useless to apply pressure on Israel because that would only make it more inflexible; i.e., that only a secure Israel can make concessions and negotiate peace. The fact that American support has only served to reinforce Israel's determination to continue its annexationist policy and to resist negotiations seems not to have affected American policy at all. Mr Carter never tired of repeating that Israel would continue receiving all the assistance it needed no matter what its policies were, and Mr Reagan seems determined to keep this pledge.

The Israeli leaders and their supporters in the United States know that as long as the military approach is the dominant one in dealing with the Middle East, they will always be able to sell Israel as America's strategic ally and most reliable partner in the region (and to continue to receive American military and financial support).

Thus despite the fact that in recent years PLO peace signals have been frequent and clear, they have been consciously and consistently rebuffed. It is now clear that the more moderate the PLO is, the less acceptable it becomes to Israel. Indeed, a truly moderate PLO has always been perceived as a more dangerous threat to Israel than a belligerent one. In this context it is not difficult to see why PLO peace policy has had such little success in Israel and in the United States.

Notes

1. Text in Faisal Haurani, *Palestinian Political Thought, 1964-1974* (Beirut, 1980), pp. 228-39 (in Arabic).
2. The PNC, in its 1977 session, approved support of and dialogue between Palestinians and 'progressive and democratic elements in Israel'. See text of recommendations in Institute of Palestine Studies, *Arab and Palestinian Documents, 1977* (Beirut, 1978), p. 97 (in Arabic).
3. T.W. Mallison in UN, 'An International Law Analysis of the Major United Nations Resolutions Concerning the Palestine Question', (ST/SG/SER.F5), p. 37.
4. Articles 12, 13, 14, text in Faisal Haurani, op. cit.
5. PNC, Political Programme (5th Session, 4 February 1969), in *Palestine Yearbook, 1969* (Beirut, 1972), pp. 66-8 (in Arabic).
6. PNC, Political Programme (12th Session, 1-8 June 1974), text in R. Hamid (ed), *Resolutions of the Palestine National Council, 1964-1974* (Beirut, 1975), p. 247 (in Arabic).
7. PNC, Final Communiqué (13th Session, 20 March 1977), text in *Arab and Palestinian Documents, 1977*, p. 97.
8. Ibid.
9. Verbal text, UN Doc. A/PU. 2282, p. 51.
10. 4 February 1981.

Part III
Current Trends in
Arab Society

Understanding Islam

Al-Sadig al-Mahdi

Definition

Islam means submission. In the religious context it means submission to Allah (God). The word is derived from the root SLM from which *salam,* meaning peace, is also derived. The general connotation of the concept is submission to Allah, and through that submission the realization of psychological peace (within oneself), social peace (within one's society), and ecological peace (within one's environment). That is so because the three realms are all subject to divine will.

The Spiritual Message

According to Islam, mankind has primordially entered into a covenant with Allah acknowledging monotheism (Al-Araf, 172). The apostles of God remind mankind of that and preach the identical spiritual message: 'We have revealed to all those Prophets who preceded thee that I am the only God and that you should worship me.' In the Quran, the word 'Islam' is used extensively to describe the message of all the apostles of God. These messages have been sealed by the last message: that of Muhammad. Man is spiritually endowed and, through faith, his spirituality may be extended so that he may transcend himself: 'O ye that believe! Fear God, and believe in his Apostle, and he will bestow upon you a double portion of his mercy and provide for you a light by which you shall walk.' (Hadith 28).

The Moral Message

In Islam, morality is based on rational criteria: altruism, universality, and reciprocity.

Altruism: 'Those who give preference to others over themselves though they are in great need.' (Hashr 9)

Universality: 'To do that which is universally approved and to avoid that which is universally rejected.' (Quran)

Reciprocity: 'Repay the aggressor in kind measure for measure.' (Quran)

The Humanist Message

Islam is positive in a humanist sense. Man acquires knowledge by four means, which are: revelation, intuition, reason and experience.

Revelation: 'It is no less than inspiration sent down to him. He was taught by one mighty in power.' (Najm 4 and 5)

Intuition: 'Obey God and he will enlighten you.' (Quran)

Experience: 'Say travel through the earth and see how God did originate creation.' (Ankabut 20)

Reason: There are more than fifty instances in the Quran where man is instructed to use his rational faculties: to infer, deduce, judge and reason. 'Without reason you cannot be properly religious.' (Hadith)

These four sources of knowledge are not opposed to each other, but complement one another in man's pursuit of wider and deeper enlightenment: 'On the earth there are signs for those of assured faith, as also in your own selves: will you not then see?' (Zariat 20)

Islam demands achievement in this world and considers it worthy of reward in the next. These beliefs transformed the outlook of the people who came to constitute the community of believers – the Umma. They drove them to heights of unparalleled achievement, an achievement characterized by dynamism, populism, purposefulness, and spiritual and moral fervour. The Umma burst into history and in eighty years spread its message over an expanse of territory larger by half than the territory amassed by the Roman Empire in eight hundred years.

The Causes of Decline

There are eight main reasons why that new world lost much of its initial vitality.

1. Political leadership was to begin with decided by popular acclaim of the worthy, but soon this populist republicanism was discarded in favour of dynastic succession. In 55 AH Muawiah made his son Yazid his successor and used force to impose his decision. Both the Ummayad and Abasid dynasties, which in turn ruled the Muslim world, espoused the principle of next of kin succession. These monarchic regimes were not without benevolence, but in due course power came to rest on naked force alone. Eventually government passed into the hands of military overlords. Despotism reigned supreme.

2. The Islamic economic system established by the Prophet in al-Madina was a compassionate one. It encouraged and rewarded effort. It prohibited all forms of unearned income, e.g. usury, gambling, etc. It rejected both luxury and destitution and catered for the needs of the poor and the disabled. Gradually, and hand in hand with the growth of despotism, a society based on privilege and social stratification emerged.

3. For some time, cultural and intellectual dynamism continued, in spite of political and economic deviations. While the body politic fell sick, Muslim thinkers and authors proceeded to develop the Arabic language, to translate and extend the wisdom and knowledge of ancient cultures, to interpret the Quran, to collect the Hadith, and on the basis of these texts to codify Muslim law. Their achievements in all aspects of human endeavour – the humanities, the sciences, technology, and art – were immense.

The schools of Muslim law, founded by the genius of individual thinkers working privately, are to this day a tribute to faithful dedicated effort. But those pioneers never intended their achievements to be the final word on Islamic law. A combination of factors, however, led to that unfortunate situation. The regime of *taghlid* (loyalty to the opinions of the founders) came to stay, and from the fourth century AH onwards people have been expected to espouse this or that recognized school of Muslim law. *Taghlid* replaced initiative.

4. The Quran is explicit about the full humanity of the Prophet Muhammad: 'Say I am but a human being to whom the

message of monotheism has been revealed,' (Quran). Again, the Prophet said, as quoted by Umsalama: 'In matters where I receive no revelation, I judge matters on the basis of my opinion.' In spite of these declarations, the Prophet came to be exalted by many like Jesus in the eyes of the Christians. This transformation had much to do with the unwarranted development of theocracy in Islam.

5. The authority of the Prophet was unjustifiably sought to chart the inevitable decline of Muslim society, with the frequent repetition of such hadiths as, 'Every year you will be worse than the previous year' – and this despite the fact that it contradicted explicit Quranic promises: 'Allah has promised those who believe and do righteousness to make them vice-regents on earth as he had done to their predecessors.'

6. Initially Sufism (mysticism) emphasized spiritual endeavour, love among believers, and love of the believers for Allah. Many a vexed soul found in Sufism a spiritual haven amid the desolations of life. In time, however, the initial inspiration was distorted by a host of beliefs which encouraged the mediation of certain pious individuals between Allah and mankind. Similarly other-worldly views were encouraged, requiring believers to turn away from this world and reject all achievement in it. The door was opened wide to mystical, magical and superstitious ideas. If *taghlid* arrested intellectual initiative, then loyalty to Sufi orders arrested spiritual and emotional vitality.

7. These factors – despotism, economic injustice, social stratification, the stagnation inherent in *taghlid,* and the world-negation of Sufism – combined to empty the Umma of mind, heart, and social purpose.

8. One good reason put forward in defence of *taghlid* is that it served as a protection of the mind of the Umma against encroaching alien ideas. Ironically, along with the aforementioned factors, it was *taghlid* which weakened the inner vitality of the Umma, leaving it a sitting prey to external enemies. A new Europe, strengthened by the achievements of the Industrial Revolution, marched its armies to encircle the world of Islam and conquer its territories one by one. The impact of Western conquest did not remain at the military and political levels, but set in motion a cultural and ideological onslaught. The Muslim politicians, businessmen, men of letters, and so on, who first came into contact with the ideas and institutions of the conquering West were most impressed. Many of

them manifested a great degree of self-hate and a great zeal to be cast in the image of the invading culture.

The Current Resurgence

In attempting to explain the current Islamic resurgence, I would identify a number of related factors.

A primary factor is the continued vitality of Islam when under assault. Throughout periods of decline, *mujahids, mujtahids* and *mujadids* have refused to accept that decline is inevitable, and in one way or another have made a reforming or revolutionary impact. More specifically, during the decisive encounter with the West which took place last century, enlightened men of this sort laid the groundwork for the current resurgence. Their ideas were developed and articulated by enthusiastic disciples.

Reaction to the West, operating at several levels of experience, has been a crucial element in the current resurgence.

Initially secularist Western ideas made a great impression, and this receptive enthusiasm was repeated, after the Second World War, for Communism. But during the last twenty years two phenomena have manifested themselves: first a sophisticated understanding of Third World relations with both East and West, both of whose policies have been shown to be motivated by domination and the pursuit of economic benefits. Second, as the internal weaknesses of both systems became more apparent, the appeal of imported ideas was blunted and people grew disillusioned with them. Today the Third World increasingly views international affairs in terms of a North-South, rather than an East-West, encounter.

Within the Third World, Muslim society has been shaken out of complacency by Western efforts at acculturation – direct efforts as in the case of Algeria and indirect as in the case of Iran, and by violent displacements as in the case of Palestine. The identity, dignity and integrity of Muslim society have been rudely violated, so that even the most drowsy have had their eyes opened to the fact that the soul of their society is under attack by aggressive enemies. This realization has helped spur Islamic resurgence.

Most non-Western societies, in their encounter with the West, have sought to modernize but not Westernize – that is to say, they have refused to lose their identity in the process of modernization.

This is why they have in their different ways reached for their roots and attempted to make the process of modernization a form of renaissance. For Muslims, Islam is not only the root of roots, it has also been throughout history the main protection in the resistance to foreign domination. Islam as a pointer to a past golden age, as a shield against foreign domination, and as the abiding source of identity and dignity for the masses, has ensured that the renaissance is an Islamic renaissance.

A further factor of resurgence has been the failure of nationalism. In the struggle for liberation from Western domination, many movements espoused nationalist ideologies extending from Kamalism to Nasserism and Ba'thism. These ideas succeeded in achieving a measure of national mobilization and political liberation, but, being either indifferent or hostile towards Islam, they failed to enlist the enthusiasm of the masses. They were, as they remain, elitist. They also failed to deliver the goods they promised. Their failures, which were in some cases dramatic, prompted the search in earnest for an alternative to nationalist ideology.

If disappointment with nationalism is a negative reason for Islamic resurgence, a positive reason has been provided by a host of Muslim writers and thinkers who turned away from the straightjacket of traditional Islamic systems, while rejecting the ideas and systems of the invading culture, and took a position which may be described as both Islamic and modernist. Men who articulated this insight in various ways were, for example, the late nineteenth-century Islamic reformer and thinker Jamal al-Din al-Afghani, Muhammad Iqbal, a founding father of modern Pakistan, and Ali Shariati, the young Iranian Islamic humanist who died in 1977.

And finally resurgence is powered by the economic and strategic importance of the Islamic world.

Oil is the life-blood of modern industry and society. The financial resources realized from oil since the 1970s have increased the economic leverage of the oil-producing countries, a majority of which are Muslim. But, with or without oil, the strategic importance of the Islamic world cannot be exaggerated: it falls in the centre of the world and through it pass vital water, air and land routes. Its strategic importance is further enhanced by great power conflicts and the game of global domination which the great powers are engaged in. Directly and indirectly this increases Muslim self-awareness and encourages a degree of Muslim self-assurance.

Thus various factors combine to explain the current Muslim resurgence.

Islam's new importance prompts a further question: what are the main features of the contribution Islam can make to contemporary society? A host of different answers might be given to this question by the various schools of Muslim thought, but I believe that the answer is, and can only be, as outlined in the following pages.

Islam in the World Today

As a religion, as a culture, and as a social order, Islam has a distinct character. Neverthess, it has never been a closed phenomenon. In metaphysical terms Islam is the culmination of a process of divine revelation which recognizes and completes the previous monotheist revelations. In historical terms, W.M. Watt rightly said: 'There is something almost incredible and because of that fascinating in the story of how the ancient cultures of the Middle East became transformed into Islamic culture.'

Islam encouraged a high degree of intellectual freedom. It sanctioned no representative or representatives of God on earth who would establish a religious command. No one was entitled to be the exclusive interpreter of the sacred texts, i.e., no legitimate basis for a theocracy existed or exists.

Islam sanctioned all the known means of knowledge: revelation, intuition, reason, and experience. It encouraged interest in the achievements of other civilizations. The Quran cited the experience of other peoples. It employed terms of foreign origin, for example *ingeel* is Greek, *sirat* is Latin, *sair* is Syriac, *gahim* is Amharic, *gehanem* is Hebrew, and so on. There was no taboo placed on the adoption of useful ideas or institutions of foreign origin. The Khalifa Omar ibn al-Khatib adopted several such ideas and institutions, for example the land tax called *kharaj* and the bureaucratic system called *diwan*. Muslim civilization incorporated the achievements of other civilizations, digested them, and employed them in the enrichment of its own culture. This development was not accidental. It followed from the very image of man in Islam.

Islam is positive in a humanist sense. Humanity *per se* is honoured: 'We have honoured the offspring of Adam,' (Quran). Allah's will permeates human history and manifests itself in it: 'Allah changeth not your state of affairs until you change yourselves,' (Quran). The Islamic principle on which all this hinges is that revelation and reason, sacred and secular, complement each other.

Islam triumphed because it delivered a divinely inspired message, and because the Islamic Umma believed the message and acted as the custodian entrusted with realizing it in human history. The early Muslims successfully applied the revealed teachings of Islam to the problems of their time. For us to re-apply their solutions, as if time had stood still, is the height of folly. But to employ their *methods* in the radically different society of today is both Islamic and rational.

Contemporary society is faced with many challenges. It may be useful to identify some of the major ones facing us as we approach the end of the twentieth century.

Undoubtedly, the scientific and technological revolution has increased man's knowledge of the natural world, enabling him to harness natural forces and extend by leaps and bounds his technical abilities. This is a commendable achievement. However, the geometric rate of technical advance disturbs two desirable balances: first, the ecological and second, the ethical. These two imbalances derive from a basic malady of modern society – the demise of traditional beliefs and values which has left a wide spiritual void in its wake. The French philosopher Pascal said: 'Man needs to believe and to love. When he is deprived of proper objects for his belief and love, he will substitute wrong ones for them.' Lacking the proper objects, much modern experience is a search for substitutes, in alcohol, drugs, gambling, and bizarre cults (after the suicide of Jim Jones and his group, it was estimated that there were about three thousand such cults in America alone). The espousal of perverted and shocking practices becomes a means to respond to monotony and alienation. An inordinate love for pets satisfies unfulfilled emotional urges. And in spite of all the substitutes, psychological and psychiatric complaints are pervasive.

Modern man is on a high wave of scientific and technological achievement, but on those lonely heights he is desperately in search of a soul and a heart. Many creeds fail to provide what he needs because they are either basically anti-scientific or completely other-worldly. And as H.A.R. Gibb said: 'No religion can ultimately resist disintegration if there is a perpetual gulf between its demands upon the will and its appeal to the intellect of its adherents.' The modern secular 'isms' also fail to satisfy because they are either negative about or indifferent to spiritual and moral issues. Islam, on the other hand, is a spiritual and moral message which encourages and welcomes the development of scientific and technological knowledge.

A second challenge is posed by aspirations to equality. Many sections of contemporary society have become acutely aware of their lack of fulfilment. Oppressed economic classes, oppressed social groups, oppressed races, women, and even previously unrecognized sections of society such as young people and children, have all become conscious of their lost rights. There now exists a politicized consciousness which no ideology can afford to ignore. World-negating creeds cannot meet this challenge. Nor can creeds like Hinduism which through the sacred caste system perpetuate a certain social pattern. The social teachings of Islam, however, as is explained below, can face the challenge successfully.

The yearning for development poses yet another challenge. People, except for some mystics, seek to better their material well-being. This basic aspiration has been accentuated in the contemporary world by the achievements of economic development and the ability of people everywhere to see for themselves how others have increased their material prosperity. It has been demonstrated for all to see that economic underdevelopment means deprivation as well as subordination. No wonder then that creeds and ideologies are increasingly being judged by their ability to effect economic development.

A further problem is that of reaching a proper balance between the individual and the state. The modern state is a more powerful machine than ever existed before. If it responds to the requirements of planned economic development, its powers are further enhanced. This prompts the question: how far can state and social power be extended without making the individual an impersonal number deprived of conscience and choice?

Then there is the question of human rights, of which modern man is more and more conscious and to which everyone at least pays lip-service. Human rights require to be maintained within national and international contexts. Ideologies will be judged by their record in recognizing and defending human rights.

Religion itself poses a problem by its manifold subdivisions. Many, often rival, creeds are to be found within all contemporary societies. The secular solution to the problem of interdenominational relations is to assume its non-existence or to expect it to fade away in time, an approach which is either unrealistic, or hypocritical, or ineffective. The other extreme – making one creed the basis of the state and society (as in the case of Israel) – is intolerant and in the long run no more effective. The principled Islamic response to this challenge is to extend recognition to other creeds, to give them denominational autonomy, and to organize the civil rights of their adherents in a just way so long as they respect the integrity of the state and society in which they live.

A last challenge that I would list is that posed by the nation–state. Secularist political thinking assumes the sovereign nation–state to be the unit of international relations. The concept of sovereignty is carried to such an extreme that the citizens of a particular state can be out of the reach of any international principle, however desirable. The nation–state regards itself as an island unto itself, often representing that jealous singularity by the symbolism of wild animals and birds: the lion, the bear, the eagle, etc. In this situation peaceful relations between states are possible only insofar as they are necessary. There is no wider principle on which to base them. Islam, however, requires the fulfilment of certain obligations between human beings transcending political divisions: a brotherhood of man. Sovereignty must be balanced against considerations of brotherhood and justice.

Needless to say, once we turn away from traditional formulations and concepts, we shall find in the Quran and Sunnah a positive response to all the challenges of contemporary society. To settle this issue, let us examine the teachings of Islam to confirm the legitimacy of change and to show that it is those who reject change and espouse *taghlid* who endanger the current resurgence and play into the hands of the secularist right and left.

The Legitimacy of Change in Islam

The spritual and moral teachings of Islam are innately based and fixed. The social teachings complement them but are flexible and dynamic. In his book *Marriage and Divorce in All Religions*, Abdullah al-Maraghi said: 'Islamic injunctions are divided into two groups: the first group is concerned with regulating the relations between Allah and man in belief and worship. These are God-given and fixed so that they may not be extended by analogy or any other means.' None the less, they are never irrational and a purpose is almost always ascribed for them. Prayer, for example, is described as a protection against evil and corruption, ablutions are described as a purification, and so on. Abdullah al-Maraghi continued: 'The second group deals with relations between men. Here the holy texts employ welfare criteria and injunctions have an explicit functional purpose. Change here is possible when circumstances change.' One example is the Prophet's saying: 'I have previously forbidden you to store meat to make it available for the temporary visitors who come to al-Madina, now you may store it.' Islamic jurists are unanimous about the welfare orientation of these injunctions. They differ, however, in defining the criteria. Some, like Imam Ashafi, think that all possible welfare has already been considered by the received holy texts, and that therefore we are not justified in citing welfare considerations not explicitly supported by those texts. Imam Abu Hanifa went further and approved preference (*istihsan*) as a means of catering for change. Imam Malik employed utility (*istislah*) for a similar purpose. Imam ibn al–Gaiem rejected Ashafi's restrictions. He quoted Ibn Agil in support of his argument: 'Ashafi said no policy is justified unless it is based on the revealed texts. This is wrong and would put the companions of the Prophet at fault. Islam approves of all policy which creates good and eradicates evil even when it is not based on any revelation. This is how the companions of the Prophet understood Islam. Abu Bakr, for example, appointed Omar to succeed him without precedent. Omar suspended hand amputation for theft during a famine, he suspended it also when he discovered that the two thieves, the employees of Hatib, were underpaid. And so on.'

With this open–mindedness we may review some aspects of modern life.

Islam and Modern Thought

The rush to condemn modern thought as a manifestation of godlessness, which we are required to heap into a pile and burn, is ridiculous. Much of modern European thought has developed in hostility to a clerically governed church which claimed to represent God and to be infallible. At one stage it denied the value of rational knowledge. Rationalism developed as a reaction to that denial.

Humanism challenged the concept of the fall of man and original sin. Materialism challenged the denial of the importance of materialist factors in society. The church's teachings on sex under-estimated its psychological and social role – many Christian teachers have described it as a necessary evil – resulting in the reaction of psychoanalysis. The rejection of the world inherent in some teach-ings of the church has encouraged the secularist thesis which denies meaning to anything not related to this time and this world. Such views may in various degrees be paralleled in some traditional concepts of Islam which established a 'churchianity' in Islam not warranted by the authentic texts. They cannot, however, be justified in an authentic Islamic context because Islam is world-positive, it recognizes rational and empirical knowledge, it recognizes the cardinal importance of material factors in history and society, it also recognizes the great psycho-socio-physiological role of sex. Far from considering sex a necessary evil, it describes it as one of the gifts which man should welcome and enjoy. Finally Islam partially satisfies the existentialist and humanist thesis by honouring humanity and ascribing to it basic goodness.

All the factors which loom so large in modern European thought are explicitly recognized by Islam, not as singular, one-eyed principles to provide the be-all and end-all bases of the human situation, but as important pieces in a mosaic which enhances their meaningfulness, in a global harmony with spiritual, moral, and aesthetic dimensions.

Islam and the Political System

Islam does not require the establishment of a particular political system. The system of Islamic government described by al-Mawardi (420 AH) in his *Al-Ahkam al-Sultania* is a theory of his own which, moreover, remains to this day an exercise in pure speculation.

There are two types of Islamic injunction with regard to govern-ment. The first type refers to certain general principles, for example the need to organize society politically, the need to base that organization on popular participation, the imperative of justice, and so on. The second type requires Islamic legislation to be applied. Any political system which fulfils these two conditions may be described as Islamic.

The traditional Islamic state and its institutions are a historical experience which is not binding. Historically, the different schools of political thought in Islam differed and blood was shed on the issue of who was entitled to be Khalifa. Any qualified Muslim, said the Khawarij; any qualified Qurashi, said Ahl al-Sunnah; the reigning Imam among the twelve Imams, said the Shia; any qualified Fatimid, said the Zaidis. If we reflect on the matter we can easily deduce that these differences are the result of political and historical considerations which have absolutely no contemporary relevance. Contemporary Muslim political thought is duty-bound to heed the two conditions outlined above and develop a modern system of government which is authentic as well as informed by all the achievements of modern political science.

Islam and the Economy

There is no particular Islamic economic system. The attempt to deduce a system from the opinions on economic matters of the different schools of Islamic law is a dangerous waste of time. In the field of economics Islamic teachings require the fulfilment of two conditions. First, certain general principles are enjoined, for example that wealth is collectively owned by mankind as vice-regent of God, that individual ownership is legitimate through effort, that it is a duty to develop and exploit natural resources, that society should cater for the disabled and destitute, and so on. The second condition requires that certain particular injunctions should be observed, for example the institution of *zakat* and laws of inheritance and the abolition of interest, and indeed of all unearned income – gambling, monopoly profits, fraud, and so on.

There are very wide and legitimate differences about how to define and carry out these injunctions. For example, Muslims are enjoined not to hoard treasure. But what precisely does this mean? Abu Zar considered anything above one's needs a hoarded treasure. Ibn Omar considered that anything on which *zakat* had been paid was not a hoarded treasure even if literally buried underground! Some thinkers have given very radical definitions. Ibn Arabi, for example, considered any income above that warranted by the circumstance under consideration a usurious, and therefore prohibited, increment. Like the economic system and institutions of the past, the opinions of the jurists who founded the schools of Muslim law are interesting historical studies, but they are not binding. Today three things must be taken into account – the two conditions outlined earlier, the views of the different schools of Muslim law, and study of the theories and institutions of modern economics. From these elements contemporary Islamic economic thought must outline an economic system which is both Islamic and modern: a system which passes the supreme test of achieving economic development and ensuring an equitable distribution of its benefits.

The Legislative Aspect

The schools of Muslim law were, in their time, great achievements. Although their founders never wanted or expected them to be binding on others, that is exactly what happened from the fourth century AH onwards. In the face of this rigidity, statesmen and administrations restricted the province of Shariah courts – where the schools of law reigned supreme – and developed parallel court systems: *Sahib al-Mazalim* for cases of administrative law, *Wali al-Jaraim* for cases of criminal law, *Sahib al-Mal* for financial cases, and so on. Imam ibn al-Gaiem condemned the evolution of such parallel systems, which are analogous to the parallel systems of Shariah and civil courts of modern times. He was quite explicit as to who was to blame for the move to circumvent Shariah. He said: 'Those who put Shariah in a straitjacket are responsible for driving policy-makers to seek those extra-Shariah improvisations.'

The received legislative texts in the Quran and Sunnah were in many cases interpreted differently by the founders of the schools of Muslim law. They also differed in the use they made of the following methods: abrogation, gradualism, particularization, consensus, analogy, custom, adoption, utility and preference. This accounts for the variety of their opinions. Further, it was considered that some regulations could be waived or enforced in the light of the aims of Shariah, for example that hardship must be avoided, that anything which causes harm must be rejected, that the lesser of two unavoidable evils should be permitted, and so on. The founders' opinions also varied even on the most specific injunctions, for example *hudod* (canonical punishments) and *faraid* (inheritance laws). The variety of opinions in these matters hinged on the different conditions for their application.

Basing themselves on the Quran and Sunnah and employing the

methods here described, the founders evolved a number of schools, eight of which have become famous: Hanafi, Maliki, Jafari, Zaidi, Shafi, Hambali, Zahiri and Ibadi. These schools are a permanent testimony to the resources of Shariah. They are authentic interpretations of the legislative teachings of Islam. There is no basis, however, for the claim that any or all of them are entitled to a monopoly of legislative authority in Islam. The very fact that they genuinely differ among themselves indicates the possibility of further different interpretations. Moreover, it can be seen that methodological and environmental differences are reflected in the views of the founders of the schools.

A serious attempt at Islamicizing the legal systems of Muslim countries today can only be undertaken by scholars familiar with the whole heritage of the schools of Muslim law, with other contemporary legal systems, and with contemporary social needs and problems, and assisted in the endeavour by economists, sociologists, political scientists and statesmen. Such a 'workshop' should base itself on the Quran and Sunnah and proceed in the spirit of a new *ijtihad* to codify civil, criminal, personal and international law. Something of this nature is already being undertaken in several places. For example a committee in Jordan (1979) worked out a complete Islamic civil code, drawing widely on the opinions of the eight schools of Muslim law. A general and agreed new *ijtihad* is now most urgently needed because the existing dichotomy between civil and Shariah systems, and the existing divisions of schools within the Shariah system itself, are alien to the unifying aims of Islam. Without this supreme effort, the case for Islamicizing the legal system in Muslim countries will fall by default.

Islamic Revolution has amply demonstrated its ability to mobilize the masses and overthrow despotic regimes patronized by this or that foreign power. Its ability to build a new social order which is Islamic as well as modern is contingent upon the transcending of the old schools in favour of the new order. Revolution or reform which dismantles the existing order and attempts to revive the old moulds will not only fail, it will also play into the hands of those who claim that Islam is outdated.

International Relations

International relations as conceived by traditional Islamic jurists are

coloured by the jurists' respective political and historical circumstances. No wonder then that their relevance to the contemporary
world is limited. The Islamic texts are explicit about what
constitutes a just cause for war: it is injustice. 'You have been
permitted to fight to deter injustice,' (Quran). When no aggression
has been committed against Muslims, then peaceful – and indeed,
cordial – relations are to prevail between Muslims and non-
Muslims. 'God forbids you not with regard to those who fight you
not for your faith, nor drive you out of your homes, from dealing
kindly and justly with them: for God loves those who are just. God
only forbids you with regard to those who fight you for your faith,
and drive you out of your homes, and support others in driving you
out, from turning to them for friendship and protection. It is such
that turn to them in such circumstances that do wrong.' (Quran)

If that is so, what, some may ask, about *jihad* – the holy war?

In his book, *The Preachings of Islam,* Arnold has shown that it is
untrue to say that Islam spread by force. The Quranic principle in
this matter is: 'There is no compulsion in religion.'

The Prophet said: '*Jihad* is continuous until the day of judgment.'
Jihad means to struggle to vanquish the forces of evil within oneself.
It means to struggle in the cause of righteousness until the will of
Allah reigns supreme. It requires the sacrifice of blood and property
for that purpose. It means going to war when the freedom of
Muslims is denied and when they become the victims of injustice
and aggression. Some Muslims say that the purpose of *jihad* is to
force Islam upon people, and in support they invoke verse five of
Tawba, which says: 'Fight and slay the pagans whenever ye find
them.' But a study of the text before and after verse five shows
clearly that the pagans in question were a particular group which
betrayed the Prophet and initiated violence. Verse four says: 'But
the treaties are not dissolved with those pagans with whom ye
entered into alliance,' while verse six says: 'If one of the pagans asks
thee for asylum, grant it to him so that he may hear the word of
God, then escort him to where he can be secure.'

Five principles constitute the basis of international relations in
Islam:

1. A human brotherhood with an honoured status in creation.
2. Supremacy of justice: 'Be just under all circumstances.'
3. Continuous preaching of Islam; if freedom to preach is

denied, or if Muslims are attacked, then a violent response is required.

4. Contracts and trusts are to be honoured under all circumstances, whoever the other party may be: 'Three are equally binding upon you whether the other party is a believer or non-believer: contracts, trusts and family obligations.' (Hadith)

5. Reciprocity in the conduct of relations when no agreements to regulate them exist.

Basing themselves on these principles, Muslim international lawyers and statesmen may elaborate a modern system of international relations.

Islam and Aesthetic Values

Beauty, like perfection, is part of the cosmic design. The text of the Quran is full of references to beauty and harmony in creation: 'No want of proportion wilt thou see in the creation of God most gracious, so turn thy vision again; seest thou any flaw? Again turn thy vision a second time, thy vision will come back to thee awed and stunned with admiration,' (Quran). The admiration of natural beauty and harmony is strengthened in the Muslim mind by the Quran. Measured, harmonious and rhyming words make poetry. Measured, harmonious and synchronized sounds make music. This may explain why art and literature have flourished under Islam. It may also explain why Muslims have pioneered measured and written music. The classic book on music for the whole of human literature is al-Farabi's *Al-Musica al-Kabir* (The Grand Book of Music). Arabic poetry excels in richness and variety – I can think of no aspect of the human predicament which is not beautifully expressed by one or two verses of Arabic poetry. The Prophet used to listen to poetry with appreciation. His own sayings were always beautifully expressed.

The question of whether Islam encouraged or prohibited listening to music and song has been the subject of several essays. Ibn al-Gaisirani (448–508 AH) wrote a classic on the subject called *Al-Samaa* (Listening). In it he said:

Al-Ghourtubi said that songs are permissible in celebrations, for example during feasts and weddings. Also they may be sung to cheer people up during the performance of hardship tasks, for example during the excavation of the ditch around al-Madina or when Angasha sang for the camel caravan of the Prophet's family . . .

Al-Gushairi said drums were beaten rhythmically when the Prophet entered al-Madina. He sanctioned the performance . . .

Al-Ghazali said in *Al-Ihya* that on the basis of both textual authority and analogy (*quias*), listening to music and song was permissible.

And so the book continues, with its arguments and supporting quotations.

Man's aesthetic experience, like his other experiences, has been and continues to be abused. Some jurists, repelled by that abuse, ruled aesthetic activity out of court in Islam, so depicting Islamic society as joyless and austere. Reflection on the text of the Quran, which is not only the primary book of guidance and instruction but also the foremost literary treasure of a highly literary language, indicates otherwise. The biography of the Prophet is punctuated with his appreciations of aesthetic values. The joyless unsmiling image of Islamic society is a figment of the anxious imaginations of some theologians.

The traditional Muslim mind feared schism and abhorred the corrosive effects of alien thought. It loathed the corruptions which invaded the body politic and feared lest that corruption find its way into strictly religious affairs. To protect itself against these fears and anxieties, the Muslim mind developed a shell in which to enclose itself. There are at least three versions of that shell: the Sunni, represented by the regime of *taghlid*; the Shii, represented by the exclusiveness of the Shia establishment; and the Sufi, represented by the esoteric regime of the Sufi Orders.

When modern secularist thought of both left and right speaks about Islamic fundamentalism, it really refers to one or other of these shells – more frequently to the first two. Many Muslims have faced up to the secular challenge and fought back with concepts embedded in the shells, but, were it not for two reasons, secular thought would have crushed the shells to powder and achieved a walk-over victory. The reasons are: first, the secular 'isms' have proved to be vehicles of acculturation and conduits of foreign domination; and second, in the search for identity many Muslim societies have reached for anything, even the shells, to avoid liquidation.

But whatever usefulness the shells may have had in the past, they do a disservice in the contemporary world and could in the long run render Islam completely vulnerable to the designs of the alien 'isms'.

I believe that, by revolutionary or evolutionary means, the Muslim will is going to break out of those shells to restore the vitality of Islam and to re-establish the dynamic role of the Umma. Muhammad is the seal of the Prophets. His message is designed for all times and all places. This means that the seed of righteousness has been implanted in the soul, mind, heart and muscle of the Umma, and that the Umma is entrusted with the fulfilment of the Will of Allah in history. This is the fundamental calling to which, through the ages, the living Umma should respond.

I am grateful to the organizers of this volume for having made the memorial of the departure of our much lamented friend an occasion for a deeper understanding of the ideological imperatives and cultural characteristics of the civilization to which he belonged.

Arab Nationalism: Decades of Innocence and Challenge

Hazem Nuseibeh

The adult formative years of Abd al-Hamid Sharaf epitomize the milieu, the idealism, the intellectual and spiritual ferment which gripped Arab patriots in the 1950s and 1960s, animating a whole generation with buoyancy and restlessness, as well as with an urgent and challenging sense of mission. From the vantage point of today one looks back with intense nostalgia at that crucial period in the evolution of the Arab nation, striving impatiently to reconstruct, articulate and consolidate itself and to usher in a new and better world.

In a real sense, the activism, restlessness and idealism of men like Abd al-Hamid Sharaf were the marks of a pioneering second phase of nationalism, powered by events and factors which had occurred since the first inchoate stirrings of the Arab national movement in the closing decades of the nineteenth century. Successes and reverses, achievements and thwarted aspirations were the legacy of the Great Arab Rebellion of 1916, which had first crystallized the deep-rooted yearnings of the Arabic-speaking world for national identity, cultural flowering and the restoration of the Arab lands to the world map after centuries of stunted growth, de-Arabization and marginal national existence.

No one who lived through the Great Arab Rebellion or has read its literature could fail to be impressed by the genuineness, the dedication and the idealism which imbued its architects. They went to the gallows with extraordinary courage and dignity. So did the rank and file, for the idea of Arab nationalism was no longer confined to the solitary intellectual, the musing poet or the vision-ary statesman, as had been the case in the incipient stages of Arab awakening. It had become a popular cause, a living force in the consciousness of the masses. Martyrs in abundance were offered at its altar and many fought for its triumph. No longer did Arab nationalism have to fall back upon the memories of ages past for vindication. The living history of the Arab rebellion was itself sufficient title deed to nationhood.

In the multi-racial composite of the Ottoman Empire, the Arabic-speaking peoples took it pretty well for granted that their common denominator was Arab nationalism. The factors making for affinity and oneness far outweighed local and regional differences in the assertion of the Arab national identity. This Arab identification became all the more pronounced when the other major ethnic group in the Ottoman Empire, namely the Turks, intensified their Pan-Tauranian Turkish nationalism, thus making a fundamental break with almost fourteen centuries of Islamic universalism and racial equality as the foundations of polity providing the sense of belonging. When in March 1924 the secularist Turks abolished the Ottoman Caliphate in the aftermath of the empire's defeat during World War I, they merely acknowledged formally what the Arab Rebellion had established in fact, namely that Arab nationality was the foundation of the Arabs' political life.

This did not mean that the Arabic-speaking peoples utterly rejected the larger communities in which they had lived in dignity and union for almost fourteen centuries – the Ummayad Empire in Damascus, the Abasid Empire in Baghdad, the Fatimid Empire in Egypt and lastly the Ottoman Empire in Istanbul, which had asserted that its claim to the caliphate was legitimate because of the abdication of the Abasid Caliph, Al-Mutawakel, in Cairo in 1517. Arab nationalists, however, would maintain that, if the abdication occurred at all, it occurred after Selim's occupation of Egypt and therefore under duress.

The Arabs have invariably held to the belief that they are the 'substance of Islam'. This, they maintain, is proved both by the lessons of history – the part played by the Arabs in the rise of Islam and its monumental civilization – and by the intimate connection between the Arab genius and the spirit of Islam. This may sound boastful, indeed xenophobic, but it connotes no intention of exclusivity. Rather, cultural Arabization is seen as only to be expected, since the Holy Quran was conveyed to the Prophet Muhammad in Arabic and Arabic was the language of the Islamic civilization which ensued. The great amalgam of many races within the 'domain of Islam' quickly rendered irrelevant any early racial overtones, in addition to which Islam as a doctrine has always vehemently opposed distinctions on the basis of race, colour or descent. The criterion is virtue and the message is universal. 'But it [the Quran] is naught else but a reminder unto all mankind.'

The fundamental break with this ages–old universalism was not made simply out of spite or as an act of despairing disenchantment. In fact the break with the Ottomans had as its principal objective the re-creation of another, smaller community which as a first step would comprise all the Arab domains in the East and eventually the whole of the Arab world from Morocco on the Atlantic to the Arab Gulf. Arab unity was taken for granted. It was an act of faith. Its achievement, however, seemed to young Arab nationalists neither insurmountably difficult nor unfeasible inasmuch as it had long been a fact of life within the Ottoman Empire, whose centralized political organization embraced almost all the Arab countries in Asia as well as those in the Arab Maghreb with the sole exception of Morocco. People moved from one province to another of that huge expanse of territory without let or hindrance, much as citizens do today in the sprawling United States of America. They were citizens in the full sense, enjoying unfettered mobility. The tremendous cohesive impact of a uniform system of government, even if sometimes unpalatable, is difficult to overestimate, as is recognized by students of international organization who see in the 'functional approach' the surest means for the attainment of a wider 'community consensus and integration'. However paradoxical it sounds, it is none the less true that the Arabs enjoyed a greater measure of unity under the non-Arab but united Ottoman Empire than they do today with their independent but separate existence in over twenty sovereign states, often at loggerheads with each other and cherishing a multitude of parochial or misguidedly perceived interests and local loyalties and prejudices which, according to what a sociologist has called the 'iron law of oligarchy', tend to be self-perpetuating.

The Arab League, created in 1944, was a poor substitute for genuine Arab integration and consensus, in that it simply ratified the vivisection inflicted upon the Arab world by its former Western allies. Even geographic Syria was cut up into four separate entities under the secret Anglo-French Sykes-Picot agreement, in a reckless division of the spoils.

It should be emphasized that the Arab national movement was to begin with confined to the Arab lands east of Suez. There is no *a priori* or ideological rationale to explain why the east and west wings of the Arab world, which belong to one common background and heritage, should have branched out on separate courses of national orientation. The explanation lies in the special conditions which accompanied the resurgence of each. In the Arab East, the 'in group' and the 'out group' were defined by the breakdown of an existing community consensus. In the western wing of the Arab world, however, the situation was very different. Egypt had been made a British protectorate in 1882; Libya was invaded and colonized by Italy; much earlier Algeria had been colonized by France; Tunisia and Morocco were turned into French protectorates. In all these countries the incitement came first from without, not from within, and it was in response to foreign imperialism that pan-Islamic solidarity developed, in combination in some instances with local liberation movements.

That after liberation the two wings of the Arab world coalesced under the aegis of the Arab League and in numerous bilateral relationships proves beyond doubt that the Arabic-speaking peoples of the East and the West belong to one Arab nation united and indivisible.

Before examining the Arab national movement in the 1950s and 1960s, it might be useful to take a glimpse at what nationalists felt and did a decade earlier, in the 1940s. I shall confine my observations to activities within the American University of Beirut, where thousands of students from virtually all Arab countries came together. Extensive political movements were at work throughout the Arab world, but the activities of the Arab national movement at the AUB were an authentic microcosm of thoughts and deeds elsewhere. During the 1940s, when I was an active adherent of the movement (within the constraints imposed by the world war), we had three major objectives, which often incited us to perilous demonstrations.

First was our determination to win independence from foreign tutelage, whether in the form of mandates, protectorates or out-right colonization. Most Arab countries during that decade were under one form of foreign dominance or another. It was, therefore, only natural that independence was the priority goal.

Secondly, we were determined to work for Arab unity, which had been thwarted by the European powers in the aftermath of World War I when they failed to honour solemn pledges to their erstwhile Arab allies struggling for independence in unity. As a result of this setback, pessimism was the prevailing characteristic of the movement, except among the idealistic young who, in their buoyant, almost naive, optimism, genuinely believed that with sufficient dedication and selflessness they could remove all impediments and restructure their Arab nation in the image of the cherished utopia.

Thirdly, having been exposed to Western culture and ideas and conscious of the relative backwardness of their own societies, Arab nationalists nursed grandiose plans for reform covering every aspect of national life. Arab nationalists conceived of reform and progress in general terms; they did not work out specific formulations or lay down precise frameworks; their ideology was devoid of 'isms' and of detailed socio–economic prototypes. They believed in a blending of what was best in the newly-discovered Arab heritage and in contemporary Western civilization and culture, and they foresaw no serious problem which might impair the process of amalgamation. By and large they accepted Western liberal democracy as the best system of government, one fully compatible with the golden era of the Arabs' past. Not surprisingly, therefore, as one Arab country after another achieved its independence in the late 1940s and early 1950s, they established political and economic systems on the pattern of Western liberal democracy.

And then came the catastrophe.

Arab nationalists of Abd al-Hamid Sharaf's generation were more than shaped by the Arab–Israeli war of 1948 – they were jolted to the roots by the trauma of Arab defeat and the forcible implanting of a Zionist Israel in four-fifths of Palestine. This presented them with a challenge exceeding by far the challenges which their forerunners had faced. It also banished for good naivety and optimism. It was a stunning eye-opener to the realities of the world as it is, so different from what they had conceived it to be. But they could no longer blame external forces as the sole villain. They had to, and did, look inwards for the answer.

Abd al-Hamid Sharaf was for many years one of my most intimate and constant friends, and told me of those days of intense dialogue on AUB's uniquely beautiful campus. I can well imagine him and his nationalist friends agonizing over a wide spectrum of problems and probing into ways and means of finding appropriate and effective responses. Their discussions must have been all-encompassing as well as passionate, and their priorities must have undergone profound reappraisal.

A first dismaying discovery for Arab nationalists of the 1950s was that the achievement of independence, excellent as that was, was merely a *means* and not an *end*; that their implacable adversary was not simply an outside colonial power whose removal would usher in the millennium. Of equal, if not of greater, importance were the intrinsic weaknesses and flaws of Arab societies which had been so shockingly and starkly revealed by the Palestinian catastrophe.

In taking stock of the situation, the initial and too superficial response was to blame adversity on leaders, regimes and institutions. Even 'devil' theories and 'foul play' were much in vogue. It had not yet dawned on the young nationalists that leaderships, of whatever persuasion, were in the final analysis merely a reflection of the societies to which the duty of governance had been entrusted. For every people can only have the quality of government which it deserves.

The leaderships which paid the price for the Arab people's catastrophic débâcle had a great deal to be blamed for, but they had also won impressive credentials in both peace and war. They had thrown off the Ottoman yoke; they had wrested sovereign independence from previously entrenched colonial powers, and, last but not least, they had built literally from scratch the mechanisms and institutions of modern government. Responsibility for their poor performance during those early years of independence must be shared in equal measure by society at large, which showed itself totally unprepared to confront the colossal challenges of the modern age. After centuries of debilitating dependence, the Arabs found themselves standing on their own feet, no longer junior partners or satellites of the larger communities of ages past. What the Arab peoples needed most to prepare them for their contemporary renaissance was freedom. What they experienced was despotic government which stifled and eventually destroyed Arab civilization and culture. The atrophy and the immobility were equally lethal to the social organism.

Naturally enough, this analysis turned Arab nationalists against the existing regimes, which for their part eyed the nationalists with suspicion, accusing them of reckless adventurism. The mutual suspicion developed into outright hostility, with the result that the flowering of democratic institutions – which, ironically, had been a platform common to both sides – was further circumscribed. When, in the early part of the twentieth century, the older generation rebelled against despotic Ottoman rule, one of the nationalists' foremost objectives had been the reinstatement of liberal constitutional government. Later generations of Arab nationalists fought with equal determination against oppressive and undemocratic foreign colonial rule. And yet, when both external adversaries had been successfully removed from the scene, the Arab nationalists of differing generations found themselves deadlocked in a struggle for power, which unwittingly but inevitably undermined their shared goal.

For the younger generation, infatuated both with their idealized vision of the Arabs' golden eras and with the advanced Western societies whose thinking, accomplishments and overall superiority they were absorbing, the invidious comparison with contemporary Arab weakness and failures became an untenable burden. Their priority shifted dramatically from Arab independence in unity to the more arduous task of nation-building – and in as short a time as possible. There was an acute awareness of the urgency of the task, with a concomitant shift to revolution from the hitherto orderly and peaceful evolution. Arab leaders as well as lethargic Arab societies had to be rebuilt from their foundations to make possible far-reaching change at an accelerated pace. This urgency explains the dizzying phenomenon of military *coups d'état*, the underground

204

revolutionary movements and the outright hostility to existing regimes throughout the length and breadth of the Arab homeland. By and large, the transformation was not desired nor prompted by power-hungry individuals and movements. Indeed, to many nationalists, the painful transformation ran counter to their basic preference for orderly peaceful change within a humanistic democratic society. But it seemed to them inevitable – there was no other way.

In fairness to the rising generation of Arab nationalists of the time, it should be said that, even if they were the intellectual apologists preaching salvation and fulfilment in revolutionary action, the revolutionary as distinct from the evolutionary process was put into practice by military men who exploited the deep disenchantment of the masses traumatized as never before by humiliation and defeat in 1948.

For the most part the revolutionary officers claimed to be saviours, although they had neither the vision nor the intellectual capacity to satisfy the yearnings of the masses for progress, unity and strength. Their monopoly of force could sustain them in power but could not achieve much else. Invariably they sought to attain legitimacy by enlisting the moral and sometimes the material support of the intellectual avant-garde represented by the Arab nationalists, the Ba'th Party, and other like-minded movements. But the participation of these movements in the real decision-making process was more token than real. These military-led revolutions seriously derailed the process of orderly nation-building within a framework of democracy and freedom – the essential building-blocks in any society.

A watershed in the 1950s was, of course, the emergence of Nasserism following the 1952 overthrow of the Egyptian regime. This momentous event is not to be compared with the *coups d'état* which repeatedly plagued Syria and posed a threat to other countries. President Nasser did not simply change a government; he set in motion a movement which left an indelible impact upon nationalists throughout the Arab world. Not only did he restore Arab national identity to Egypt itself, hitherto torn between self-contained Egyptian nationalism on the one hand and, on the other, the pull of a much wider Islamic community. But he also pitted secular Arab nationalism against a formidable Muslim Brotherhood, and prevailed.

Furthermore, President Nasser's brand of Arab nationalism was not confined to asserting Arab national identity and unity but was dedicated to far-reaching social and economic changes. Thus he gave an ideological thrust to a movement hitherto devoid of any specific social content. But, in its early stages, Nasserism was undoubtedly non-ideological and ambivalent. Its principal objectives were:

1. the removal of backwardness, corruption and appalling social disequilibrium;

2. total removal of the lingering vestiges of foreign rule, both tangible and intangible;

3. a process of nation-building on as yet undefined and uncharted patterns, systems and mechanisms, but with modernization as the ultimate goal.

It should be emphasized that, in the Arab East, the nationalists were divided over whether or not Arab nationalism should have a philosophy to sustain it. Some thinkers believed that the formulation of a systematic, forceful and clear-cut national philosophy was a prerequisite of genuine Arab revival. Others believed that a philosophy was required merely to preserve the cause from being torn asunder by alien ideologies or falling victim to inner petrification. They asserted that, to be more enduring, it should be anchored in the heart and not in the head. They argued that it should be sufficiently flexible to accommodate ever-widening intellectual horizons and to avoid a hardening of its emotional base around certain assumed truths. These were pragmatic empiricists, simply advocating Arab nationality as the foundation of the state, in contradistinction to the ideologues, the mystical and the moral visionaries of Arab nationalism.

The issue remained unresolved by the rising generation of Arab nationalists, who instead agreed on the need to resuscitate the best in the Arab-Islamic heritage and to blend it with the best in modern Western thought and institutions. Such a process, they believed, would inevitably lead to a new and higher synthesis.

With the advent of Nasserism, different ideological systems which had been kept in abeyance or had not existed before began to surface, and naturally enough fell out with one another. The Arab nationalist comrades of Abd al-Hamid Sharaf could no longer maintain a neutral stance. Most came from conservative or middle-class backgrounds and did not, therefore, regard a socialist, centrally controlled economy as the best, still less as the only, avenue to modernization and progress, as was asserted by the Nasserite movement. They certainly lauded Nasser's identification with Arab nationalism, seeing it as a vindication of their deeply cherished belief in the unalterable unity and common destiny of the Arab nation. They were elated by his fiercely independent steward-ship of Arab policy unfettered by external powers be they of West or of East. They were willing to see his socio-economic formu-lations fastened on to their own undefined programmes for unity and progress, but they did not elevate his socio-economic ideology to the status of a doctrine or an absolute truth.

The discussions of Abd al-Hamid Sharaf and other Arab national-ists at the microcosm of the AUB must have mirrored the same divisive forces which then prevailed throughout the Arab world. All were agreed on the imperative necessity of shaking Arab society from its torpor and on promoting far-reaching structural progress, social justice and modernization in order to catch up with the advanced world. But in their view there was more than one avenue to this goal. It was at this juncture, I surmise, that the young Arab nationalists experienced a serious disagreement, even a split. Such is the price which must be paid by a movement still in its embryonic stage, as it seeks to build a nation on new principles of allegiance.

When community consensus was based on the principle of an Islamic polity, there was always a monumental and ages-old edifice united in diversity to fall back upon. Why did the Arab revival not anchor itself to that great legacy, with its strength and proven durability? The truth is that the interpreters of that legacy, traditionalist and rigid, had become almost incapable of changing their methods or outlook. Yet mechanisms of change existed and were sanctified in Islamic doctrine, such as constant reinterpre-tation, laid down and mandated through the vehicles of social change such as analogy, or the consensus of the community, a concept akin to that of the 'general will', as well as other mechan-isms of adaptation. But these possibilities were neglected and interpretation became inflexible. As things were, Arab nationalists had to look elsewhere for solutions to pressing and changing problems, and turned to the legacies and accumulated experiences of other modern societies.

Today atrophy poses a tremendous obstacle to the various movements of so-called pan-Islamic fundamentalism, whose proponents, in their own rigidity and lack of understanding of the real and innermost spirit of Islam, find themselves hard put to answer adequately the problems of the modern age. Strong as their emotional appeal may be – as evidenced by their resurgence today – they are still their own worst enemies. Islam is, after all, a dynamic religion imposing hardly any constraints on mankind's restless search for the best and highest. This Islam demonstrated in its first surge fourteen centuries ago across half of the then known world.

I must at this point explain that the Arab nationalist movement has never been inspired by the jingoism, the kind of self-centred egoism, or the excesses which have afflicted nationalisms in several other parts of the world. Its driving force was from the start a force for integration and wider community consensus co-terminous with the limits of the Arabic-speaking world, in a spirit of solidarity with the far wider Islamic world, and in friendly cooperation and amity with the rest of humankind.

I have attempted to give a mental portrait of an Arab nationalist in the 1950s and 1960s, outlining the intellectual influences which shaped his mind and suggesting his response to them.

In the early 1960s, Abd al-Hamid Sharaf's intellectual and ideological development stood him in good stead as he embarked upon a brilliant public career, with all the dedication, the sense of purpose, and the intellectual integrity of which a resurgent nation is so much in need – and which, alas, seem to be faltering in a world beset by self-seeking materialism, selfishness and outright indifference to the common good.

Abd al-Hamid started his career at the Ministry of Foreign Affairs. He was unassuming, forthright, disciplined, and determined to put all his energies and skills at the service of Jordan within the overall matrix of Arab union. He was totally self-reliant, never taking advantage of belonging to one of the prestigious branches of the Hashemite ruling family. His independence of mind and expression, his devotion to duty, and his articulate and realistic perception of the world around him enabled him to rise rapidly in the political hierarchy until, at the age of only forty, he attained the highest position – the premiership of Jordan. In the different cabinet posts entrusted to him earlier, he was invariably imaginative, innovative and reformist, qualities which shine all the more brightly in the inertia and conformism too often to be found. His diplomatic career at the United Nations and in other international forums was exemplary, and he is still remembered with profound respect by the many diplomats and statesmen who came to know him and to appreciate his friendliness, his articulacy and his incisive mind.

He was deeply attached to his family, his wife Leila and his two sons, Nasser and Faris. Notwithstanding the heavy pressures of work, he always radiated a genuine, tender love and caring. It was stimulating to listen to and share in the intellectual encounters between him and his wife, an intellectual herself. But for all their heady excitements, these meetings had none of the stringency or strain which sometimes overshadow the satisfaction, open-mindedness and sense of proportion that make life livable, enjoyable and down to earth.

What a tragedy that the life of a man of such talent and promise should have been cut short so abruptly and at so early an age, before he had the chance to come to full flowering and fulfilment in the cause in which he so ardently believed!

He was an Arab humanist and nationalist who kept his vow and never allowed expediency to compromise his vision and belief. His like-minded Arab compatriots and countrymen are justifiably proud that he vindicated the best of their hopes and expectations in a period of trial. This must be a profound source of consolation as well as of inspiration.

Arab Society and the West

Malcolm H. Kerr

The era of Arab–Western relations that began with the British occupation of Egypt in 1882 and ended with the death of Gamal Abdul Nasser in 1970 was fraught with continuous political conflict with the Western world and a great deal of anger and disappointment. It began with an act of Western domination, and ended at a moment of Arab humiliation. Yet it was also a time of remarkably vibrant faith among Arabs in the general desirability of Western culture and the value of maintaining an intensive political dialogue with Westerners; and so, for liberal intellectuals of both societies, it stands in retrospect as something of a golden age at least in comparison with all that has followed.

The encounters of East and West are of a different order now, and the perspectives of Arab society have shifted. Contacts between Arabs and Westerners now commonly take place on the mass level, and the business at hand has less to do with cultural or political exchange, and more with buying and selling. Many Arab intellectuals disillusioned by events in Palestine, Lebanon, and elsewhere, seem to have lost their belief in the usefulness of political debate and to have sunk into a resigned cynicism. Still others, convinced that Western civilization has little to offer them except the destruction of their cultural identity, have turned to religious fervour and to an attitude of rejection towards both the West and their own secularly-minded fellow citizens.

Many persons like Ābd al-Hamid Sharaf and myself who have experienced something of the old era of Arab–Western cultural encounters in the privileged atmosphere of the American University of Beirut in the 1950s could not fail to regret the change. 'Arab–Western relations' was *our* subject. It consisted, if not exactly of our own private relationship, then of our awareness of the thoughts and deeds of a stable of familiar figures on whom our minds could take a firm grip, heroes of the past hundred years who had personified movements of nationalism, literary revival and religious reformation such as Tahtawi (1801-73) who helped introduce European ideas into Egypt, the Islamic reformers Afghani and Muhammad Abduh, Faisal I of Iraq and Nasser. We also had our villains, Cromer, Balfour, Eden, and Ben-Gurion. We had our revered texts, such as George Antonius's *The Arab Awakening,* and our revered professors, such as Constantine Zurayk and Nabih Amin Faris. Still other scholars stood on slightly more distant pedestals: Arnold Toynbee, H.A.R. Gibb and Albert Hourani.

The issues were few and the lessons to be learned relatively simple, which is not by any means to say that they were invalid. At the heart of it all was the implicit belief that the problems of the Arab–Western relationship were matters of personal conscience to be settled by a handful of key personalities: the usurpation of Palestine by the Zionists, the insistence of British and American leaders on unequal treaties with Arab regimes, the quest by Muslim intellectuals for a synthesis of the Islamic heritage with Western science and humanistic liberalism. Left to ourselves, Abd al-Hamid and I could have quickly solved all the problems; without our help, the statesmen and thinkers might take a little longer, but we always hoped that they would soon acquire the goodwill and understanding that would assure them success.

Of course we were naive, if only in underestimating the capacity of statesmen for folly and of thinkers for obfuscation. But what was more important was that even as we debated, the stage was expanding and our small cast of heroes and villains was being crowded out by a new mass of faceless participants, too numerous and too amorphous to be either controlled or held accountable. Mass politics and mass consumer culture had arrived. It was no longer a question of Western and Arab leaders settling on the right solutions to the old problems, for the solutions no longer lay in their hands, if indeed they really ever had; and the old problems had evolved into newer, more complex ones to the point of being beyond any designated solutions. But attitudes lingered on, as they so often will, long after the realities had changed.

The spirit of the AUB was, and is still today, one of celebration of the essential harmony of Western and Arab-Islamic culture. In an earlier era, when the school was still titled the Syrian Protestant College, the values propagated to students had been explicitly those of Christian evangelism, but in the twentieth century they had become distinctly ecumenical. This theme was evoked in countless rituals and gestures. In the College Chapel services, Muslim and Christian students could sing together such conveniently vaguely worded hymns as 'Faith of Our Fathers' or 'O God Our Help in Ages Past'. In the Cultural Studies course, an intensive two-year programme in the history of civilization, students found no difficulty in listening to an American instructor deliver a lecture on the life of the Prophet Muhammad; a Muslim lecturer on Christianity, if only he were available, would have been equally welcome. In the Departments of History and Arabic Literature, it was taken for granted that Arab Christian professors' work should be devoted to honouring the achievements of classical Islamic civilization.

Despite its American origins and sponsorship, the AUB has been prized in the region as a resource of Arab society, offering an internationally valued product – an American-style education, with a humanistically oriented curriculum emphasizing creativity, individuality, and ethical responsibility – in an Arab environment. It was, as one author of a book about the AUB called it, a mutual concern.[1] Some of the pioneering national universities, such as those of Cairo and Alexandria, were launched at later dates with similar values; certainly Ahmad Lutfi al-Sayyid and Taha Husayn, who were so instrumental in the early evolution of these institutions, saw them as bearers of the message of the underlying unity of Western and Arab-Islamic culture, a theme explicitly laid out by Taha Husayn in a well-known work.[2] Indeed the entire Egyptian *Nahda*, or cultural revival of the late nineteenth and early twentieth centuries, that culminated in the establishment of the first state universities, devoted as much of it was to elaborating the theme of the authenticity of Egypt's own Islamic and Arab cultural heritage, offered at least an indirect endorsement to the idea of East-West cultural unity: the classical Islamic culture was scientific and humanistic, and transmitted these values to medieval Europe whence they were handed down to the modern Western world.

In short, several generations of Western-educated Arabs were raised on the explicit idea of cultural ecumenicalism, and this has had profound social and political consequences. It has meant that whatever the level of political conflict with the West, and however bitter the disappointment in Western policies, the educated Arab elite have been almost unanimous in separating culture from politics, and in upholding their strong ties with their counterparts in Europe and North America. Even those who have come to consider Western governments irredeemably hostile in the interests they represented, have continued none the less to believe in the value of private relationships with the sub-society of liberal Western intellectuals. In fact, however, the idea of cultural ecumenicalism has also pervaded the nationalist political attitudes of educated Arabs as well, in the sense that they have perceived a universal harmony of material interests alongside the harmony of social values. Encouraged no doubt by liberal intellectuals in the West, they have tended to believe the best, rather than the worst, about the real political interests of Western societies that the governments ought to represent. After all, was not nationalism initially a European idea? Surely what was good for the Arabs – namely independence, dignity, and progress – was no real threat to the West. If the history of political relations had been largely an unhappy story of conflict and frustration, the hope always remained that friendly persuasion would ultimately prevail, once the right cast of characters arrived in office in each country. In fact, this attitude seems even to have survived, rather incongruously, in the minds of a good many Arab radical intellectuals and politicians who profess to consider it naive to hope for a change in American Middle East policy, yet who continue to seek out dialogue with visiting American scholars and politicians.

The humanistic scholars of the AUB tradition lived in the mainstream of liberal or orientalist scholarship, an ethos that has latterly come under attack by some critics as implicitly patronizing and ethnocentric but which, in its more positive guises relevant to the present discussion, was moved by a spirit of intercultural brotherhood. If there was one theme of intellectual inquiry that consistently concerned the members of this school, it was the impingement of Western civilization on that of Islam in modern times, and the patterns according to which the societies of the Near East had responded to this impingement. They recognized that this continuing historical experience of interaction with the West had been crucial to the shaping of the present-day character of the region, and that the effects had been felt on many different levels: philosophical, political, economic, psychological, aesthetic, and moral. People disagreed sharply on certain of the lessons to be drawn from this experience, but agreed on the premise: that the encounter of West and East had only casually affected the outlook and processes of Western society, while by contrast the impact on the peoples of the Near East had been traumatic, and had severely tested the mechanisms of adaptation and survival in their society.

One unresolved issue arising from these discussions was whether the overall effects of Western impingement and Near Eastern trauma had been primarily liberating or oppressive in the long run. The issue was set forth in a vivid passage by Toynbee, a scholar whose moral and intellectual vision of the modern world was much appreciated at the AUB and who had once served as a visiting professor there:

> Savages are distressed at the waning of the moon and attempt to counteract it by magical remedies. They do not realize that the shadow which creeps forward till it blots out all but a fragment of the shining disc, is cast by their world. In much the same way we civilized people of the West glance with pity or contempt at our non-Western contemporaries lying under the shadow of some stronger power, which seems to paralyse their energies by depriving them of light. Generally we are too deeply engrossed in our own business to look closer, and we pass by on the other side – conjecturing (if our curiosity is sufficiently aroused to demand an explanation) that the shadow which oppresses these sickly forms is the ghost of their own past. Yet if we paused to examine that dim gigantic overshadowing figure standing, apparently unconscious, with its back to its victims, we should be startled to find that its features are ours . . . The shadow upon the rest of humanity is cast by Western civilization . . .[3]

The interesting questions here are the nature and source of the light and the character of its recipients in Toynbee's imagery. Is the light something independent, external to both West and East, some inexorable dispensation of grace that falls upon men everywhere, however passive or incompetent or undeserving they may be, so long as they do not stand in each other's way? In other words, are political self-determination, social autonomy, and economic self-sufficiency not only necessary but sufficient conditions for the flowering of a civilization? More specifically, in the Near East in modern times has the progress of Arab-Islamic civilization been blocked by the Western impingement?

Nowadays an affirmative answer would be rather commonplace, but not quite so a generation ago. The liberal orientalists' conventional wisdom assumed that the dynamic and progressive civilization of the West had come into contact with an ossified Islamic society whose days of vitality had long since passed. Having discovered the Western world, however disagreeable the circumstances, the Muslims were thought to have little choice but to learn from the West, to imitate, to borrow, to search out the secret of its progress, in order somehow to catch up. One way or another some key elements of this thesis were almost universal among orientalists and widely accepted by Arab scholars too: for instance, the assumption that the example of Western material progress had spurred other peoples to search for the means of such progress for themselves.

Much of the orientalists' attention was traditionally devoted to the question of the response of Eastern peoples, not to the darkness that the Western shadow had cast over them, but to the flood of light that it was thought to have beamed. The stock expression was 'the challenge of the West', a phrase that implied a threat but more especially an opportunity – to grow, to transform or rediscover oneself, if not in the image of the West then at least thanks to the force of its example. But how healthy could the growth process be in such an artificial environment? Perhaps this process of self-rediscovery, under the continuing pressure of an external stimulus, was not only painful but altogether impossible and even absurd. How could people rediscover themselves in someone else's image? How could they create anything authentic within their own society, in emulation of someone else's example?

Scholars at the AUB did not fail to raise such critical questions.[4] Although they and many other Arab scholars of the mid-twentieth century had been influenced by the orientalists and had, in many cases, sat at their feet as graduate students, they were far from falling in with the smug assumption set forth above, that the light of modern civilization, and the only light that shone, was all generated in the West – or anywhere else. For even if the assumption was not necessarily belied by the Arabic classics to which they were devoted, which were after all antique, it was certainly belied by the reality of the *Nahda*, a movement to which both Egyptians and Lebanese had contributed greatly and in which even the Syrian Protestant College had played a small but proud part. From their point of view, Toynbee's image was on the mark; a universal light from an external source, beaming on mankind generally, but differentially received according to the relatively advantageous positions of nations. The world's cultures ultimately owed their existence to a common source of divine inspiration, but they must each be developed locally. If there was such a thing as the unity of world culture, it had meaning only through the interaction of multiple national cultures.

It must not be confused with the dominance of Western culture. Such was the outlook prevailing at the AUB: a compound of liberalism, mysticism, and lingering missionary spirit. But Toynbee, in the passage quoted above, was speaking not only of culture but also of politics. The passage continues:

The conjunction of great effect on other peoples' lives with little interest in or intention with regard to them, though it is common enough in human life, is also one of the principal causes of human misfortunes; and the relationship described in my allegory cannot permanently continue. Either the overshadowing figure must turn its head, perceive the harm that unintentionally it has been doing, and move out of the light; or its victims, after vain attempts to arouse its attention and request it to change its posture, must stagger to their feet and stab it in the back.

Prophetic words! Here in a nutshell we have much of the political ethos of Arab nationalism of the entire modern era, in what a secularly and intensely politicized Arab elite perceived as repeated efforts to arouse the attention of the West to the intolerable injuries 'unintentionally' inflicted in a score of colonial and post-colonial settings, and to request it to desist. For it was all a mistake, to be put right by better information, attentiveness, and goodwill. According to this elite view, the things the Arabs wanted were limited, simple, and reasonable, but they were perhaps obscured from the perception of the West's leaders because the latter were accustomed to coordinating a wide variety of concerns around the globe, and tended too easily to suppose that the Arabs should fit themselves into them.

While Arab nationalists projected their lines of communication and optimistic expectations (however misplaced) between the states-men and intellectuals of East and West, they created other links within Arab society, between the secularly educated class and the traditional mass of the population. Building on a foundation of ideas already promulgated by the Islamic Salafiya reformist move-ment of the nineteenth and early twentieth centuries, the Arab nationalists did much to convince members of all classes of Arab society that their backgrounds, needs, and destinies were held in common. In particular they strove to persuade the common man that he could identify with his privileged, westernized fellow citizen even if he did not understand his lifestyle, and could trust him to represent his interests in national and international politics.

This accomplishment was no simple matter. As in many other formerly colonized societies, the intellectual elite and the common people have each had distinct and sometimes even contradictory reasons for their opposition to foreign domination. For many nationalist intellectuals a critical attitude to traditional culture came naturally, for it was seen as the reflection of a 'rotten present' that had paved the way for foreign domination and cried out for reform. Yet if he was to have any message with which to gather mass support, he must find something central in his culture to defend, and not just some distant mythological past. The masses, for their part, were ready to react against colonialism precisely because the traditional culture which shapes their daily lives had been disrupted by the intrusion of foreigners and foreign ways, a reaction recently illustrated in the Iranian revolution. They would hardly be available to nationalist leaders if all the latter could tell them was that their folkways were outmoded.

This is the kind of contradiction that the Arab nationalist move-ment was so remarkably successful in overcoming during much of the twentieth century. On the populist level, which was the crucial political testing ground, the nationalists were able to produce an effective message of compromise between the worlds of traditional

Islamic culture and secular modernity. It was especially with reference to religion that this compromise was so conspicuous and so lasting as an operative system of political beliefs.

The compromise was not without its limitations. Some political groupings such as the Muslim Brethren in Nasser's Egypt were repressed and contained rather than accommodated. The intellectual compromises between secularism and Islamic tenets were more satisfying emotionally than philosophically. In retrospect, perhaps we should speak of a coexistence rather than a compromise that had been achieved between the two cultures. But for a long time many people believed that a genuine harmony had been worked out.

Mostly secular in their own orientation, Arab nationalist intellectuals often made efforts to find points of support in the Islamic religious tradition for the proposition that the nationalist gospel was friendly to the values of common people. Even Christians could view the Prophet Muhammad as the historic father of Arabism, and Islamic history as the core of Arab history.[5] Likewise, the most ardent nationalist social reformers made a practice of assuring the public that their actions and programmes – land reform, nationalization, promotion of social services – were endorsed by the principles of the Quran or the exemplary behaviour of the Prophet and his Companions.

On the other side of the picture we find representatives of Islamic progressivism over the past century seeking to persuade the faithful to believe that the true Islamic message, correctly understood, was supportive of science and learning, of constitutions and parliaments, of socialism and national liberation. These symbols went in and out of fashion, of course: here it might be a multi-party system, there a one-party dictatorship; here the cause of evolutionary moderation, there of revolutionary militancy. But that did not matter, for the important thing was not what one might logically conclude if he weighed all the detailed scriptural evidence, but rather the message that Islamic piety was a practical, flexible, adaptable outlook, dedicated to the cohesion and welfare of the community of believers.

And on the part of secular nationalism, the important thing was that the advocates were mindful of the need to carry the community with them. Thus both sides were ready to meet in the middle.[6]

In this manner Arab nationalism sought to span the chasm that might otherwise have divided the adherents of religious tradition

and those of secularism. Nationalism nationalized religious sentiments and symbols, and reconditioned them in the service of what
was at least nominally a secular ideal. It had come to serve as a new
civic religion, without actually displacing or even challenging the
old one. For Islam, like Christianity, is a universalist faith, and its
creed offers itself as a complete and eternal guide to life. One cannot
be both a Christian and a Muslim. Nor can he be both a Communist
and a Muslim (or Christian), not so much because of specific
doctrinal incompatibilities but because neither Christianity nor
Islam nor Communism can admit for itself a secondary status in the
hierarchy of systems of social principles. But with nationalism there
was no such contradiction: Arab nationalism and Islam seemed to
achieve a comfortable symbiosis of mutual appropriation and
support, in which neither really challenged the claims of the other,
even if logically one might expect them to do so, and even if
individuals might privately adopt any uncompromising position
they wished.

Admittedly, whether this practical compromise between secu-
larity and religion was an accomplishment or a shortcoming on the
part of the Arab nationalist movement was a matter for debate.
Some said that it prevented progress, that an organized, energetic,
uncompromising attack on established religion and its superstitions
and social stultifications would have liberated the mentality of the
society and prepared it for various large challenges, such as eradicat-
ing disease and illiteracy, or building canals and factories. Some
believed that this lay behind the success of the Chinese and Soviet
regimes in mobilizing their populations: the forcible replacement of
one universalistic social ethic, weighted down with tradition, with
another of their own.[7]

This was not a surprising viewpoint. It was indeed hard to build a
coherent and dynamic programme of social action around the mere
idea of nationalism, which was not only tradition-bound but was,
after all, only an answer to the question of social identity rather than
the question of what must be done. There were at least vague
implications that something needed doing, that society required
reform; but there was no programme inherent in nationalism. All
this was true, and no doubt it cost Arab society something.

But if this reasoning was plausible, it fell short of being convincing. For it was the nationalist message, and its link with religious
culture, that held Arab society together fairly successfully during a

disruptive period of history. It channelled hostilities outside, against an external foe, rather than letting them develop within. In this connection it is not surprising that comparing Egypt and Lebanon in recent times, we find that it is Egypt, with its terrible problems of poverty and overpopulation, that has held together as a passably harmonious society; while prosperous Lebanon, idealized by all the world, educated, sophisticated, happy and secure in its beautiful mountain villages, has undergone a tragic orgy of destruction.

No doubt there are many possible explanations; but one central consideration is that it was in Egypt that a coherent sense of belonging to a unified society, Egyptian and Arab and mostly Muslim, took root a long time ago, while in Lebanon the question of identity was too delicate to be seriously discussed between the various communities.

To sum up our argument this far, Arab nationalism has rendered important services to society. The nationalist ethos has made it easier for the educated classes to relate effectively both to the West, despite the long history of political conflict, and to the common people of their own society, despite the gulf of cultural differences. In addition, national independence has been achieved almost everywhere; the privileged legal status of foreigners in Arab countries has been ended; and in many states, programmes of economic and social progress have been fairly successful. As for the cause of Arab unity, while success could hardly be claimed on the political level, social and economic integration across state boundaries has proceeded apace, particularly under the impact of the oil boom and the great upsurge of labour migration.

Today, however, there are a number of reasons to question whether the ideas of Arab nationalism will continue to yield the same benefits, under the stress of several unsettling changes in the orientation of some members of both elite and mass society, away from consensus and towards a dangerous polarization. The symbiosis of traditional and modern culture favoured by the liberal reformers, the faith in the underlying oneness of human values, no longer commands broad support. Instead there appears to be a growing assumption that the Islamic and secular ways of life are not really compatible.

Despite the persistence of unresolved political problems with the West, the secular representatives of Arab society have been undergoing a curious process of de-politicization, which has served if anything to anaesthetize their sensitivities to these conflicts. Two preoccupations in particular have arisen to distract the Westernized elite from the old nationalist concerns.

The first of these is technocracy. Here we refer to the way in which high technology and sophisticated organization have come to dominate so much of the business of government, from military to economic to educational and cultural affairs. The Arab world has come full force into the technocratic era, and its technocrats, regardless of the particular regimes they represent, are members of an international network and ethos that they share with their fellow technocrats in the Third World and the West. The ethos is one of efficiency, productivity, innovation, organization: in short, the antithesis of the world of political strife.

Of course the Arabs continue to face serious problems of inequality at all levels of their international relationships, and one might suppose that the inequality would sustain a continuing urge for political militancy. But in this the Arabs have company throughout the Third World; the problems are rooted largely in the way the world's economic affairs are organized, and cannot be resolved by any amount of ideological zeal. Increasingly, a technically trained leadership seeks technical solutions. As Elbaki Hermassi has aptly remarked, Algeria's technocrats are mindful that 'synthetic ammonia cannot be manufactured by enthusiastic peasants'.[8] Nor, he might have added, can peasants or anyone else in the Third World control the world market terms for synthetic ammonia, but at least the experts can negotiate them in company with their counterparts throughout the world, not in the arena of mass politics but in the quiet atmosphere of corporate boardrooms and ministerial offices.

To the technocrat, the old ideals of populist reformism and a special Arab destiny, preached so fervently by the Ba'th Party in the 1940s, 1950s and 1960s are parochial, romantic, and irrelevant to the great questions shaping the world's future: wealth and poverty, progress and backwardness, maintenance or reform of existing world commercial and financial mechanisms, and the success or failure of developing countries in coping with what the technocrat sees as the growing homogenization of world material culture on

which all modern life must increasingly be based. His circle of
company by which he is conditioned in his thinking is made up of
the international set of his fellow experts, not his less educated
fellow citizens; his passions are directed to projects and budgets, not
nationalist causes.

A second reason for de-politicization is the oil revolution. The
leaders of oil and non-oil states alike are consumed with the effects
of the new concentrations of public funds: lending and borrowing,
buying and selling and investing. Large numbers of private
individuals are consumed with the business of seeking their
fortunes, through migratory employment or contracting. While
inevitably some writers focus on the notion that the oil regimes
have a natural motive to preserve their separate political status,[9]
what may be more significant is the subtle way in which the
de-politicizing impact of oil has also seeped through to many non-
oil-producing states: many features of the new social and economic
structure of the oil states are replicated to some extent in the
neighbouring countries, and with them a similar pyramid of privilege and an attitude of impatience with ideology.

If the non-political technocrat is replacing yesterday's nationalist
intellectual as the predominant representative of the priorities of
Arab governments *vis-à-vis* the outside world, it might equally be
said that within the Arab world the role-model for educated youth
is no longer the revolutionary army officer or the crusading journalist but the well-dressed businessman with his briefcase, boarding a
jet bound for Kuwait or Jeddah in search of a lucrative deal. Another
image of changing times is provided by the profile of students
attending the American University in Cairo. Once an enclave of
American culture patronized by Coptic and Levantine minorities,
and largely ignored by the Egyptian Muslim upper class, the AUC
remains an enclave but is now heavily populated by the sons and
daughters of the latter group. Rather than enrolling in the national
universities, many now prefer the AUC as a stepping stone to
careers in foreign-owned banks or commercial agencies.

Technocrats, businessmen, and the Westerners with whom they
deal, share a common impatience with political controversy, as well
as a common distance from mass society and popular culture. The
electronic age and the oil revolution have brought them together, as
members of a rising new cosmopolitan class of experts and entre-
preneurs from around the globe, bound together by the same

ultra-modern techno-commercial culture: the same ambitions, the same skills, the same English lingua franca, the same hotels, restaurants, and offices, the same indifference to humanistic questions, the same instrumental ethics, and the same remoteness from ordinary men in their own or other countries.

If this new tendency has invaded the outlook of the Arab (and Western) educated elite, the man in the street seems to have been moving in an opposite direction. This can be characterized as alienation from cosmopolitanism and therefore from the secular–traditional symbiosis that nationalism promoted in the past. The Iranian revolution, with its rejection of the legacy of Muhammad Mossadegh no less than of the Western dominance he had fought, represents an extreme version of this reaction, but an active and powerful one that must be taken seriously as a putative model for neighbouring countries.

It is not difficult to detect a number of reasons for the current of Islamic resurgence sweeping numerous Arab and other countries, in terms of developments occurring within the local society and in its relationship with the West. Certainly it has much to do with the crisis that uncontrolled social and economic change has imposed on the daily lives of millions of ordinary people. More often than not, rapid 'development' is in large part a mere reflection of an increase in the money supply, bringing with it inflation, shortages of housing and transport, conspicuous consumption, corruption, crime, the presence of a large and privileged class of foreigners, and police repression.

The foreigners coming to the Arab world are a different lot than before, and they are in much larger numbers. They come with less interest in the country and its people, with less desire to stay, and with a greater devotion to making quick money. Many of them are working–class people with rough manners who know or care little about Islamic cultural norms regarding female modesty or the consumption of alcohol. The encounters of such people with the local population can bear more resemblance to highway collisions than to social introductions, and can only reinforce the conviction of many of those who meet them that traditional social standards must be protected at all costs from barbarous alien influences.[10]

The Islamic resurgence is a broad and varied movement that cannot easily be explained. It does appear, however, that an important aspect of this movement is a new and strongly felt reserve about the validity of acquiring foreign ways of life, a reserve directed against the local westernized elite as much as against Westerners, and an insistent reassertion of the indigenous culture. In the mildest version of this attitude, it will be claimed that a primordial attachment to religion is the only meaningful basis of social identity available to the masses, while the upper classes with their secular education tend to have more in common with foreigners than they do with their own fellow citizens. According to this view (readily shared by the typical Westerner who has recently arrived in the Arab world), the two cultures need not be in any direct conflict: they can coexist very peacefully and fruitfully by respecting certain practical principles of segregation, as is done for example in the conservative oil states. But a symbiosis is out of the question.

A more extreme view is the one expressed by some spokesmen of militant Islamic movements, to the effect that Islam is the sole legitimate source of identity not only for the masses, but for the elite as well; that the secularizing influences on the elite are insidious forces of alienation; and that the very presence of Western cultural patterns constitutes as ominous a danger to the health of Muslim society as military domination did in the past. This view amounts not to a mere call for segregation but to a cultural declaration of war, against the West but more especially against the indigenous elite. The Iranian revolution and the seizure of the Great Mosque in Mecca in 1979 are both expressive of this view. On both sides of the newly emerging polarized society – the radicalized masses, the commercialized elites – the driving pressures are deep-seated and long-term. If the polarization so far is not acute, it may yet grow more severe. The ideas of liberal nationalism are still very much alive within intellectual circles, but these circles are politically isolated, and as an integrative force in Arab society the future of the ideas is doubtful. This is a dangerous situation, since it implies that the future ability of the best-educated citizens to relate to the mass of the population is also doubtful, and the latter will find no effective interpreter to organize their concerns in a coherent programme and articulate them to the outside world.

If the problem is to be overcome, it may be because a new and more dynamic set of ideas – a new political religion – will arise to take the place of the old. Perhaps this will be a new *Nahda*, less Western oriented and more authentically rooted than the old one.

But this will take time, and the shape it will assume cannot be foretold. In the meantime, there is a need more urgent than ever before for the surviving liberal Arab intellectuals, the bearers of the torch of intercultural dialogue and tolerance, to receive all the fraternal support their Western liberal counterparts can give them, as they seek to clarify the new challenges and contribute to their solution.

Notes

1. John Munro, *A Mutual Concern: The Story of the American University of Beirut* (Caravan Books, Delmar, NY, 1977).
2. Taha Husayn, *Mustaqbal al-thaqafa fi misr* (Matba'a al-Ma'arif, Cairo, 1938), trans. Sidney Glazier, *The Future of Culture in Egypt* (American Council of Learned Societies, Washington, DC, 1954).
3. Arnold Toynbee, *The Western Question in Greece and Turkey* (London, Constable, 1922), pp. 1-2, quoted in Elie Kedourie, *The Chatham House Version and Other Middle-Eastern Studies* (London, Cass, 1970), pp. 366-67.
4. See for example Constantine Zurayk, *Nahnu wa al-ta'rikh* (We and History), (Beirut, Dar al-'Ilm lil-Malayin, 1959).
5. Constantine Zurayk, *Al-wa'i al-qawmi* (National Consciousness)(Beirut, 1949), pp. 109-18, translated in Sylvia G. Haim, *Arab Nationalism: an Anthology* (University of California Press, Berkeley and Los Angeles, 1962), pp. 167-71.
6. The best source for detailed review of these viewpoints is Albert Hourani, *Arabic Thought in the Liberal Age, 1798-1939* (Oxford University Press, London, New York, Toronto, 1962).
7. See for example two books by Sadiq al-'Azm: *Al-naqd al-dhati ba'd al-hazima* (Self-Criticism After the Defeat)(Dar al-Tali'a, Beirut, 1968), and *Naqd al-fikr al-dini* (Criticism of Religious Thought)(Dar al-Tali'a, Beirut, 1969).
8. Elbaki Hermassi, *Leadership and Development in North Africa* (University of California Press, Berkeley and Los Angeles, 1972), p. 207.
9. Hasan Naf'a, 'Al-qawmiya al-'arabiya wa al-tafakkuk fi al-watan al-'arabi' (Arab Nationalism and Disintegration in the Arab World), *Al-Mustaqbal,* January 1982, p. 9. Naf'a refers to the oil regimes as 'the natural enemies of pan-Arabism'.
10. A similar process is meanwhile working in reverse in the West most notably in London, where the man in the street is undergoing a rude exposure to the influx of armies of shoppers and holiday-makers from the Arab Gulf states.

Social Trends

Michael Gilsenan

In 1937 *The Times* of London delivered a magisterial commentary
on social trends in Egypt. 'The Egyptian outlook,' it remarked with
gratification, 'is good.' Not unreservedly good perhaps. For if 'new
ideas, new economic influences have produced great changes in the
minds of the young generation', the writer felt obliged to register
the headmasterly qualification that 'some of their results have
admittedly been regrettable'. 'Still,' and here the voice resumes a
brisker tone, now that 'the great political problem has been solved'
(he refers to the achievement of independence by Egypt) Egyptians
can turn to wider economic and social problems. 'On balance the
changes have been beneficial', and, just to put the final seal of
approval on the events of the time, The Thunderer speaks to its
readers in the quintessential language of the English boarding
school: 'The physique of the middle class has greatly improved with
the growth of athletics, and Egyptians . . . are playing an increasing
part in international sport.'[1]
　One bows in awe before this sublime illustration of the imperial
worldview.
　If this authentic voice of its time now strikes us as irresistibly
incongruous and revealing of nothing so much as of its own
speaker's social universe, it may serve all the better as a terrible
lesson to anyone presuming to give an account of social trends in the

Arab world. He is likely to reveal far more about himself than about his subject.

It should also remind that same anyone, however, that many of the half-noticed developments remarked on with such a patronizing regard forty-five years ago are very much at the root of contemporary Arab society. Those 'new ideas, new economic influences' have made their mark. But merely identifying what is changing, never mind how and why and in what directions, is a far more complex question than the editorialist thought and it can be formulated and answered in many ways. But all the answers, from whatever perspective, will have to decide just how heavy is the tradition of all the dead generations that, as Marx so sombrely proclaimed, weighs like a nightmare on the brain of the living.

Dealing with the 'what?' question is difficult enough, as fellow social anthropologists know only too well. For if Arabs as individuals and as members of social groups and classes have different understandings of the social relations in which they are enmeshed, and different conceptions of their cultural and social realities, anthropologists see things in no less diverse ways. We often disagree about the extent to which fundamental social patterns have shifted and are shifting in the modern Arab world. We also frequently, indeed usually, differ as to how social and cultural processes are connected. We have opposed ideas about the nature of such connections. These various ideas lead us in turn to focus on and select as central material or subjects which for others might be relatively marginal.

Let me give one very relevant example. Some writers take culture, values and beliefs as an area of life that has a high degree of autonomy and continuity which persists despite major transformations in politics and the economy. They tend to see culture as above all a shared set of concepts and symbols. Others, and I am among them, stress what they regard as the very uneven but fundamental changes that are occurring in cultural practices of many kinds: etiquette, ways of socializing, speech forms and modes of address, rituals, relations between the sexes, the divisions between private and public spaces and so on. Writers of this persuasion relate these changes to developments in society as a whole. This kind of approach tends to emphasize that there are very disparate and unequally shared ideas and practices of what people regard as right behaviour, the traditional, the place of religion in life or even what they mean by religion, or the right to power and the legitimate ways to exercise it.

If anthropologists like myself are uncertain about identifying social trends and the direction in which Arab societies are moving, this is hardly surprising. It is not merely the result of our particular theoretical positions. Perhaps as seldom before those societies contain both explicit and concealed tensions, specifically around the highly charged field of the view groups and classes have of themselves and their relations.

It seems to me that ambiguity and conflict have particularly arisen over what I shall call the founding terms of life. I mean those conceptions, vocabularies and ways of linking them in thought and action that construct what people basically take to be how things really are or should be.

Such terms concern not only religion and kinship and family in whatever forms. They also entail basic problems in the cultural conventions of interpreting, accounting for and predicting the actions of others; how people understand their social relations, what expectations they have of others, and what they consider to be obligatory action in times of crisis as well as of routine. I believe this cultural and social unease to be a widespread and growing trend in Arab societies. It takes all kinds of specific appearances in different places no doubt, but it is a general trend none the less.

What has struck me again and again in the course of some five years' fieldwork in the Middle East is that social rules and codes and judgments were being invoked with such self-consciousness, and often such stridency and insistence upon their unambiguous authority, precisely because they are becoming extremely ambiguous. They can no longer be taken for granted, or treated as though they are unproblematic and self-evident.

This is my first general point. No one can presume on a relatively stable matching up of social and cultural forms. It may exist in certain dimensions but it cannot be assumed. Cultural practices are no longer simply 'there' in some way that is ingrained and regarded as natural. You cannot make the same assumptions as before, nor can you act as if things are unquestioningly and unquestionably just so. Honour, wealth, political power, patterns of consumption, genealogical claims and solidarities no longer go together in more or less predictable ways. At the same time they are by no means totally fragmented and split apart, nor is there a new system which has replaced an old one. Things are much more complicated than that.

Underlying this trend is a second general process. Class relations are both changed and intensified. They are changed in part because the control of land and agricultural production is no longer the fundamental element in political and economic power, though it is still of real importance. In many societies of the Arab world agriculture is declining and has been for some time, both in its contribution to GNP and as a source of wealth and class relations of domination. Cities are where the money is, where the connections are, where the services of the state are concentrated, and where property, rents, business and commerce, construction, the share and finance markets, and, not least, the new patterns of consumption and status can be realized.

Members of the older dominant group who cannot participate in this world are becoming inexorably declassed. They must either limit themselves to fading influence in the rural areas, where they are often being replaced by members of the urban bourgeoisie investing in capital intensive agriculture, or to an increasingly fictional status and social position whose realities are likely to consist in a grudged or willing dependence on more successful kin or one-time rivals.

This is therefore a third general and closely associated trend. Relations between town and country are being moved ever more decisively in favour of the towns in social, political, cultural and economic terms, with enormous consequences. Class relations within the rural-based dominant group, and between them and the more dependent strata are changing, as are the links with the ruling strata located in the urban centres. 'The country' and 'the land' mean rather different things now to what they signified before in cultural as much as economic or political ways.

These are the three main trends that I want to discuss here. Each of them has many elements, none of them is new, though there are certainly recent developments that have had great effects. All of them have been in train since at least the latter half of the last century, but I need not go into the historical record in any detail for our present purposes. Above all, they are closely intertwined in ways that are sometimes clear, often obscure, and frequently contradictory.

Class and Paradox

The foundation of the ruling Arab bourgeoisie is always taken to be
a combination of the large estate-owning rural notables of the late
nineteenth century with the leading merchants of the towns. The
former predominated in that relationship, but can do so no longer.
Their national influence has declined except where they have been
able to enter into the newer middle classes based originally in
business and the liberal professions, and more recently in the cadres
of the state administration, industry and corporations, and the
armed forces. To this we might add the educational elites who have
taken advantage usually of university education abroad. In this
generation they are still often in medicine, a traditional profession,
but also in subjects such as the pure and natural sciences and in
engineering and technology.

Visibly distinct from these strata are the new rich, formed in the
days of the petroleum boom and the opportunities for financial
dealing in construction and service industries. It is particularly here
that the public forms of wealth and its display are celebrated with a
growing and almost baroque enthusiasm that earns the opprobrium
of the old and liberal bourgeoisie as much as the amazement, and
resentment, of the poor. It is of this level of society that an
intellectual Arab friend of mine recently remarked: 'They are highly
educated, but they have no culture at all.' This is perhaps a typical
intellectual's jibe, but it picks up a none the less important theme of
cultural dislocation that I shall come back to later.

As much as any one level may be said to do so, they highlight the
growingly obvious nature of social divisions, and they do so by
ways and means that were not part of the older social forms. They
are all the more significant in societies where the services sector of
the economy is the most dynamic and expanding.

This numerically small class contributes little to a country's infrastructure and is less anchored in social relations than those in
agriculture and industry. It is a group apart, a group for whom
conspicuous display is an uninhibited form of expression and is thus
the focus of some hostility and criticism on the part of those of
different classes, both upper and lower, who might otherwise have
very distinct social attitudes. The *nouveaux riches* symbolize something essentially artificial. Rather than being a sign of development,
they are glittering and even provocative champions of money-in-

itself, of dependency rather than autonomy, of a kind of life that is in, but no longer seems of society. They are peripheral, and yet at the same time integral to the direction these societies are taking.

This characterization has all sorts of implications at other social levels. It bears a particular relation to two other social classes, though the use of the term 'class' here is even more problematic than usual.

The first is the petty bourgeoisie, an unsatisfactory ragbag sort of a term but I shall use it. The shopkeepers, small businessmen, clerks, low-grade government officials, teachers, most of the high school and university students, minor employees and functionaries that make up this very heterogeneous mixture of social groupings and occupations is more and more crucial in modern Arab society. Its sheer scale is enormous and the diversity of its social and cultural relations and attitudes is considerable.

If there is a trend that can be discerned here amidst all the conflicting forces that operate on people in these strata, I think it is one towards a greater dissatisfaction with the state and tension with the dominant state and technocratic cadres and professional 'westernized' middle classes. The social position of the petty bourgeoisie is highly precarious in many cases. Neither the colonial nor the nationalist periods which saw a tremendous upsurge in this class rendered their conditions of life more stable.

As economic conditions develop now in ever more state and finance capital dominated forms, and with the increasing role of the new rich – not a contradiction in the Arab world – many sections of the petty bourgeoisie feel that they have less and less participation in the crucial political, economic and cultural institutions. These avenues appear, indeed, to be yet more securely closed off, though the army is still a road some take.

Small wonder, then, if groups such as the Muslim Brothers are finding and have always found their best recruitment in times of crisis from these social groupings. A rhetoric that looks backward meets a life situation that seems to be going backwards; a timeless utopian vision reaches those for whom history appears to be blocked if not actually in reverse. A growing sense of disjunction and precariousness finds its reassurance in an ideologically unproblematic and stable conception of society in which salvation is spelt out with apparent clarity. Any general unease about 'identity' and just what is the nature of one's cultural and social place and tradition can be quieted in the confused simplicities of this version of religion.

As more and more is changed, so 'tradition' becomes a new issue and a new refuge. For a class that has had to learn its culture in a world where *what* to learn and *who* will teach it have not been very clear or successfully answered questions, the Brothers are, almost literally, a godsend. As community breaks down a dream world of solidarity beckons seductively.

To the younger generation who have grown up in the aftermath of the high nationalist period of the 1950s and early 1960s rather than its heyday such movements as the Brotherhood may even be seen as not nearly radical enough. They want to cleanse society, and are sometimes ready to adopt the most extreme sectarian line. Real paths to development being closed, they are ready for the unreal options, of right or left. They are more part of society and less identified with it. Their fathers were both dependent on the state for jobs and economic direction and in material and political interest, and at the same time could never achieve either political or economic freedom from that same state to which in many ways therefore they felt opposed. The sons and daughters have absorbed both the failures and limitations of nationalism and have found the elephantine state apparatuses far too heavy and sluggish to respond to their urgently felt needs in all dimensions.

The other stratum I want particularly to mention here is that of the poor urban masses. Migration at often very high rates from the countryside increases their numbers all the time. They are the key to the 'informal' or 'black' economy of the cities. Thrust out to the edges of society, they are vital to its functioning. Posing huge social and economic, not to say political problems, society yet could not manage without them in the day to day. Seen on the one hand as the sources of disorder and as beyond ordinary controls, they may furnish the means and manpower of opposition in the street to radical critics of the regimes, or to the regimes themselves.

They may play highly disruptive or very conservative roles, or both at the same time. The growing *bidonvilles,* shanty towns and slums seem to be the antithesis of urbanity to the bourgeoisie, yet they almost constitute cities in themselves with their order and hierarchies. Not infrequently people here share places of origin and kinship ties with others from the same village or region. A new kind of localism develops at another level. It is growing.

The urban poor are further and further from cultural participation in the life of society as conceived by the higher classes.
Moreover, those same higher classes have less and less comprehension or apprehension of the social world of this large mass of the
people. The bourgeoisie is in a similar position in this respect to the
old colonial officials who were not too sure what the natives
thought, how they lived, or what they were up to down there in the
old city.

The Country in the City, the City in the Country

I have spoken briefly of migration, and clearly this is a major trend
affecting the social life of many levels of Arab society today. If the
cities are dominant and class power is shifting this is in part because
of the movement into the urban areas of large numbers of the rural
population. What needs to be stressed is that this is not a unitary
phenomenon that takes the same form and has the same explanation. There are many different kinds of emigration and they need
to be understood in some of their diversity.

The traditional idea of a rural world that can no longer support its
population and therefore as it were pushes out the surplus, the poor
and landless and displaced small artisans, into the towns has some
truth in it. Share-croppers who have no land of their own and who
can only cultivate small plots may find the already hard life of the
peasant and agricultural labourer, which is what they will often also
be, increasingly hard.

But it is not so for everyone. The so-called 'middle peasantry'
has often done and is doing quite well. At this level where people
own or cultivate anything from roughly ten acres upwards and
frequently employ labourers on a wage basis, emigration means
something more than a flight or a refuge. Cooperative schemes
have assisted in their consolidation. They are the chief beneficiaries
of government assistance in the countryside, and they have a corresponding social status and influence. Emigration for them expands
the economic range of the family from a more secure base, places
children in the petty bourgeoisie of the citites and perhaps in the
officer class or the lower levels of the state services. Diversification
is the name of the game, and a wider range of possibilities is open to
them than to their share-croppers.

The latter, too, have tried to diversify: a brother cleaning cars in a garage, a daughter working as a maid, another brother making cheap furniture in a small workshop, a third selling black–market goods from a cart, a couple of children helping on the land or acting as camel drovers. And all of them are liable to find themselves without work at more or less a moment's notice. The informal economy is staffed by people from this level. To them the city represents a haven, a chance, a culture of kitsch films, more open sexuality, money in however tiny amounts, and a greater degree of freedom from the obligations of kin ties and paternal discipline.

They may even, at times of economic crisis, see the city in a far rosier if more unreal light than those who come from the middle peasantry and rural petty bourgeoisie. For the latter find themselves in situations where they may have to settle for less than they expected and hoped for when they left the rural areas. Rents are getting higher, and they must choose between living on their own or in too much company. It is far more difficult to raise the funds necessary for marriage than they imagined; stable jobs, that goal of every individual from this stratum, are rare commodities.

They may end up in a more fragmented and contradictory situation than their poorer village age-mates. Looking down on the lifestyles and culture of the lumpen masses, and above all concerned with making something of themselves and having a trade or, oh dream of dreams, a secure government post, the possibility of achieving neither is a terrible menace. And they are educated, to a greater or lesser degree informed, to a greater or lesser extent participant in the social and cultural world of the middle classes, or at least observers of it.

If times are hard they stand to lose more than anyone else, and with them so do their relatives in the countryside. Here is the link with movements such as the Muslim Brothers again. For those who come from villages and small provincial towns to the larger urban centres find themselves excluded from an equivalent social and economic position to the one their families may have at home.

In these current circumstances the city may come to be seen in exactly the light that the 'fundamentalists' shine upon it – a centre of immorality, injustice, corruption and alienation. This is exacerbated by the trend towards the splitting up of the city into separated zones of social and cultural life in which class is increasingly and obviously the key factor. This process, which has its foundations in the colonial period, now has a more indigenous development. It makes of the main cities a patchwork of neighbourhoods and quarters, suburbs and *bidonvilles* that can be quickly identified in social terms.

The older areas are tending to ever higher population densities and to a breakdown of services of the most basic kinds. The working-class areas are often both quite new and already decrepit. One is in the city, but in another sense farther away from it than ever before. It is a temple of commodities which are out of reach, of manners that cannot even be satisfactorily aped, of a culture one does not understand. It offers everything but gives nothing.

Under these circumstances family life can no longer be organized according to once conventional codes and practices of dividing private from public, either in the home or outside it. At the same time there is no crystallized new family culture. People are in a kind of unending transition between an old and a new, but it is a transition that never seems to achieve itself in a resolution of a structured, modern and different form.

A more radical kind of emigration has been a very important social trend. Going right outside one's own society, to the Gulf or Saudi Arabia for instance, has been of great significance over the past twenty years or so. Initially mostly restricted to the more skilled, it has also become a route for even the poorest agricultural and urban skilled workers. The exchange of capital for labour between the petro-rich and the population-rich has become a major trend in the life of many Arab societies.

The social and cultural effects are considerable. There is a kind of *gästarbeiter* syndrome in the Arab world itself and for good and ill this now touches the lives of many people at the lower levels of society. For the bourgeoisie of course, the architects, doctors, middle men and bankers, movement is part of a way of life as well as a profession. For the peasant or labourer or lorry driver it is both necessary and disruptive.

The remittances and the consumer goods are seldom translated into productive forms, but tend to go into social and ritual consumption in which newer symbols of local status, furniture, television, a car, compensate for the dislocation that made them possible. They extend the urban world in terms of what are taken to be its characteristic objects, tastes, and values into the village and the small town. They stand for the new proximity of city and country, separated by so many factors yet joined ever more tightly in a hierarchy in which the latter is subordinate to the former.

Cultures and Traditions

Villages and villagers are therefore both less and more themselves: less as they are incorporated in the national political and economic spheres in more direct and multiple ways; more as the social distance between them and the city grows, despite the emigration that only seems to integrate them. The state is omnipresent, yet relations are cast in a personalized, patron–client kind of mode in which the individual is the key, and the contact is the vital resource. This is not the traditional kind of person-to-person tie, whatever that was, but something that looks like it yet occurs in a quite different context.

The newest patterns may take the oldest forms. The successful landowner who has considerable local political clout and city investments in property is the one who will be the champion of 'traditional' ritual forms of social life at weddings, saints' days, Ramadan and in the everyday world of social encounters. Tradition is rather more expensive than it used to be. It is now a commodity too, one might cynically say, and certainly it is more a subject of argument and ambiguity than an unquestioned natural certainty.

If there is a cultural crisis, or as it is often described, a crisis of identity, it is one which assumes very distinct shapes for different classes. And it is not a metaphysical question as it is so often taken to be. It is rather a series of intensely practical problems that are experienced by people in their everyday lives. It may be converted into mysticism and metaphysics, but that in itself is a process to be explained and not something inherent in the tensions and contradictions of some supposed Arab 'mentality'.

If Sufi Brotherhoods seem to be having a resurgence, for example, this is a trend that grows out of very concrete circumstances in my view, and not just some kind of atavistic or primordial instinct reasserting itself. It is part of a wider phenomenon which I shall call for want of a better term particularism. This may take religious or 'confessional' or regional, or urban or village forms. It is a pattern of withdrawing into smaller units such as village and town quarters or social clubs and religious brotherhoods even as the base of their social links and relations becomes obscured.

A further and crucial area of withdrawal concerns the place of women in contemporary Arab societies. There are signs indicating that the gains which were made during the past fifty years or so, limited though they were, are being lost. Where women are integrated into market production it is mostly in terms of agricultural production, where the work is predominantly seasonal, their wages are lower, and they function as a pool of surplus labourers.[2] This is a role which maintains their dependence. As social distinctions grow, those whose wives and sisters work in the fields or in domestic service in the towns are thought to be shamed in comparison to those whose women are restricted to the home and to highly regulated kinds of social contacts within restricted circles of kin.

Social trends that lead to new patterns of display and consumption also lead to a reinforcement of women's subordination as a mark of 'honour', family standing and class position. It is notable that even in a country such as Algeria, where a more radical conception of the role of women came out of the war against the French colonial power, there is a swing back to a much more conservative view on the part of the state, in some degree responding to pressure from below. Middle-class women and some sections of the intelligentsia may protest against this, but it looks as though the overall trend will be too strong for them.

As people try to draw the cultural and social lines more clearly in a global situation where they are not and cannot be clear, male–female relations are bound to be a major area of preoccupation and insistence on the absolute clarity of what is in fact a highly unstable set of relations. Domestic culture, if I may put it in those terms, becomes more self-consciously male centred as its codes and practices become more objectively difficult to sustain. A certain view here of what Islam demands may be invoked to guarantee the rightness of such 'traditional' controls. The rhetoric of honour and shame is strengthened by the social changes now occurring rather than being weakened. This appears to me to be a culturally and socially backward trend with major consequences for social life as a whole.

Conclusion

Put at its most general level one could say that the fundamental question for people, particularly for those at the lower levels of Arab societies is: what appearances go with what realities?

It has frequently struck me in the course of anthropological fieldwork in Egypt and the Lebanon that people were not quite sure, not instinctively certain about what a given action meant, what particular statements should be taken to signify, how to respond to specific words or deeds, what to do to convince others of one's own intentions or the position one wanted to be seen to occupy. I exaggerate of course. But I do so to make the point that constantly imposed itself upon me; that people are often in the position of, as it were, commenting upon their own actions and doings from an ironic distance, as though they were playing on the existence of social and cultural contradictions and oppositions of whose existence they were only too aware but which they felt they could neither control nor resolve.

This is a wildly general observation, but to me it begins to approach a very basic element in contemporary Arab societies. The founding terms of life, to go back to my original formulation, are at issue. But not yet in ways that promise resolution.

Notes

1. *The Times Book of Egypt* (The Times Publishing Company, London, 1937), pp. 3-4.
2. See for example Judith Tucker, 'Egyptian Women in the Word Force: an Historical Survey' in MERIP Reports, No. 50, Washington DC, 1976, pp. 3–9.